Believing the News

Believing the News

Edited by Don Fry

A Poynter Institute Ethics Center Report

ISBN 0-935742-11-5

Printed in the United States of America

Cover by Sally Wern Comport
Photos by Gulfstream Communications, Inc.
Book design and production by Billie M. Keirstead

Copies of this publication may be ordered at $3.00 each
from The Poynter Institute, 801 Third Street South,
St. Petersburg, FL 33701.

**For Bertrand Harris Bronson
who never lets misinformation pass**

About This Book

In January 1985 a distinguished group of journalists came to St. Petersburg for a seminar sponsored by The Poynter Institute to discuss the credibility of newspapers and television. They had been invited to discuss and debate the merits of a charge made the previous year that television was in a major way responsible for many of the credibility problems of newspapers. That allegation had been made by newspaper publisher Creed Black in his farewell address as president of the American Society of Newspaper Editors. Black's thesis was that many readers and viewers were unable or unwilling to distinguish between the two main branches of the media and that when readers said they were angry at the press it was often television news with which they were unhappy.

The Institute, without taking sides, thought Black's charge was worthy of further discussion and convened the seminar of leading writers and executives of both media to thrash it out. The group gathered at an unusual and highly charged moment. On January 23, the eve of the seminar, the jury in the suit by former Israeli Defense Minister Ariel Sharon against *TIME* announced that the magazine had indeed defamed Sharon by implying that he had "consciously intended" to permit Lebanese Phalangists to take revenge by deliberately killing non-combatants in two Palestinian refugee camps. Twenty hours later, in the midst of the three-day seminar, the jury announced that the paragraph which contained this allegation was false. Not for another month would the jury rule that, while some *TIME* employees had been careless and negligent with the facts, the magazine was not guilty of actual malice and thus not of libeling a public figure. The suit by General William Westmoreland against CBS was in trial and more than three and a half weeks from settlement. Both cases were very much on the minds of the seminar participants. But that did not prevent them from proving that the best way to attack any major societal problem is to put first-class minds against it.

Over two and a half days of intensive debate, both in and out of the seminar room, the discussion ranged far beyond Creed Black's original charge. The early hours were marked by a sharp division between the newspaper and TV people. That was followed by a successful search for common ground and then, under the skillful leadership of moderator James David Barber, basic, if not total, agreement on some prescriptions for all journalists.

The Poynter Institute is pleased to have sponsored the seminar and is especially hopeful that publication of the proceedings and related materials in this book will spark further discussion by journalists, students, teachers, and all who believe in the essential nature of a free society, fully informed by a free and responsible press.

Robert J. Haiman, President
The Poynter Institute

Participants

JAMES DAVID BARBER, whose doctorate in political science is from Yale University, is James B. Duke Professor of Political Science and Public Policy Studies at Duke University. He is co-director of Duke's Center for the Study of Communications Policy, which is particularly concerned with the relationship between news and democracy. He is the author of several books including *The Pulse of Politics: Electing Presidents in the Media Age, Race for the Presidency,* and *The Presidential Character.*

MARILYN BERGER has been NBC News White House Correspondent, *Washington Post* diplomatic correspondent and UN correspondent for ABC. She has also served as diplomatic correspondent for *Newsday.* She had her own program on WNET in New York and also moderated *The Advocates* on WGBH in Boston.

CREED BLACK is chairman and publisher of the *Lexington Herald-Leader.* During his career he has held news editorial positions at *The Nashville Tennessean, Savannah Morning News* and *Evening Press* and the *Wilmington* (Delaware) *Morning News* and *Evening Journal.* He was managing editor and executive editor of the *Chicago Daily News* and was vice president and editor of *The Philadelphia Inquirer.* His address in 1984 as outgoing president of the American Society of Newspaper Editors was the stimulus for this seminar.

LOUIS D. BOCCARDI is president and general manager of the Associated Press. Boccardi joined the AP in 1967 after serving as assistant managing editor of the *World Journal Tribune.* At AP he served as managing editor and executive editor. As vice president, he was the AP's senior news executive.

DAVID S. BRODER is national political correspondent and columnist for *The Washington Post*. His twice-weekly syndicated column is carried by 275 newspapers across the nation. He joined *The Post* staff in 1966 and was named an associate editor in 1975. Broder, who won the Pulitzer Prize in 1973 for distinguished commentary, is generally regarded as one of the country's most influential political columnists.

DAVID BURGIN was recently named editor of the *San Francisco Examiner*. Prior to that he was editor and vice president of *The Orlando Sentinel*, after serving nearly four years as the first editor of another Tribune Company newspaper, the Peninsula *Times Tribune* in Palo Alto, California.

JOHN CHANCELLOR, an NBC correspondent for more than three decades, is now resident commentator of the *NBC Nightly News*. He began his career as a reporter for the *Chicago Sun-Times*. For NBC News, he has been midwestern correspondent, foreign correspondent in London, Vienna, Brussels and Moscow, and, for nearly 12 years, an anchorman of the *NBC Nightly News*. He also has been director of the *Voice of America*.

MICHAEL GARTNER is former president and chief operating officer of the Des Moines Register and Tribune Company. Prior to joining the *Register*, Gartner held various writing, reporting and editing posts at *The Wall Street Journal*, serving as front page editor from 1970 until 1974. Gartner also is a lawyer and the author of a syndicated column on words.

DON HEWITT is executive producer of *60 Minutes*, now in its 18th season. In his 36 years with CBS News, Hewitt has been closely associated with the production and direction of broadcasts dealing with virtually every major news event which occurred during those years. He is the recipient of seven Emmy Awards and in 1980 was named Broadcaster of the Year.

LARRY JINKS has been senior vice president for news at Knight-Ridder Newspapers since January 1983. In this role, he has corporate responsibility for the news and editorial quality of KRN's 30 daily newspapers and the Washington Bureau and news service. Before assuming his corporate position, he was executive editor of *The Miami Herald* and editor of the San Jose *Mercury-News*.

DAVID LAVENTHOL is publisher and chief executive officer of *Newsday* and a group vice president of newspapers for the Times Mirror Company. Laventhol became publisher of *Newsday* in 1978, following nearly eight years as editor. He came to *Newsday* from *The Washington Post*, where he was an assistant managing editor. He previously had worked for the *New York Herald Tribune*, the *St. Petersburg Times*, and the *Washington Star*.

BARBARA MATUSOW, a veteran television journalist, is the author of *The Evening Stars: The Making of the Network News Anchor*. She has worked in radio and television news at CBS and NBC in a variety of positions, including newswriter, assignment editor, and producer. She is senior contributing editor of *Washington Journalism Review*.

JACK NELSON is Washington bureau chief for the *Los Angeles Times*, and previously served as an investigative reporter for the Washington bureau and chief of the Atlanta bureau of the *Times*. Nelson won a Pulitzer Prize in 1960 and the Drew Pearson Award for Investigative Reporting in 1975. He appears frequently on the public television program *Washington Week in Review*.

MARTIN F. NOLAN has been editor of the editorial page of *The Boston Globe* since 1981. He joined *The Boston Globe* in 1961, and in 1969 was named Washington bureau chief. In 1966, he was a member of the team that won the Pulitzer Prize for Meritorious Public Service. He has been a frequent panelist on *Face the Nation, Meet the Press,* and *This Week With David Brinkley*.

EUGENE PATTERSON is chairman and chief executive officer of the *St. Petersburg Times* and president of its Washington publication, *Congressional Quarterly*. After several years with the old United Press, Patterson served as editor of the *Atlanta Constitution* and managing editor of *The Washington Post* before assuming the editorship of the *St. Petersburg Times*. He won the 1966 Pulitzer Prize for editorial writing. He is a former president of the American Society of Newspaper Editors.

RALPH A. RENICK recently resigned his position as news director of WTVJ-TV in Miami and vice president in charge of Wometco Television News Operations. Renick now is a candidate for the Democratic nomination for governor of Florida. Renick's 6:00 nightly program, *News 4 with Ralph Renick*, was the nation's longest continuously-running news report, more than 35 years.

VAN GORDON SAUTER is executive vice president of CBS/Broadcast Group. Reporting to him are the CBS News Division and the CBS Television Stations Division. He also has been president of CBS News and CBS Sports. Sauter joined CBS in 1968 after spending nine years as a newspaper reporter in Massachusetts, Detroit and Chicago.

TONY SCHWARTZ is a contributing editor at *New York* magazine. He previously was a television reporter for *The New York Times* and was also a media critic for WCBS in New York.

JOHN SEIGENTHALER is editor and publisher of *The Tennessean*, Nashville's morning newspaper. He was given the additional assignment of editorial director of *USA Today* when the Gannett paper started publication in 1982. The *Tennessean*, during his tenure as editor and publisher, has won many national awards, including the Pulitzer Prize.

SANDER VANOCUR is senior correspondent for ABC News, which he joined in June 1977. In addition to his regular reporting on ABC's *World News*

Tonight, he has contributed to its "Special Assignment" series. During his 14 years with NBC News, he served three years as White House correspondent before being named national political correspondent.

JUDY WOODRUFF has been chief Washington correspondent for *The MacNeil/Lehrer NewsHour* since 1983. Ms. Woodruff previously served as NBC News's White House correspondent, after which she became chief Washington correspondent for the *Today* show. In addition to her work on *NewsHour*, Ms. Woodruff is the anchor for public television's *Frontline* documentary series.

ROY PETER CLARK is director of the Writing Center at The Poynter Institute. He is a graduate of Providence College and has a Ph.D. in English from the SUNY at Stony Brook. He was a professor of English at Auburn University where he taught writing, language and literary criticism. He worked at the *St. Petersburg Times* as a writing coach and also served as reporter, feature writer and film and theater critic before joining the Institute faculty.

DON FRY is associate director of The Poynter Institute. He graduated from Duke with a degree in English and received a Ph.D. from Berkeley. He was a professor of English at the University of Virginia and at SUNY at Stony Brook, where he also was chairman of the Department of Comparative Literature and Provost for the Humanities and Fine Arts.

ROBERT J. HAIMAN is president and managing director of The Poynter Institute. Before joining the Institute as president in 1983, he worked 25 years for the *St. Petersburg Times*, the last seven as executive editor. He is a director of The Times Publishing Co., a past president of the AP Managing Editors Association and a frequent visiting lecturer at the journalism schools of universities in the U.S., Canada, and Europe.

Contents

Introduction

Surveys show that many Americans distrust the news media. Media executives and commentators respond along a spectrum bounded at one end by helpless handwringing and at the other by defensive bravado. Some quietly implement improvements, and some ridicule their concern. Some blame the media, the government, the times, and even the public.

The Poynter Institute Seminar on Credibility responded to the concern expressed by more thoughtful journalists by assembling a panel of expert practitioners to discuss the issues connected with credibility and to suggest paths for improvement. Rather than tackle the large and amorphous topic of news and belief, the seminar responded to a specific charge by Creed Black in his 1984 address to the American Society of Newspaper Editors, entitled "Our Image Problem: A Paradox," reprinted in this volume as Essay 6. Black chided newspapers for their inattention to public distrust, and concluded that most of the image problems of newspapers stem from what he perceived as the sins of television news: arrogance, unnamed sources, mixing fact and opinion, and superficiality. The participants sparred briefly and comically over the relative faults of the two media before accepting Van Gordon Sauter's metaphor of a shared boat that will not sink as long as both ends keep rowing.

As various speakers introduced new aspects of credibility, especially in relation to differing media, the discussion quickly showed that simple definitions of problems and easy answers fail to address the interlinked complexities of actual journalistic practice. The participants watched their peers learn and grow before their very eyes, some more than others. One theme repeatedly emerged: credibility grows out of the traditional techniques of responsible journalism.

Credibility problems result from mismatches between journalistic practice and public expectations. People expect certain standards of behavior among civilized citizens, and they demand civility even from powerful organizations. When citizens charge the press with unfairness, bias, arrogance, and greed, they presuppose a higher standard than they might apply to their associates, their friends or even themselves. This presumption flows from the perceived power of the press to do harm to less-powerful individuals and organizations. The public expects restraint in the use of power, but they perceive abuse everywhere around them, not just by the press, but also by governments and large corporations.

Of course, the public does not see the routine care and restraint of the press: the tragic stories downplayed, the gory photographs rejected, bias edited out of stories, inaccuracies caught and corrected before presstime. They do not understand the inner workings of journalism, even such basic distinctions as news versus commentary, or the strict boundaries maintained between advertising and editorial divisions. They cannot know these things because the press assumes they do not want to know them, and therefore does not explain them to its public.

The very processes of reporting news distort reality as ordinary human beings experience it. People swim in a flow of events, not necessarily causally connected. The press sees the world in terms of stories, interrelated happenings with beginnings and ends, with apparently extraneous details left out. The reader or viewer, seeing the flotsam and jetsam of real lives made brief and orderly, tends to respond, "But there's more to it than that."

The presentation of news in writing or speaking pictures violates the ordinary citizen's perception further. Words fail us in capturing the complexities of human experience. A verbatim quotation loses the cushioning of its spoken context, loses the tempering of gestures, both vocal and physical. Pictures telescope and juxtapose disparate events, and selecting them for dramatic impact magnifies atypical occurrences. News media cannot tell the truth truthfully enough to satisfy

John Chancellor shares an anecdote with Creed Black.

their audiences, no matter how professionally they perform. Their media fail the media.

Every thoughtful journalist knows these limitations of newstelling. But the audience does not, and expects something like the truth from newspapers and television. The best journalistic practice will never totally overcome these inherent obstacles. Unfortunately, journalistic practice seldom approaches its best.

Most charges against the press involve a perceived arrogance coupled with deliberate rudeness. The public sees reporters in action, crowding around upset victims, demanding instant answers to rudely phrased questions. Photographers snap flashguns in the face of a mother watching her child die in a fire. Editorials cast snide aspersions on well-meaning civic boosters. Movies such as *Absence of Malice* depict journalists as vultures willing to do anything to promote themselves with a good story.

Television now shows the press in action, right before the viewers' eyes. To see reporters abusing subjects 25 years ago, one had to be present at the scene or enjoying a fictional account. Now the nation can watch live as Sam Donaldson shouts questions at the President over the noise of helicopter blades. Donaldson looks rude, and the President looks presidential. A clever White House has learned to manipulate the public's disposition toward seeing journalists as crude. Revving up the helicopter causes Donaldson to raise his already stentorian voice to a shout, and television magnifies what becomes an ugly scene. The showman President shakes his head wistfully, and smiles.

But the press *is* arrogant by its very nature. One cannot intrude professionally on people's lives without seeming intrusive. One cannot pay close attention to events without developing superior knowledge of events. One cannot organize daily experience without gaining a certain sense of power over events. One cannot belong to a meritocracy without feeling selected. Arrogance comes with a sense of superior vision, a by-product of privileged access to information.

The American press has cultivated a macho style that encourages such arrogance. The insistence on "just the facts," the traditional bullying tone of desk editors, the specious avoidance of emotion, all the characteristics associated with the phase "Green Eyeshade," enhance the innate feelings of superiority of writers and pictors. Some commentators seem to regard mere discussion of credibility problems as demeaning the "manliness" of the press.

Recognizing the necessary arrogance of the press does not doom the media to destructive habits. Leaders can channel arrogance for good purposes, such as investigative reporting. More importantly, leaders can mitigate arrogant signs by educating reporters and editors, by promoting escape from dinosaur behavior.

Participants in the seminar focused on the televised presidential news conference as particularly damaging to the image of the press. Journalists see prominent reporters asking "creampuff questions," and accepting mushy answers to let the next questioners have their turns. The public sees strident reporters rudely picking on their popular President.

Another group of credibility problems falls under the category of fictionizing. Many readers and viewers regard parts of the news as simply made up, particularly in details such as quotations. The participants attributed much of this extreme skepticism to the use of unnamed sources. Reporters use such sources for a number of reasons, some legitimate and some not. Young journalists tend to think of anonymous sources as indicative of inside information, a sign of their ability to ferret out the real scoop. At the other extreme, government officials use cloaked attribution to float trial balloons, make untraceable allegations, and inflate their own importance as real insiders. The audience often equates the unnamed source with the bylined writer. The participants agreed on the damaging effects of anonymity, but saw no way to eliminate it, particularly in today's political climate. They could only suggest minimizing the use of unnamed sources, as well as adding general identifications of sources and some indication of potential motives.

Cynics often view the press as an arm of the elusive but omnipresent government, or at least in collusion with it. The White House has steadily increased its control over Washington (even world) news, attempting to reduce the press to a conduit for publicity releases. Unfortunately the media find it easier and cheaper to swallow White House news than to go hunting in the departments. Van Sauter suggested that the public sees "the media and the politicians...involved in a dance, a dance that only they understand," a suspicion that William Greider's conversations with David Stockman seemed to confirm.

The public faults the media for mixing opinion with supposedly objective news, echoing Black's charge about television. The recent ASNE survey showed that 23 percent of respondents regarded the front page as containing more opinion than the rest of the paper. News stories often seem objective because of their style: the rather flat, fact-dominated, passive, and overly-attributed mode associated with the Associated Press wire. But bias can sneak in through selection and play of details.

Readers (and some journalists) equate analysis with bias. As Judy Woodruff noted, "We all know by now we can't just report the facts as we see them; there's more to journalism than that." Modern journalism

Sander Vanocur and Don Hewitt scrutinize news stories.

must transcend mere reporting. Writers must explain complex issues and personalities, and such explanation requires analysis. By applying the same controls used on straight news, reporters and commentators can keep analysis relatively unbiased, but readers need appropriate markers to distinguish analysis from straight reporting.

Some commentators believe that readers and viewers find the news simply incomprehensible. Clearly understanding must precede belief. James David Barber points out that stories contain vocabulary well over the general audience's head, and Jack Nelson objects to the intense focus on tiny incremental developments in government reporting as confusing. Reporters do tend to write for their peers, for their subjects, and even for themselves. Editors can insist on explanatory journalism, written with the needs of the audience in mind. Writers need to "take a step back" now and then, as David Broder says, to review sequences of reported events, and to put them into clearer and larger patterns. Such breathers and long looks tend to clarify the writer's thought as well as the audiences' comprehension. The recent movement toward improving writing in American newspapers has already contributed to raising consciousness of clarity and fullness.

The news media set the agenda for the nation's attention, but some participants raised the question of how well the coverage matches the real interests and needs of the audience. The emphasis on breaking news causes the press to miss the real impact of slow developments over decades, such as school integration, the shift to the suburbs, and the effects of abortion. News traditionally focuses on government, which ranks rather low on the average citizen's agenda.

The advent of *USA Today* with its deliberately upbeat tone has renewed the debate over the negative emphasis of news reporting. One study showed that negative stories dominate by a 20-to-1 ratio. Since few citizens could survive a life with a 20-to-1 ratio of negative occurrences, the news seems incredible, or worse, inflicted on the public by overly-critical writers. Viewers often take mere questioning of the President in televised news conferences as badgering, a reaction exacerbated by the popularity and apparent civility of President Reagan.

Traditional definitions of news guarantee a negative emphasis. Take Melvin Mencher's first guideline for news: "News is information about a break from the normal flow of events, an interruption in the expected." That sentence defines news as abnormal. Most people regard themselves in a rather optimistic light, and see their lives as a series of neutral or positive developments, with occasional negative bumps. Even when good news breaks, traditional reporting practice demands balance, presenting potentially negative consequences. Balance and the weighing of evidence require relentless skepticism, which the public dislikes.

Everyday citizens complain that the press injures people by invading their privacy, especially by displaying their grief in misfortune. Yet everyone knows that grief sells newspapers. Television brags about its ability to take us to the crash scenes, or to show us live interviews with hostage relatives. Despite the public's annoyance with the press's intrusiveness, they do want to see the human side of events, reactions by real people. Often the grieving relatives themselves will call the media to invite them for an interview.

Finally, the public feels frustrated by its inability to talk back to large organizations, especially to the press. Citizens want to make their views known, to correct what they see as errors in coverage and interpretation. The sheer volume of letters to the editor can overwhelm the space available on the op-ed page, and television has never devised a satisfactory outlet for viewer response in any large numbers. This frustration often leads to unnecessary libel suits, where the plaintiff seeks a magnified voice in the courts.

So the very processes of newsgathering and publication, both in newspapers and television, clash with the expectations of the audience. The qualities we value in a good reporter (aggressiveness, skepticism, dogged accuracy, etc.) may necessarily seem obnoxious to the civil citizen.

If credibility problems seem endemic, can the press solve them, and should it even try? The skeptics and some of the more aggressive executives say no, and bluster ahead as they always have. But the seminar participants in general felt that some reforms might have a mitigating effect on the public's attitudes.

The group endorsed greater efforts toward explaining journalists and journalism to the public, to promote understanding of the limitations of news. They suggested ways to tone down some of the more egregious practices, such as over-reliance on unnamed sources. They endorsed the traditional values and safeguards of journalism as thoroughly tested methods of providing the news with spirit and restraint. Despite their high rank and visibility in the profession, they also seemed to admire a certain humility which might lead to a more realistic posture with their audiences. David Broder recommended a message to readers something like this: "What we are dropping on the doorstep is a brief, hasty, incomplete, necessarily distorted version of some of the things that are fit to print," followed the next day by this message: "We've learned some things since we've last come into your home....here's how we'd like to revise and update and correct what we told you yesterday."

* * *

The following transcription captures the essence of the speeches and discussions over the two-day seminar, except for the unrecorded individual caucuses. Editing reduced the original taped record by 40 percent, mostly by deleting redundancies, asides and procedural explanation. I have edited heavily to convert slightly formal conversation into informal prose, while attempting to preserve the personal tone of exchanges. To promote clarity, I have frequently expanded first-name and pronoun references to full names. I apologize for any faulty attributions.

Don Fry
August 1985

Journalists Sink Teeth Into Issue of Credibility

By CHARLES STAFFORD

The men and women who bring you the news have their yearnings.

John Chancellor does not want you to like him; he wants you to believe him.

Marty Nolan does not want your affection; he wants your respect.

What they want most—Chancellor, Nolan, their colleagues and bosses—is for you, the viewer, the reader, to believe in the credibility of their work.

Twenty-one of them, lions and lionesses of newspapers and television, were in retreat Friday and Saturday in a meeting room in St. Petersburg. They came at the invitation of The Poynter Institute for Media Studies because they know from opinion polls that the American people don't much care for them. They came to talk about how they can improve their credibility with readers and viewers.

It was an unusual conclave because television and newspaper people don't care all that much for each other. But Dr. James David Barber, Duke University political scientist, moderated the discussion and helped this contentious group to reach a measure of accord.

Near the end, Poynter Institute's Roy Peter Clark summed up these "shared values and opportunities for collaboration":

• Help redraw the lines between fiction and non-fiction so that we can convey information with authority, with more emphasis to verification and attribution.

• Cultivate more enlightened criticism of the media from many quarters.

• Collaborate in the training and continuing education of journalists.

Charles Stafford is a national correspondent for the St. Petersburg Times. This article originally appeared in the St. Petersburg Times (January 27, 1985) A1, A10. Reprinted by permission.

- Use each other's media to enhance our efforts to inform the public.
- Fight our image as arrogant and insensitive by revealing ourselves and our reporting and operation to readers and viewers.
- Carry on discussions of ethics in ways that enhance rather than undercut our efforts to serve the public.

There was a good deal of growling at the beginning.

Creed Black, publisher of the *Lexington* (Ky.) *Herald-Leader,* had expressed this concern last May in his valedictory address as president of the American Society of Newspaper Editors:

"The public lumps the printed press and television together in something called the 'media' and makes little if any distinction between the two. The result is that we are blamed for the sins and shortcomings of what television—which remains basically an entertainment medium—calls news."

He came to the meeting at the Don CeSar to defend his premise that "newspapers are being tarred with the brush of TV's transgressions."

Van Gordon Sauter, executive vice president of CBS Broadcast Group in New York, told Black that a Lou Harris poll last year "found that television news enjoys a higher confidence than the print press."

He added: "Candor requires me to note here that television should not be the primary source of information in our society...because of its limitations as a medium....But as they said to me in the gaming rooms of my youth, you play to the strength of the hand you are dealt.

"Under any circumstances, there is an absurd preoccupation today with journalists' standing in the public opinion polls."

"Creed," said Don Hewitt, executive producer of CBS News' *60 Minutes,* "neither of us is so good nor so pure nor so untouched by profit motives that we can afford to be so damned goody-two-shoes. You're not that good, we're not that bad, and cut it out, will you? It's becoming very, very unbecoming."

From that opening, the group moved into a "you-don't-understand-us" phase.

"The television set is a little stage in everybody's living room," Hewitt said. "On that stage they watch Michael Jackson, Joe Montana, Ronald Reagan, John Chancellor, Ralph Renick, Mike Wallace, back to Meryl Streep. It is so different from what you guys do that to try to have some kind of blanket rules for the way the print reporters work and the way television reporters work is ridiculous...."

"We may be bad, but I think it is a miracle that we do as well as we do in a medium that people bought to be entertained. They bought that newspaper to be informed. Everything on television is a show. The news is a show. *Beverly Hillbillies* is a show. The Super Bowl is a show. The assassination of Sadat, when we broke in to do that, was a show. That's the nature of our business."

"Television brings the (news) process into the home and it's not a pretty sight," said Marilyn Berger, former TV and newspaper reporter. "To make an omelet you have to break an egg, and to get news sometimes you have to be not very pretty about it. The least pretty people in one of the biggest stories in America...were the boys who broke Watergate, and they didn't do it by being gentle. They were not television reporters. It's the same process."

Now, you see, the people began to come together, to find a commonality.

"The television is the instrument, a mindless instrument, that has helped create the problem of credibility," said NBC's Chancellor. "I don't say the television journalists do it, I just say the electronics have done it. And the main culprit in my mind is the televised press conference.

"Before television, reporters asked tough questions of people in those news conferences and then went back to the office and wrote the story and smoothed it over. All press conferences before television must have seemed to the readers like very civilized encounters. When television came along...the public suddenly saw people asking nasty questions of the President of the United States. That is simply a technological change. I don't think they (people) like what they see because they are not journalists and they don't know that these sometimes very, very hard questions have to be asked."

"It strikes me," said David Broder, *Washington Post* columnist, "that the distinctions that are relevant are not between press and television, but between good journalism and bad journalism."

Television reporters, he said, are much more visible than newspaper reporters.

"They see Sam Donaldson at work," Broder said. "They do not see Lou Cannon at work. If they saw Lou Cannon or Sy Hersh working on the phone, cajoling, berating, threatening, intimidating, bluffing someone to try to get one more piece of information out of him, they might cite that example. I don't think our behavior patterns are very different."

Now came an "it-isn't-all-the-media's-fault," moment.

"We've been beating up on ourselves when we should devote a little bit of time beating up on the U.S. government," said Chancellor. "This administration has done more to make us look bad, we have walked into more traps as journalists, than I have ever seen before. This administration is hiding more things from the public than any administration I can remember, and when good journalists uncover these things, it is made to look intrusive. When the *L.A. Times* or *The Washington Post* or one of the other big papers comes out with a hell of an exclusive story, an awful lot of Americans now are getting angry about that because we are prying into the secrets of government."

Chancellor said the White House is involved in what he called "the Ronald Reagan cupped-ear gambit."

"The press is deliberately and systematically kept away from him so that when the President walks across the colonnaded walkway near the Rose Garden, all you hear is a bunch of monkeys screaming at him when they could easily have been brought right up and the President could have stood and talked in a conversational tone. That is killing us, and it's not hurting Ronald Reagan one bit and they know it."

Having found common ground and a common adversary, the group now began looking at the common problem of credibility.

Louis D. Boccardi, president of the Associated Press, told the others, "I think there is a serious credibility problem. Anonymity is a serious issue that affects both sides. There is a problem of public perception of unfairness, (invasion of) privacy. We are not going to solve the credibility issue by continuing to bludgeon each other."

Hewitt asked him to define credibility, what it is journalists want.

"We want a greater public acceptance of our role in society and acceptance of the fact that a lot of time we are going to bring them bad news," Boccardi said. "I think we want them to trust and believe what we say. I think we want them to believe that we try to do what we do fairly. I think we want them to feel we are responsive to their news and information needs rather than arrogantly pursuing an agenda that we...set."

"It's not whether we're liked," said Nolan, editorial page editor of the *Boston Globe*. "God help us, who would like us? As H. L. Mencken said in the 1920s, 'Nobody likes the press. We have all the best seats right up front.' Nobody is going to like us, love us, but the matter of whether they believe us or not, that's important."

"I think that at some point across the 35 years when newspapers learned that television was not going to kill them, somewhere in time, the public got a look at us, and they didn't like what they saw," said Eugene Patterson, chairman of the Times Publishing Co. and The Poynter Institute. "Television put us into the living rooms of America, the people who previously had been anonymous by-lines. It worked a particular magic in the breasts of all of us down where the ego resides.

"We all like to be recognized, we like to be known. Television has that fatal attraction. It can make you famous."

Attack journalism was born, he said—"let the public see how big we are and how we can shove people around."

He suggested that journalists take a lesson from President Reagan.

"He can get away with anything he wants to... because the people trust him," Patterson said. "He's a friendly fellow; we're perceived as being very unfriendly people. He seems to wrap himself in the flag at all times; we're regarded as unpatriotic when we question him. We bare our fangs and curl our lips...and the public sees that because we're on television just like Ronald Reagan is. They never see him do that. He cups his ear and listens to Sam yell at him. He smiles. He never gets angry at anybody, and as a result the people trust him. And as a result of our incivility, people don't trust us....

"I think that instead of simply criticizing Mr. Reagan for having gained the trust of the American public, we ought to analyze ourselves in contrast with him. I think we (should) lower our voices a little bit."

And what else? What other things can be done? The group came at last to the search for solutions.

Restricting the use of anonymous sources was high on the list. It can't be wiped out, they agreed.

But Jack Nelson, Washington bureau chief of the *Los Angeles Times,* said: "One of the answers to that...is wherever you can, explain the motive of the anonymous source. If you are quoting a source on Capitol Hill about one of the Reagan administration's programs, you say 'a critic of the program.' "

Nolan said many people come to reporters with information and, after having imparted it, say they want to be anonymous. "My favorite rule is, 'You peddle it, you get your name on it,' " he said.

Most of the group thought there should be more effort to inform readers and viewers of how the news is gathered and why information is sought.

"They want to know what the hell that process is," Broder said. "They are no longer ready to accept that what we are handing them somehow comes down from the divine source and is immutable. They want to know how it got there."

Concern was expressed for intrusion in people's privacy even while it was agreed that much of it cannot be avoided.

"Inevitably there is the response, 'Why are you playing God?' " said John Seigenthaler, editorial editor of *USA Today* and publisher of the *Nashville Tennessean.* "It's very tough to say, 'Well, that's what we do.' But that's true. Stories hurt people and sometimes hurt innocent people. I think we can sell that. I don't think we can sell the idea that we're playing games. Too often, I think, we do play games."

Everyone wanted more accuracy—including spelling and grammar—and more lively writing.

"The only cure for it is to hire people who are professionals and to make sure they remain professionals," said ABC News's Sander Vanocur. "We have got a lot of dogs in television who are not professionals. The emphasis should be on professionalism in both print and television. I think that will go a long way toward resolving the problem, and I don't think you can codify it."

Michael Gartner, president of the *Des Moines Register,* said an eye must be kept on the business ledger.

"You can't be journalistically vigorous," he said, "unless you are financially strong."

And so it came to an end, a pride of lions and lionesses in substantive agreement, which was summed up by Nolan.

In his best Irish brogue, he read a description of the role of the newspaper that was written by Mr. Dooley, pen name for a Chicago writer at the turn of the century.

"The phrase I love: 'Comforts the afflicted and afflicts the comfortable,' " said Nolan. "Whatever our ethics problems are, whatever our credibility problems are, we are going to have no trouble if we remember that it is our duty to 'comfort the afflicted and afflict the comfortable.' "

Believing the News

Friday Morning

JAMES DAVID BARBER: We begin with a challenge and response, hoping for a diagnosis of what the problem is. The title of this whole affair is "News Credibility," that is, the credibility of all of news, as you do it. Later on, I hope we can develop some creative ideas for improvement.

We begin in the hope of John Stuart Mill that out of the clash of truth and error some knowledge might result, with a certain difference of opinion that has emerged, represented first by Creed Black and then by Van Gordon Sauter and Don Hewitt.

CREED BLACK: I'm reminded of one of my favorite Gene Patterson stories. Several years ago, Gene and I were both officers of the American Society of Newspaper Editors, meeting in Washington. For three straight evenings, we found ourselves in the company of then Vice President Hubert Humphrey. By the third evening, at a little reception before our closing banquet where the Vice President was to speak, we all felt that we knew the Vice President quite intimately. And at one point I noticed Gene Patterson had Mr. Humphrey backed up into a corner, pointing his finger at his chest, and giving him all kinds of instructions on how to run the country. Finally in desperation Humphrey said, "Pardon me, Gene, but I think I've taken enough of your time."

I almost feel the same way. You all have read copies of my speech [see Appended Essay 6]. What I want to do in just a few minutes is not repeat the speech and not to do a critique of television news, but to cite a few examples to support my thesis that newspapers are suffering because of a tendency on the part of the public to lump newspapers and television together in something called "the media," and to confuse the two. In my speech, I said that I first became aware of this problem 20 years ago in the so-called "free press, fair trial" issue when the New York Trial Lawyers Association issued a report saying that they thought there was very little hope for any reliance on voluntary restraints by the television industry in the future. That was 20 years ago, and it's interesting to look at the situation today to see if there has been any change, if there has been any restraint.

Last year when I was ASNE president, one of the letters I got came from the editor of the paper in Charleston, South Carolina, Arthur Wilcox, who said that he was sitting there looking at a stack of letters crammed with bitter complaints about the press and its interpretation of the First Amendment. He said that the cause of this outpouring of anger was the arrest of someone charged with a series of rapes, murders, robberies, and violence, and that the police came to the newspapers and the television stations locally and asked them not to publish photographs of the suspect until they had an opportunity to put him in the lineup to see if they could get an identification. Everyone went along with this request, he said, except one television station, which felt compelled to broadcast the picture. The next day, the police came into the television station, arrested all the members of the news staff, marched them off in handcuffs, and charged them with obstruction of justice. He said the prosecutor then staged a press conference denouncing the media in general, and the television station in particular, for standing on First Amendment rights in order to justify a ratings grab. The editor went on to say that, as we would have expected, the newspapers defended the television station's rights to do what they did. But he said, "We're a voice crying in the wilderness. We're drowned in outraged complaints. The public doesn't give a damn about First Amendment rights."

Mr. Wilcox said that, as a result of this TV station's irresponsibility, his mail was filled with complaints about the press. That's "press" in the generic sense. Also note that the prosecutor denounced the media in general.

You say that's a little station back in the backwaters of Charleston, South Carolina. But we had a similar incident recently involving one of the networks, ABC. The *Good Morning America* show had a staff member who contacted the families of six jurors in the

DeLorean case, while they were still deliberating his fate, to try to arrange their appearance as guests after they rendered the verdict. A spokesman for the U.S. Attorney in Los Angeles said the action raised questions of possible jury tampering. The judge felt obliged to reiterate a previous order barring any effort to talk to the jurors. And finally ABC, through a memo to the *Good Morning America* staff, warned after the fact that no such contact should be made without approval from the Broadcast Standards and Practices Department. ABC explained that the *Good Morning America* program is part of its Entertainment Division, not its News Division, a subtlety that would be lost on the general public.

More recently, another thing drew my attention to this problem, the reaction I got and others got after the Grenada incident. Here, for instance, is a letter to the editor of our newspaper: "It's noteworthy that the two groups of people who seem to complain the loudest and longest over the occupation of Grenada were the politicians in Congress and the news media, especially the big three television networks. The news media are elected by nobody. These self-appointed TV geniuses are steamed up because they were kept off Grenada for three days. Just think, we were spared the arrogance of their inspecting, dissecting, analyzing, and criticizing every move, and the passing of their profound judgments while at the same time rounding up all of the anti-American stories they could find."

Here were two references in this letter to the news media, yet there was no further mention of newspapers. All the criticism was directed at TV. The response I got and our editors got was not isolated. Well before I made this ASNE speech, I had a letter from H.L. Stevenson, who at that time was executive editor of United Press International, who wrote this: "In the aftermath of Grenada, I got some pretty hostile reactions from questioners at the Rotary Club in Columbus, Indiana, after a speech. I think the anti-press attitude is running pretty deep in mid-America and elsewhere. A number of TV transgressions are cited, and they in turn tar everybody."

The reaction that Stevenson got and that I got was being seen elsewhere. Here's a little item from the *U.S. News Washington Letter,* reporting on a survey in which 92 percent of its readers who responded, supported the military on the decision to ban correspondents from the Grenada invasion. Some newspapers, the letter said, notably *The New York Times* and *The Washington Post,* came under fire for being too liberal, elitist, and slanting stories. But, the newsletter said, reader lash fell mainly on TV newscasters, notably Dan Rather of CBS. He and others were called, "too opinionated, arrogant, themselves censors." Other readers said, "TV news is show business, aims only for ratings." They also got complaints about hyper hyping of TV specials, as with *The Day After.*

Haynes Johnson wrote in *The Washington Post* that after Grenada he'd been deluged with letters. But it went beyond the military exercise to form a powerful indictment of the press, and suggested a public climate exists for moves that would restrict the way the press operates. Newspapers, Haynes said, could take no comfort from the kinds of comments expressed about them. But, as with this *U.S. News Washington Letter,* he found from his mail that the greatest criticism involves television, its superficiality, its stress on personality, its hype, its penchant for presenting film footage that grabs you. As one reader put it, "I believe your TV cousins are so caught up in superficial visual images that excite and titillate and grab, that they just don't have time to consider to present difficult, even boring concepts. So they don't try to present them at all. Or if they do, they do a superficial, misleading job of it."

Here's another example of the way our critics blast away at the media in generalities and then zero in on TV when they get down to cases. This is a series of five ads some of you may remember seeing from our old friend Herb Schmertz, that ran in 1983. The kicker line on this Mobil Oil series read, "Are the media giving us the facts?" There were five ads in the series. The first was called the "Myth of the Villainous Business"; it dealt solely with the way businessmen are portrayed on TV. The second one was called the "Myth of the Informed Public"; it was a continuation of the theme of the first one, dealing again with TV's portrayal of businessmen. The third was called the "Myth of the Crusading Reporter"; it discussed investigative journalism, both in newspapers and on TV. The fourth, called the "Myth of the Open Airwaves," obviously was devoted exclusively to TV. The final one, the "Myth of the Threatened First Amendment," covered libel suits against both newspapers and TV. So we had five ads in the series, three of which were devoted exclusively to TV, not one exclusively to newspapers.

Finally, here's a letter from a professor of international affairs at the University of Kentucky. His thesis was that there had been major changes for the worse in the media over the years, and he offered the following documentation.

The first enclosure was an article from *Political Science Quarterly* Magazine, in which a political scientist made these points as summarized by this letter writer. "TV news is now highly politicized. The media are no longer merely a mirror held up to society, rather the TV media in particular are active participants in the political process. Third, the increasing dominance of TV news is directly linked to the growing weakness of our political parties."

The second piece of documentation he offered was a *Christian Science Monitor* article on the Lichter-Rothman survey on the television elite, noting that dominant people in TV news are overwhelmingly liberal. And putting these two pieces together, the professor wrote, "We have a mass media not merely assuming the traditional adversarial role toward all political leaders, but rather a mass media and most especially the TV media fully engaged as active, hostile participants against a somewhat conservative president such as Reagan." Once more then, we find the brunt of the media critics' documentation directed not at newspapers, but at the perceived transgressions of television news.

Just recently there was an interview in *U.S. News & World Report* with Ben Wattenberg. Some of you may have read his new book, *The Good News Is the Bad News Is Wrong*. This article summarizes the book.

The final question asked Ben Wattenberg in this interview was, "Why, despite all the positive factors you have cited, is there widespread feeling that the U.S. is not as great a country as it once was?" Answer: A great deal of the blame should go to the media, television especially, for negative reporting. That is what I had in mind when I said that I think that newspapers are being tarred with the brush of some TV transgressions.

One of the problems I see is that what the networks call news is, in fact, a mixture of news, analysis, opinion, and speculation. I'm going to distribute a page here called "The Television News" with items reprinted from the three networks, all taken from the month of November [see facing page]. When I found out that Don Hewitt had subscribed to my paper, I decided I would subscribe to his transcripts. So we read the transcripts for the month of November, picked out some items, and have tried to convert this to newspaper style to give you an idea of what some of this stuff might look like on a newspaper page. All of these came from the month of November with one exception; there's a Chris Wallace story on there about Reagan that goes back to last April, because I happened to see that newscast, and I was so outraged by that one that I wrote for the transcript at the time.

BARBER: Creed, I wonder if you would comment on this mockup, "The Television News," a little bit. What was it that you had in mind?

BLACK: I hope it's self-evident. But one footnote to all of this. In the speech I said that television news isn't always news, but a mixture of news, analysis, opinion, and speculation. CBS is very ably represented here by two eloquent spokesmen. But I was interested to find out from *The New York Times* recently that CBS seems to agree with me. One of those editor's notes by Abe Rosenthal and Seymour Topping said, "The TV View column on page 21 of the Arts and Leisure section today discussing the influence of news anchors asserts, 'In fact there's less news on the *CBS Evening News* than on the other networks. CBS feature

THE TELEVISION NEWS

Vol. 1, No. 1 | November 1984 | 1 page | Priceless

Bush bumbling idiot

By John Severson
NBC News

WASHINGTON — "Thank you. Thank you," Vice President George Bush said.

At the beginning of this campaign, George Bush was given the easiest job of his political career: Say something nice about Ronald Reagan.

"We are number one again, thanks to President Reagan's leadership," Bush said. "You know what the Tigers did to the Padres. That's exactly what Ronald Reagan did to Walter Mondale and that's what's turned this country around.

"... call it cheer-leading, or I hear the criticism a little bit, you know," Bush said.

And when he isn't cheer-leading, he's tackling Walter Mondale.

"Mr. Mondale, the sky isn't falling. The future looks bright," Bush said.

Bush has not tackled the issues. His speeches are filled with slogans.

"More jobs mean more opportunity," Bush said.

He generally has gone to safe places where Ronald Reagan is popular, often to high schools, and to audiences who seem more mesmerized by the fanfare than by Bush himself. In the beginning, he simply ignored Geraldine Ferraro. In the end, he has been patronizing.

"And I don't want to be patronizing. But I do want to say something here," Bush said.

His campaign has been pockmarked with rhetorical excesses and silly mistakes.

"You guys, let me give you a little lecture," Bush said.

(He has) ... become a lightning rod, the subject of a harsh Washington Post editorial.

"I'd rather have a poll showing head-on-head with Ferraro, showing me whipping her, than I would worry about some editorial that's in the Washington Post," Bush said.

Doonesbury has ridiculed him.

Are you personally insulted by the Doonesbury ...," a reporter asked him.

"No. I haven't had time to read 'em," Bush said.

In his mind, the high point of the campaign was the debate. Afterwards, he said he kicked a little ass. That's now become an unofficial campaign slogan.

"I did a little kicking of my own," a woman said.

Campaign officials say party polls show that Bush is more popular than ever and he thinks it's been a very successful campaign. But party insiders are not so convinced. There may have been a political price for his cheer-leading. Nobody knows for certain where George Bush stands on a number of important issues, or if he can stand by himself in 1988.

George Bush lectures reporters

Ferraro up for sainthood

By Bob Kur
NBC News

NEW YORK — (Walter Mondale's) selection was bold and calculated. If he were considered dull, she would add excitement; if he represented the past, she symbolized the future and opportunity. They knew three-and-a-half months ago what they'd say in a commercial this week: "The important thing is not how she's made us feel about her, it's how she's made us feel about ourselves and about the country."

And there's no denying the feeling. People want to see and touch her. She's a hot political property, often seen by more people in a day than George Bush is in a week.

"You are absolutely marvelous. My goodness," Geraldine Ferraro said.

Her style is as unique as her homespun approach on issues. Pentagon spending, for example.

"They had a six, a seven thousand dollar coffee pot that they bought. Now, I wanna tell you, lemme tell you, I'm not just speaking to women here, you know, none of us would spend that kind of money on a coffee pot. Right?" Ms. Ferraro said.

Expectations were high. Mondale was counting on Ferraro's special appeal to help him with special groups of voters, women, parents, and blue-collar ethnics. But Mondale's choice was as risky as it was bold.

"Life, yes; Ferraro, no; life, yes; Ferraro, no," hecklers chanted.

Her position on abortion created diversion. Questions of inexperience persist, though she passed her big test. But headlines about her family finances and her husband's business broke any early momentum and caused her family anguish.

For three months, Geraldine Ferraro has known that win or lose next week, she'd make history — and she has.

Test your telepathic powers with today's news quiz

Editor's note: Think you're pretty smart? Well, read this story. Then try to answer the simple questions at the end of the story. Warning: It's not as easy as it seems.

By Dan Rather
and Rita Braver
CBS News

BUFFALO, N.Y. — A federal grand jury today indicted the giant General Nutrition Company. The charges: marketing an untested product as an illness curing drug in the company's more than 1,000 retail stores.

The government calls it one of the biggest scams in the $180-million-a-year health food industry. Products are labeled as food supplements to avoid federal drug testing requirements, but the products are really sold as drugs, with heavy sales pitches and literature suggesting miracle cures. That is illegal, and today an indictment charged General Nutrition Incorporated, the nation's largest health product chain, with using the scheme to sell Evening Primrose Oil. Federal officials say the identical scheme is used by other companies, too, to push hundreds of such products.

"In the presumed medication which is given to the public with a — a tacit understanding that it can do something that it cannot do is a danger regardless of whether it's water, whether it's harmless. It's a danger because there's the possibility that other treatments will be avoided," United States Attorney Salvatore Martoche said.

General Nutrition had no comment today. Government officials say the real danger is that people often buy so-called food supplements rather than seek legitimate medical treatment. They say this case could discourage a whole range of bogus claims and put an end to futile hopes and wasted money. For example, this Oil of Evening Primrose sold for $21.99.

☆ ☆ ☆

Today's questions: What is Oil of Evening Primrose? What disease is it used to treat? What ill effects can result from using it as a medication?

U.S. mulling attack if crates hold MiGs

Reagan administration warns Soviets not to send jet fighters to Nicaragua

By Dan Rather
CBS News

NEW YORK — U.S. intelligence officials tell CBS News tonight that a Soviet freighter is on its way to Nicaragua, and that it may be carrying MiG-21 jet fighters. Pentagon Correspondent David Martin reports that the freighter left a Black Sea port last September, shortly after President Reagan met with Soviet Foreign Minister Gromyko. The U.S. officials caution that they do not have proof that MiGs are on board, but they do have satellite photographs which show that, at the time the ship was being loaded, a dozen crates similar to those used to transport MiG-21's disappeared from the pier. The Reagan Administration has warned Moscow not to send fighter aircraft to Nicaragua. If those planes are on the ship, one U.S. option being considered is a surprise attack to destroy them.

(Editor's note: That's all, folks.)

Reagan makes no news

By Chris Wallace
NBC News

COLORADO SPRINGS — White House aides were selling Americana today and they had a scene to make a campaign manager weep for joy. The President, 1,000 Air Force cadets, and the Rocky Mountains. And not a protestor in sight.

Mr. Reagan got right in the spirit of things, siding with the Air Force against its service academy rivals.

"The Air Force Academy is 7,250 feet above sea level, and that's far above West Point and Annapolis," the President said.

It was a day for the traditional values the President likes to talk about. He told the cadets they must defend freedom and he mentioned the one program he always cites when talking about the future.

"America's future will be determined by your dreams and your visions and nowhere is this more true than America's next frontier, the vast frontier of space," the President said.

Then Mr. Reagan stood in the sun for almost 90 minutes and shook hands with every one of the 997 graduating cadets, as they accepted their diplomas in two lines. Finally, the traditional end of the graduating ceremony.

The President did not make much news on this trip. But news wasn't the point. What the White House wanted was pictures, so that while the Democratic candidates are seen climbing around toxic waste dumps, Mr. Reagan is seen urging on Olympic athletes and Air Force cadets.

News/views in brief

Tell a vision

No matter whose particular political vision prevails this election year, we don't want to overlook the continuing power of one vision we all agree on, and that is the vision of the American ideal — economic opportunity and social equality, guaranteed by a Constitution of democratic principles. What keeps that vision alive and growing from one generation to another is the vote. Tuesday, your vote decides between the visions of the moment, between Ronald Reagan and Walter Mondale, and your vote ensures the enduring vision of the American ideal.

—Dan Rather, CBS News

Seems like yesterday

Not since the legendary belly dancer Little Egypt who wowed the paying customers in Chicago in 1893 has a World's Fair amounted to a whole lot.

— Sam Donaldson, ABC News

Mondale noble, humble

In these final days (Mondale's) campaign has acquired a Don Quixote style, crossing the country chasing ethnic votes with a kind of nobility and humility and an over-abundance of hope.

— Betsy Aaron, ABC News

Deep waters, Watson

How shall we treat these various leaks and trial balloons that have been sent up from the White House this week?

As one insider said today, don't take it too seriously. At this stage, most of those decisions aren't made until later. So some of what we're seeing is posturing. Some of it maneuvering. Expect major cuts, but Congress will most likely decide exactly what they'll be.

— Dan Rather and Bill Plante, CBS News

Much improvement

There are some straws in the wind, and they are only that, of a renewed interest on the part of both the superpowers in easing tensions. At the White House today Larry Speakes, the spokesman, expressed willingness to provide the Soviets with more details of the American proposal for so-called umbrella talks on arms control. ... That kind of talk at least is very much an improvement on the past rhetoric.

— Peter Jennings, ABC News

And now, a reminder

During a successful reelection campaign the President made a good deal of reminding Americans they are better off now than four years ago. Today, the Catholic Bishops were reminding Americans that not everyone is able to agree.

— Dean Reynolds, ABC News

Bloody good show

And most (Sikhs) did not want Mrs. Gandhi killed either, but things like that always seem to happen in India. It's probably too late now for a political solution, and this will end the way things like this always end in India — never. The blood boils, then spills out, then what's left of it simmers.

— Steve Kroft, CBS News

Today's afterthought

By the way, there is another development out of Washington tonight. Marvin Kalb has learned that Secretary of State Shultz and Soviet Foreign Minister Gromyko have agreed to meet in January to discuss arms control. Marvin has details on that meeting and some new goals that the administration is considering.

— Tom Brokaw, NBC News

Here's what we say 'they' say

Flash! Economists agree

President Reagan, the day after his election victory, reassurance for taxpayers on tax simplification.

"... That it would not result in any individual having his taxes raised by way of a tax reform," the president said.

But economists say that just isn't so.

—Irving R. Levine, NBC News

Experts also agree

Most experts agree that deinstitutionalization (of the mentally ill) was a good idea. It was just poorly executed.

— Harold Dow, NBC News

Hey, critics! Look here!

This was not the first time an American ship has drifted into Cuban waters, but it is the first time a U.S. aircraft carrier was sent in to assist. U.S. officials say it was the only prudent thing to do given the Cubans' unpredictability. But critics are likely to call this a major overreaction to a minor incident at sea.

— Rick Inderfurth, ABC News

Even if asked

Few doctors would say that keeping a sick infant alive for three weeks is a great accomplishment.

— Robert Bazell, NBC News

The tea leaves say

Many experts look for unemployment to go back up in coming months and Americans face other economic problems, too, such as record budget and trade deficits. But the dangers lie mainly in the future and voters don't usually look very far ahead.

— Dan Cordtz, ABC News

Only the shadow knows

There's no question of that and they have on their side Defense Secretary Weinberger who is pushing for a 100 percent foolproof, verification scheme. But it is not believed that that kind of scheme can work, that that kind of an agreement can be achieved. So, the State Department, led by Adelman at this point, is pressing for arms control without agreements. It's a very difficult thing. It's very controversial. But they feel if there's going to be arms control at all, it's going to happen this way.

— Marvin Kalb, NBC News

Name your poison

CBS News

NEW YORK — The EPA said today that Rohm and Hass, maker of the most widely used pesticide for apple trees, has suspended sales. The company will determine if the chemical poses a danger of birth defects in children of farm workers. The EPA says the company found the pesticide caused birth defects when given orally to test animals.

stories have a way of dragging on.' " "In fact," according to this editor's note now, "according to spokesmen for CBS in the Television Information Office, the public relations arm of the broadcasting industry, the question of news content on television is subjective. They say it's hard to distinguish the feature from the news report." I think that's what this mockup page is saying to us.

If crates hold MiGs
Reagan administration warns Soviets not to send jet fighters to Nicaragua
By Dan Rather
CBS News

NEW YORK—U.S. intelligence officials tell CBS News tonight that a Soviet freighter is on its way to Nicaragua, and that it may be carrying MiG-21 jet fighters. Pentagon Correspondent David Martin reports that the freighter left a Black Sea port last September, shortly after President Reagan met with Soviet Foreign Minister Gromyko. The U.S. officials caution that they do not have proof that MiGs are on board, but they do have satellite photographs which show that, at the time the ship was being loaded, a dozen crates similar to those used to transport MiG-21's disappeared from the pier. The Reagan Administration has warned Moscow not to send fighter aircraft to Nicaragua. If those planes are on the ship, one U.S. option being considered is a surprise attack to destroy them.
(Editor's note: That's all, folks.)

The lead story, a CBS story, started the whole Nicaraguan crisis over the MiGs. This is all of it. By the next morning, it had been pretty well knocked down in the newspapers. Interestingly, our editorial page editor was in Central America recently and in Nicaragua. And the correspondents for both *The New York Times* and the *Post* told him that as soon as CBS broke this story, their home offices were on the phone to these correspondents saying, "Gee, we've got to have this story about the MiGs." And they both said, "There aren't any MiGs down here." I don't believe any newspaper would go far with a story like this on such a flimsy basis. At least there would be more of it.

Reagan makes no news

By Chris Wallace
NBC News

COLORADO SPRINGS—White House aides were selling Americana today and they had a scene to make a campaign manager weep for joy. The President, 1,000 Air Force cadets, and the Rocky Mountains. And not a protester in sight.

Mr. Reagan got right in the spirit of things, siding with the Air Force against its service academy rivals.

"The Air Force Academy is 7,250 feet above sea level, and that's far above West Point and Annapolis," the President said.

It was a day for the traditional values the President likes to talk about. He told the cadets they must defend freedom and he mentioned the one program he always cites when talking about the future.

"America's future will be determined by your dreams and your visions and nowhere is this more true than America's next frontier, the vast frontier of space," the President said.

Then Mr. Reagan stood in the sun for almost 90 minutes and shook hands with every one of the 997 graduating cadets, as they accepted their diplomas in two lines. Finally the traditional end of the graduating ceremony.

The President did not make much news on this trip. But news wasn't the point. What the White House wanted was pictures, so that while the Democratic candidates are seen climbing around toxic waste dumps, Mr. Reagan is seen urging on Olympic athletes and Air Force cadets.

The "Reagan makes no news" story came from last April; I happened to see that newscast. I was so struck by it at the time that I wrote for the transcript because I see it as a classical example of a correspondent getting in all his own licks without really giving you much of an idea of what was going on there. The AP and *The*

New York Times and others carried a straight story on what the President said out there. The *Times* even carried the full text of his remarks. But after all of this, we come to the last paragraph, and Mr. Wallace tells us the President didn't make much news.

Bush bumbling idiot

By John Severson
NBC News

WASHINGTON—"Thank you. Thank you," Vice President George Bush said.

At the beginning of this campaign, George Bush was given the easiest job of his political career: Say something nice about Ronald Reagan.

"We are number one again, thanks to President Reagan's leadership," Bush said. "You know what the Tigers did to the Padres. That's exactly what Ronald Reagan did to Walter Mondale and that's what's turned this country around.

"...call it cheerleading, or I hear the criticism a little bit, you know," Bush said.

And when he isn't cheerleading, he's tackling Walter Mondale.

"Mr. Mondale, the sky isn't falling. The future looks bright," Bush said.

He generally has gone to safe places where Ronald Reagan is popular, often to high schools and to audiences who seem more mesmerized by the fanfare than by Bush himself. In the beginning, he simply ignored Geraldine Ferraro. In the end, he has been patronizing.

"And I don't want to be patronizing. But I do want to say something here," Bush said.

His campaign has been pockmarked with rhetorical excesses and silly mistakes.

"You guys, let me give you a little lecture," Bush said.

(He has)...become a lightning rod, the subject of a harsh *Washington Post* editorial.

"I'd rather have a poll showing head-on-head with Ferraro, showing me whipping her, than I would worry about some editorial that's in *The Washington Post*," Bush said.

Doonesbury has ridiculed him.

"Are you personally insulted by the Doonesbury...," a reporter asked him.

"No. I haven't had time to read 'em," Bush said.

In his mind, the high point of the campaign was the debate. Afterwards, he said he kicked a little ass. That's now become an unofficial campaign slogan.

"I did a little kicking of my own," a woman said.

Campaign officials say party polls show that Bush is more popular than ever and he thinks it's been a very successful campaign. But party insiders are not so convinced. There may have been a political price for his cheerleading. Nobody knows for certain where George Bush stands on a number of important issues, or if he can stand by himself in 1988.

Ferraro up for sainthood

By Bob Kur
NBC News

NEW YORK—(Walter Mondale's) selection was bold and calculated. If he were considered dull, she would add excitement; if he represented the past, she symbolized the future and opportunity. They knew three-and-a-half months ago what they'd say in a commercial this week: "The important thing is not how she's made us feel about her, it's how she's made us feel about ourselves and about the country."

And there's no denying the feeling. People want to see and touch her. She's a hot political property, often seen by more people in a day than George Bush is in a week.

"You are absolutely marvelous. My goodness," Geraldine Ferraro said.

Her style is as unique as her homespun approach on issues. Pentagon spending, for example.

"They had a six, a seven thousand dollar coffee pot that they bought. Now I wanna tell you, lemme tell you, I'm not just speaking to women here, you know, none of us would spend that kind of money on a coffee pot. Right?" Ms. Ferraro said.

Expectations were high. Mondale was counting on Ferraro's special appeal to help him with special groups of voters, women, parents, and blue-collar ethnics. But Mondale's choice was as risky as it was bold.

"Life, yes; Ferraro, no; life, yes; Ferraro, no," hecklers chanted.

Her position on abortion created diversion. Questions of inexperience persist, though she passed her big test. But headlines about her family finances and her husband's business broke any early momentum and caused her family anguish.

> For three months, Geraldine Ferraro has known that win or lose next week, she'd make history—and she has.

The items on Bush and Ferraro aired on the same evening shortly before the election on NBC. I think that some person might read a little bias into the contrasting portraits of the two candidates. The Ferraro one is self-explanatory. The questions that were left unanswered in that piece ought to have been apparent to any editor.

The News/Views in Brief were things that struck us as a little bit opinionated. I sometimes wonder when I hear some of these, particularly some by the stand-up correspondents who give their reports and weave their opinion in and out, what place that leaves for our friend John Chancellor and Bill Moyers and others, who are giving what is strictly labeled as commentary.

Today's afterthought

By the way, there is another development out of Washington tonight. Marvin Kalb has learned that Secretary of State Shultz and Soviet Foreign Minister Gromyko have agreed to meet in January to discuss arms control. Marvin has details on that meeting and some new goals that the administration is considering.
—Tom Brokaw, NBC News

I was amused by the way "Today's afterthought" was introduced, starting off, "By the way," the first announcement on this network that Gromyko and Shultz were going to meet.

Here's what we say 'they' say

Flash! Economists agree

President Reagan, the day after his election victory, reassurance for taxpayers on tax simplification.

"...That it would not result in any individual having his taxes raised by way of a tax reform," the President said.

But economists say that just isn't so.

—Irving R. Levine, NBC News

Experts also agree

Most experts agree that deinstitutionalization (of the mentally ill) was a good idea. It was just poorly executed.

—Harold Dow, NBC News

Hey, critics! Look here!

This was not the first time an American ship has drifted into Cuban waters, but it is the first time a U.S. aircraft carrier was sent in to assist. U.S. officials say it was the only prudent thing to do given the Cubans' unpredictability. But critics are likely to call this a major overreaction to a minor incident at sea.

—Rick Inderfurth, ABC News

The tea leaves say

Many experts look for unemployment to go back up in coming months and Americans face other economic problems, too, such as record budget and trade deficits. But the dangers lie mainly in the future and voters don't usually look very far ahead.

—Dan Cordtz, ABC News

Even if asked

Few doctors would say that keeping a sick infant alive for three weeks is a great accomplishment.

—Robert Bazell, NBC News

Only the shadow knows

There's no question of that and they have on their side Defense Secretary Weinberger who is pushing for a 100 percent foolproof, verification scheme. But it is not believed that that kind of scheme can work, that that kind of agreement can be achieved. So, the State Department, led by Adelman at this point, is pressing for arms control without agreements. It's a very difficult thing. It's very controversial. But they feel if there's going to be arms control at all, it's going to happen this way.

—Marvin Kalb, NBC News

Look at the section at the bottom, "Here's what we say 'they' say." As you read through these transcripts, you're struck, or at least I was, by the authoritativeness with which TV reporters and commentators and correspondents cite unnamed experts, and say, "economists agree." I don't think economists agree on anything. Some economists may. "Experts also agree." Who are these experts? This is a problem with newspapers too; it's the problem that we all have, too much dependence on unnamed sources. But in reading these selections, because the TV reports are so brief, I find that you don't get any backup, any substantiation for these assertions in most newspaper stories, which run much longer. In the upper paragraphs, it may say something of this kind, economist or analyst or experts. But then in the body of the article, there will usually be some names attached.

Name your poison

CBS News

NEW YORK—The EPA said today that Rohm and Haas, maker of the most widely used pesticide for apple trees, has suspended sales. The company will determine if the chemical poses a danger of birth defects in children of farm workers. The EPA says the company found the pesticide caused birth defects when given orally to test animals.

You'll find a little box down there in the corner, "Name your poison." Just another one, like the news quiz. Here's an item about a pesticide being taken off the market, and we never find out its name.

DON HEWITT: What's the point of "Today's Afterthought?"

BLACK: The point is the introduction to it, the casual phrase, "By the way."

HEWITT: I notice you conveniently left out the rest of Marvin Kalb's story, which seems to me to be selective editing.

BLACK: No, there was plenty more to the story that Kalb had to report. I'm not complaining about it being too brief. My point was that this is pretty big news, that Secretary of State Shultz and Foreign Minister Gromyko are finally going to meet after all this time, to talk about arms control. And we're told casually by Tom Brokaw that "By the way...."

JOHN CHANCELLOR: The MiGs story broke the first day on the ABC evening news, quoting administration sources, but not by name, as having said that they thought those crates might contain MiGs. The following day in Los Angeles, where the President was staying at the Century Plaza Hotel, a senior White House aide took three reporters to lunch and said, "I have the following information for you." It seems to me that any news organization, having been taken to lunch by this senior White House aide, would have run the story.

BLACK: Well, did this story follow that?

CHANCELLOR: I think Dan Rather's story was on the night of the lunch. And when he says, "U.S. intelligence officials tell CBS News...," I don't know where that came from. But I know our NBC story was out of the White House, directly out of the White House across the shrimp cocktail. The day before was the ABC story. It came out of the Pentagon.

BLACK: Well, the following morning, John, here's *The Washington Post* lead on it. The Bulgarian ship is unloaded, military helicopter, anti-aircraft weapons, and radar in the past 10 days, blah, blah, blah. Finally, way down in here, it quotes the networks as reporting this MiGs business. Even after that, the papers were not reporting it that way.

BARBER: We turn now to Van Gordon Sauter, who has a different point of view.

VAN GORDON SAUTER: My charge was to respond to Creed's speech. I will defer responding at this time to "The Television News," which is a marvelous idea.

Let me begin this morning by telling you the story of two trappers in the Shoshone Mountains, who, after weeks of operating alone, stumbled across one another in the late afternoon. While far happier going their solitary ways, they decided to share camp. There was an abundance of pelts in the mountains, so they were not really competing for economic survival. They did, however, use radically different techniques. And the older trapper, who used a more traditional system, was convinced his younger colleague with the new techniques was going to disperse the beavers and reduce the catch. That night, there was a sudden uproar in the brush, a loud crashing noise. The old trapper shouted that it was a furious and famished bear who had identified the men as a good dinner. He began to put on his boots. The younger trapper, in no way convinced that doom was imminent, asked his colleague, "If that bear's going to eat us, why are you putting on your boots? We can't outrun the bear." The old trapper responded, "You don't understand our situation here. I don't have to outrun the bear. I only have to outrun you."

As it turns out, there was no bear in the brush. It was a lost and indignant elk. The trappers were safe. I suggest to you this morning that Creed Black has not identified a bear, that his attitude is unseemingly selfish, and putting on his boots to run away and abandon television is both unnecessary and unwise. There are indeed disquieting noises in the brush. But I fear that we are conjuring up demons that don't really exist.

The Harris organization since 1966 has been tracking the confidence of the American people in the leaders of our major institutions. Virtually all institutions have shown declines. But I suspect that is the product of a better educated, better informed, and slightly more cynical society. It also has something to do with what is perceived as a highly successful presidency.

And finally, it should be noted that the media has discovered the media. The veils have vanished. But while there is a lot of talk these days about the big media, it is not a tangible experience of the American people. We don't read the daily big media, nor do we watch the big media station. If queried about this so-called "big media," the American people will immediately presume it to be distant and powerful and wealthy, and express reservations about it, just as they express reservations about big religion or big insurance or big education or the big NFL. In the real universe that each individual occupies, there is no big media.

There is, however, a small media, the tangible and reliable media that the individual uses everyday for whatever service or convenience it provides. For most Americans the small media is made up of a newspaper, some television, radio, and magazines. In the minds of those who use it, it performs well. But even in the 1984 survey, Harris found that television news enjoys a higher confidence rating than the print press. The frailties that Creed attributes to television news, frailties that he contends are depressing the image of the press, don't exist in the Harris studies. If anything, those in television could say the figures indicate that the print press is undermining the reputation of television news.

Let me take you to, of all places, Fayette County, Kentucky, home of the city of Lexington, the *Herald-Leader* and its chairman and publisher, Creed Black. They like the media down there. And while Creed may find this fact distressing, I have to report that they liked television more than they liked their newspaper.

Less than two weeks ago, we conducted a telephone interview with a random sample of 670 adults in Fayette County who read the newspaper and watch television. Nearly all those individuals consider the Lexington *Herald-Leader* as their main newspaper. They said quite clearly that television is their principal source of news. If faced with the choice of having only one source of news, more would choose television than a newspaper. Television was the first choice of both those who regularly watch television and those who regularly read newspapers. This cross section of Fayette County also regards television as being more serious and professional. It considers television stories clearer and more understandable. Television also leads newspapers, but by a narrower margin, at being fair in its reporting. They also feel the newspaper is more likely to make mistakes than television. However, they believe that the newspaper is more willing to correct its errors. Perhaps they have just had more experience with newspaper errors. Either way, Creed, you do quite well down there on both sides of the error category.

But if Fayette County is representative of the larger world, and I have no doubt its national sales representative contends that to be the case, then there is encouraging news. A great majority believe the quality of reporting has improved both in newspapers and on television. Eighty-seven percent of the people said television news reporting is fair. Eighty-four percent said newspaper reporting is fair. Seventy-nine percent said newspaper stories and television stories have the facts straight. Discussing stories where they had a personal knowledge of the events, 81 percent of the respondents said television news is accurate, and 79 percent said the newspaper is accurate.

On the basis of this survey, I would say to you, Creed, that it is myopic, self-serving, and ultimately self-destructive to dash about the country proclaiming that television news is damaging the credibility of newspapers. There is no credible evidence of this. If anything, the evidence speaks to the reverse.

Now, for all I know, the newspaper editorial hole may be smaller. Circulation growth may be sluggish in mature newspaper markets, and the time spent reading a newspaper may be slipping. But the answer to newspaper problems of appeal, economics, or ego doesn't rest with television bashing.

We have in this society, through the brilliance and the chaos of the free enterprise system, an ideal system for informing the American public. And there are six tiers to the system. First, radio with its immediacy, then television with immediacy and cinematic revelation, and then the newspapers with their broad information base, and then the weekly news magazines with details and scope and quality writing, and then the monthly publications with the editorial perceptions afforded by widely-spaced deadlines. And finally, the books, with documentation and perspective.

Used correctly, this system would result in a remarkably well-informed society. But the system is not used correctly. Part of the problem rests with our audience and part with the journalists. Candor also requires me to note here that television should not be the primary source of information in our society, both because of its limitations as a medium and because of the way it is positioned within a commercial broadcast system. But, as they said to me in the gaming rooms of my youth, you play to the strength of the hand you are dealt.

Under any circumstance, there is an absurd preoccupation today with journalists' standing in public opinion polls. There is also a paranoid sensitivity to criticism of journalism. The fact that criticism exists today can hardly be surprising. It has been there for years, indeed centuries. In the 1700s, Samuel Johnson described newswriters as "men without virtue, whose compositions required neither genius nor knowledge, neither industry nor spriteliness." In the 1800s, John Quincy Adams said journalists were "assassins, who sit with loaded blunderbusses at street corners, firing them off for hire or for sport at any passenger they select." And in this century, Ben Hecht and Charles MacArthur talked of journalists' peeking through keyholes, running after fire engines like a bunch of coach dogs, waking people in the middle of the night to ask what they think of Mussolini. And for what, the authors asked. So a million hired girls and motormen's wives will know what's going on.

If there is indeed a problem of credibility, and no matter what its size, we only have one directive. Reporters and editors and managers should forget the polls and get on with the assigned tasks: accurate reporting, fair reporting, and reporting that responds to the vital issues and concerns of our audience, its joys and needs, aspirations and apprehensions. If journalistic organizations do as they promise, if they are fair and accurate and relevant, then the public will respect them and use them. And the journalists can abandon their festive seminars of self-immolation.

In closing, I would like to note that, some time ago, I sent to Creed Black the *CBS Evening News* transcripts to which he has so generously referred. He in turn sent me 30 editions of the newspaper. I must admit that I lacked the time or the energy or the curiosity to read them. I sat down recently to write a protest to Dick Reeves about his selective extractions from an *Esquire* article about me in which I discussed television moments. And then it became delightfully apparent that I really didn't care what Dick Reeves said, let alone thought. Indeed, I wrote a letter to an old neighbor of mine in Paris, who will help Dick and his wife Cathy find a pediatrician for their baby when they move there next week.

I suspect those who work in television are increasingly uninterested in the anti-TV bias of many newspaper people. We have read more than our share of newspaper criticism of television news. With notable exceptions, it is done by insipid, ill-informed people who reflect the disdain or fear their editors feel toward the medium. Most of the material is petty gossip or snide derogatory articles, sourced by anonymous insiders. The major issues are rarely ever touched, apparently left for the adults to discuss at their journalistic seminars.

We have a media critic at CBS news. Ron Powers won a Pulitzer Prize for TV criticism while on a Chicago newspaper. He's good. And at times he really hurts. The morning after Ed Bradley's controversial interview with Mayor Washington at the Democratic Convention, Powers delivered a scathing review of Bradley's work. Ed Joyce and I took some scar tissue for that one. But we're man enough to hire a second media critic; Peter Boyer, who has been the Atlanta bureau chief of the *Los Angeles Times*, will be joining us shortly. I once denounced him in front of several hundred people at a CBS affiliate meeting for screwing up the *Times* coverage of a libel trial. But he's an excellent reporter, a superb television critic, and I'm sure that he's going to find many occasions to cane and tar us.

I don't see much of that in the newspapers. A few have ombudsmen who tend to be painfully polite. But I don't see newspapers subjecting themselves, or other publications, to the same scrutiny, the same subjective judgment, passed with such regularity on broadcast journalism. On the basis of the evidence, it is inescapable that the newspaper editors are wedded in a clubby, chummy, self-protectionist cabal to spare one another critical judgment.

Wouldn't it be interesting to see a newspaper editor assign a skilled journalist and writer to be its media critic, to write not just about television but about other publications, including the publication he or she works for? Wouldn't it be interesting to see how the editor would respond to the writer's subjective judgments about the motivation or skills or shortcomings of the paper, its executives, its editors, its journalists, to report all that inside stuff about zits and warts just as they report about television news? I suspect that such a column would be replaced after the first edition by a canned article on how beef stew has an important role in dinner menus during winter months.

In spite of all the separatist and adversarial talk, in spite of whether we like it or not, we print and TV people are in the same boat. My shoes are dry. My end of the boat is not sinking. And despite all the unnecessary agitation at Creed's end of the boat, it's not sinking either. Frankly, at this stage I don't care what Creed and his colleagues say about television news or how loud they say it, just as long as they keep rowing. Thank you.

BARBER: Thank you, Mr. Sauter. Now, Don Hewitt has kindly volunteered to add his views.

HEWITT: I don't have a newspaper. But I have some tape I'd like to show you. A couple of weeks ago Dick Reeves, in a column that ran in the *Los Angeles Herald Examiner*, among other newspapers, was horrified that *60 Minutes* had used a re-creation, even though we told our viewers exactly what they were looking at. I called Dick, and I reminded him that re-creating, drawing word pictures, describing exactly what it was like, are the stock and trade of reporters. Sometimes, if you do it well enough, they give you a Pulitzer. And Dick said, "I know that. But television is different."

I don't need Dick Reeves's or Creed Black's newspaper to tell me that. I knew that 37 years ago when I got out of print and went into broadcasting. Of course, television is different!

Creed, you seem to think that print got there first and has the exclusive right to call itself journalism. Well, I would remind you that town criers were there before the penny press. And maybe we got there first. But it's not worth quibbling about. I'll put it a little more gently than Van Sauter just did. I really don't give two figs what Creed Black thinks of us, just as I'm sure that he doesn't give two figs what I think of his newspaper. It is what it is. We are what we are.

But Creed, if you're not too happy about what you call being tarred with television's brush, I'm not too happy about being tarred with yours. I've been subscribing to the paper. You may get your jollies by saying that television is in no small part show biz. But it's your *Lexington Herald-Leader*, not CBS, that runs Sidney Omarr's Horoscope, Omar Sharif's Bridge Game, Garfield the Cat, Blondie, Beetle Bailey, Mary Worth, Ann Landers *and* Dear Abby, 39 column inches of recaps of television soap operas, and a column called "Miss Manners" that last week told me when it's proper and when it's not proper for someone to bathe naked in my hot tub.

Now, don't get me wrong. I like all that junk. I mean I think that's pretty good stuff. I'm not complaining about the junk. But if I ran all that junk, I wouldn't go around quoting Charlie Kuralt about the "very depressing state of affairs around 6 o'clock in the evening all over America....Urgent electronic music plays, the lights come up and an earnest young man or woman says to a camera, 'Good evening, here is the news,' most often an attractive young person who would not know a news story if it jumped up and mussed his coiffure."

Now, inasmuch as you are so fond of quoting Charles Kuralt on this subject, may I show you some videotape of people "breathlessly introducing on TV what is often not news at all." This time they're your words, not Kuralt's.

[Here followed a five-minute videotape of bits from local television broadcasts. The next few quotations capture the flavor of the tape, cut 80 percent.]

> Good evening. I'm Barbara Hamilton. Walter Cryon has the night off.
> Here's the early morning sequence of satellite pictures that shows clouds advancing through our area.
> One of the best basketball players I've ever seen.
> Okay. Thanks Mike. When we come back John Flanders will have another look at the extended forecast. So stay with us.
> Good evening. I'm Mark Ryan. Well, last night was a real good night for the local teams. But tonight it looks like they had to pay the piper.

HEWITT: There you are, Mr. Black. There they are, a typical sampling of the young men and women who bring you the local news each night in America. Do you know what all those well-coiffed, electronic-music-accompanied people have in common? They all work for Knight-Ridder stations. Every one of those people works for the Knight-Ridder News Organization. That's how Knight-Ridder handles television news.

If you know so much about what's wrong with television news, why don't you take the lead in doing something to shape up the Knight-Ridder broadcast operation? That's your own outfit. The people you've been talking about all over America, a lot of them work for Knight-Ridder stations. I don't mean to be rude, but it's called minding your business. And from what I've seen, there's an awful lot of business for Knight-Ridder to mind.

You're not the only ones. Not too long ago, in writing a follow-up to the Christine Craft story, *The New York Times* said local television news is influenced by show business values. Those journalists who make it on camera as celebrity anchors, and you've just seen them, aren't there simply because of their journalistic skills, but because they lure people to their channels, just as surely as Clint Eastwood lures them to his movies. What *The New York Times* didn't say was that *The New York Times* owns three local television stations complete with what it calls "celebrity anchors."

And if a news director at one of its stations didn't make sure his anchors lured viewers to his channel just as surely as Clint Eastwood lures them to his movies, that news director would soon be looking for a job, and so would every Knight-Ridder news director soon be looking for a job. It's called the Clint Eastwood School of Journalism.

How did we get on your enemies list? I think it's because you think we want to crash your club. Newspaper people have long believed that getting a job at a newspaper was akin to joining the priesthood, that journalists, not our kind but your kind, are not hired but ordained. And that we who broadcast the news instead of printing it are somehow not worthy.

I grew up around New York City at a time that was called the heyday of newspapers. As I recall it, when I was a kid, there were 12 dailies in New York City. Today there are three. New Yorkers know more about their city, more about their state, more about their country, more about the world than they did when those other nine papers were alive. And with the exception of the *Herald-Tribune*, I don't think the death of any one of them was a great loss.

Now, truth to tell, New Yorkers are not better informed today because of television; they're better informed today because of both of us. And it amazes me that you guys don't know that. Van Sauter tried to point it out a minute ago. It is the combination of newspapers and television and radio that's made a better informed country.

If gays have recently come out of the closet, isn't it about time that you guys came out of the city room? There's a whole world out there. And somehow you seem to live within these little warrens, these city rooms, and you don't know what's going on out there. An informed public, if they're smart, will use you and will use us.

Do I think you do a good job of covering the news? You bet I do. Do I think you do a better job than we do? Sometimes yes, sometimes no. If reporters want to go on thinking they're the real journalists and we're only playing at it, that's okay with me, as long as we don't take what they say too seriously.

One of the things I do take seriously is this constant sniping at us by publishers who should know better. The fallout is beginning to poison all of us, high-priced anchor and ink-stained wretch alike. If newspaper publishers spent less time criticizing television news and more time trying to put out a good newspaper, we'd all be richer, and the public would be better served.

Creed, neither of us is so good or so pure or so untouched by profit motives that we can afford to be so damn goody-two-shoes. You're not that good. We're not that bad. And cut it out, will you? It's becoming very, very unbecoming.

BARBER: Thank you, Mr. Hewitt. Could you just be a little more explicit about what we were to perceive from the videotape?

HEWITT: That was a living representation of what Creed talked about in his speech, all these well-coiffed, cutesy-looking youngsters who have electronic-music backgrounds. There they are. That particular reel was made up of the digest of the local news shows on five Knight-Ridder stations.

BLACK: Following my speech, one of the news directors of one of the TV stations in Lexington wrote a letter making that same point, that Knight-Ridder has these local TV stations. I don't see that it matters. I'm not responsible for Knight-Ridder's television stations. I'm responsible for the publication of the *Lexington Herald-Leader*. And Van, I thank you for that market research. I want to get more of that.

HEWITT: I'm saying that electronic music and those well-coiffed people bring in a lot of the revenue that pays a lot of the salaries of a lot of people in the Knight-Ridder organization who go out and make speeches about how terrible that is. Why don't they clean up their own house before they go out and talk to the world?

EUGENE PATTERSON: To get Don's point, you have to know that the *Lexington Herald-Leader* is owned by Knight-Ridder.

HEWITT: Oh, I thought everybody knew that.

BARBER: Well, now, Creed, would you like to comment on that? Or do you agree with what's been said?

BLACK: Well, I think that much of it is irrelevant. We have one of our vice presidents, Larry Jinks, here. And perhaps he'll take the word back to Miami that Don Hewitt thinks that I should be put in charge of all of our television stations.

Don and Van both, I think if you'll read my speech a little more carefully, I certainly tried to acknowledge the shortcomings of newspapers. I agree with you that the public is better informed because we have television news than it was when we didn't have it. I think that all of us in this business want to see the public get as much information as they can from all sources. I do think newspapers could be better. As you said, television news can be better.

All I was doing, and I tried as honestly and faithfully as I could, was to report on what I felt was a very significant public reaction that I had picked up in my year as ASNE president. We can talk about all kinds of polls and statistics. Van, I'm not too hung up on the criticism; I think it goes with the territory. I said in my speech the same thing you did, that criticism is as old as the institution itself. You can go back to Thomas Jefferson and see what he said about it. I think one of the differences is they didn't have public opinion polls in those days, and the editors didn't know how poorly they ranked.

But it was significant to me in that year that I kept getting this same feedback all the time, that when people would complain about the press and the media, I'd say, "Well, what do you mean? Can you cite specifics?" And nine times out of 10 they'll come back to television. That was the point I was trying to make.

I have some positive suggestions to make. I think we want to come out of this conference with something useful. David, maybe I should save those suggestions until some more appropriate time?

BARBER: I think that might be best. Let's diagnose and then cure.

BLACK: Well, one last point. Van, for all of your statistics on your market research on Lexington, I would say that if the *Lexington Herald-Leader* were not published this morning or tomorrow morning, the television and radio stations there would be hard pressed to get their daily product out. In the morning, if I haven't read our paper, I can listen to the morning radio or even the five-minute local newscast interspersed with your morning network program, and I can tell you right then what's on the front page of my paper, because that's where that stuff came from. We've got three television network stations in Lexington, plus a good public station, plus half a dozen or more radio stations, and those all combined don't have a news staff as large as ours. I think we are doing a better job than television and radio combined.

HEWITT: You're doing a different job. That's the whole problem here. You're equating different with better. Let one big story happen in America right this minute, and everybody in every newsroom in America is sitting in front of a television set. So it's a two-way street. Go to a political convention, and what are political reporters doing, except the good ones like Marty Nolan and David Broder? They're sitting there watching television. It's a two-way street. We complement each other.

BARBER: We can now open it up to a broader discussion and comments from others here. Anyone like to join in?

SANDER VANOCUR: I'm trying to put this in some kind of historical perspective which precedes Spiro Agnew, of whom Gene McCarthy, when asked his reaction, said, "I agree with everything he says. I just deny him his right to say it."

In your speech, you mentioned the 1968 convention. I think that was a great crossover point, and I still don't know why. I remember I had to substitute for John at a speech before some Hughes Aircraft executives right after early September 1968. And I was assigned the blame for what happened in Chicago. I tried to explain that the closest I had got to it was when I dropped John off at the Blackstone Hotel on Tuesday night, that what they saw on their television sets was what I occasionally saw when I came in to get the batteries recharged. They would not take that. It's as close I've ever come to being booed off the public platform. Somehow in '68, there was a crossover line. It was directed against us, but you were caught up in the backwash, too.

You didn't develop that idea in your speech very much, though you cited it. And I'm curious as to why not.

BLACK: Well, I don't know that I look at it quite the way that you do, Sandy. The only point I was trying to make in my speech was that I think that was a period when people were looking for scapegoats. The same thing happened in the Vietnam situation. I don't look at it as some historical watershed, because this criticism of the press goes back forever. The thing that puzzled me, that made me raise the question was that I think newspapers are so much better. I quibble again over the word "better," Don.

But John and Sandy and others here have had experience in Chicago journalism, and know how flamboyant Chicago papers were, how much yellow journalism there was, and in the not too distant past. I don't think that we have nearly as much journalism of that kind in the country today. Since World War II, in almost every case where there's been head-to-head competition, the newspaper that has done the best is the one that has taken its responsibilities most seriously to inform the public, to do what you said, Don, to realize that there's a world out there of people who want to be informed, and to try to inform them. The papers which have tried to compete with television on its own terms as an entertainment medium are the ones that have gone down the tubes.

DAVID LAVENTHOL: I worry about legislation that would limit the way in which we do business, both newspapers and television. But in general, a good percentage of the public sees nothing wrong with legislation to require print journalism to do a better job than it's doing now. I think that's very serious.

The media, however you slice it, have accumulated much more power and much more influence over what's happening in our society than they ever had before, even in the days when there were 12 newspapers in New York. And part of it is the intrusiveness and national presence of television. But part of it is the fact that in most communities, newspapers have near print monopolies, even as here in St. Petersburg, or where I am up on Long Island. There are very few cities where there isn't just a single newspaper. In Lexington, Kentucky, there's just a single newspaper. I think people feel frustrated and lacking in alternatives in how they can communicate.

The reaction, particularly of the television people here this morning, is typical of the way that people in the media react when facing criticism. People in television and people in newspapers pull out their howitzers, and they fire away. I don't think that's going to get at the kind of problems we ought to be discussing here. It tends to infuriate the party that isn't represented here, the people who read and view us, who can't understand why we have to get into these positions rather than dealing with the real concerns that affect their lives.

BARBARA MATUSOW: Sander Vanocur raises the historic perspective, but it's really worthwhile to go back quite a bit farther than 1968. I'm sure a lot of you remember the press and radio wars of 1933 and 1934, in which the American Publishers Association got together and agreed that they would no longer run any radio schedules unless it was treated as paid advertising. Subsequently the Associated Press, United Press, and International News Service got together and decided they would sell no news whatsoever, or let any of their news whatsoever be used by radio stations.

I don't think it was any accident that this happened in 1933. In 1932, radio had a smashing success reporting the election returns. Radio was also finally beginning to be perceived as an economic threat to newspapers. It was taking away listeners. More importantly, it was taking away advertisers. So the newspapers got together to counter that threat.

Interestingly enough, CBS started its own news gathering organization at that time. It hired stringers in all the major cities and started doing a pretty nice job, and that brought down really much more serious repercussions, scared CBS, scared NBC. And they ended up agreeing that they would not run any news bulletins longer than five minutes in length. They had to be at 9:00 in the morning and 4:30 in the afternoon. Commentators could not use any material that was less than 12 hours old. They were supposed to speak about generalities. A little service was gotten up to feed wire material to broadcasters. No item could exceed 30 words in length. The broadcasters were so frightened that they participated in this agreement. However, it didn't last very long. Everybody started breaking the embargo, and so forth. But that's an old and not very honorable war. It goes back a long way.

Don Hewitt makes a good point about the sanctity of the newspaper club, but I don't think that you can ignore the whole subject of the economic threat. This hate/hate relationship, even in terms of how it's been phrased this morning, seems to be more in terms of newspapers attacking, and TV defending. I think newspapers are the ones that perceive the threat and attack television.

BARBER: I discern three positions emerging. One, that there's no serious credibility problem. Second, from David Laventhol, that there is a serious problem for both print and TV, for all media. And third, that there is a serious problem, and it's the fault of television but not of print.

TONY SCHWARTZ: I'd like to take what David Laventhol was talking about a step further. I have been on both sides of this, in fact, on three sides in a sense. I've been a newspaper reporter; I've been a television critic; and I have, albeit very briefly, been a television journalist/critic. In my experience as a critic at *The New York Times*, I have dealt before with Don Hewitt's and Van Sauter's increasing hostility to the kind of criticism that they feel is being leveled at them. With the perspective of two years away from having been a critic of what it is that they do, I find myself much better able to understand what their backs are up about, while not always being sympathetic to it. They represent the most vocal at this point of many, many television journalists who are feeling what they feel. Number one (and this obviously focuses first on *The New York Times*, where I had the direct experience, but I think it applies rather generally), newspapers are generally disposed to dislike television news. I think the economic argument is in fact the first one. There is the sense of a very direct threat to the survival, fair or not, of newspapers from television.

The second point is a psychological one. Unfortunately, most newspaper editors are genuinely ignorant about television news. Though decreasing numbers of people in television grew up working in newspapers, almost no newspaper editors have ever worked in television.

In general, putting aside the top 10, 15, or maybe 25 newspapers in this country, very few newspapers have much more to be proud of than the comparable local news operations in their cities and towns. They are very often substantively in the same game. They're not in the game of righteous journalism and dissemination of information. They're in the business of making money, which is part of the business of television.

Now, so much for having been sympathetic to the television people's argument. I reject Van's point about the fact that CBS has chosen in hiring Ron Powers to do in some way vastly more than most newspapers are doing in terms of taking a critical look at themselves. It seems to me from watching Ron Powers, that by and large (with no disrespect to him, I think he's a very good journalist), I don't think that his basic impulse is to look closely at CBS. I think that it is rare. I don't mean that he avoids CBS, but I think it is rare that he takes it on so directly. I think you've chosen a very unusual situation in Ed Bradley.

I feel precisely the opposite, that not only does television need more criticism, but newspapers also need more. What is lacking in newspapers and on television in regard to the public, who after all matter most in this, is a sense that newspapers or television equally are willing to look self-critically at themselves. We sit at these conferences and argue with each other. But we're not here with the public.

The New York Times now runs, for the first time as far as I'm aware, these short and rather obscure buried editor's notes that rarely take account of what it is they've supposedly done wrong in any substantive way. I rarely see a newspaper that does anything more than make the simplest and most obscure correction. I rarely, if ever, see the national evening newscast or the local newscast take account of what they do wrong when they do something wrong, even if it is only an error of judgment and not of fact.

Now, I want to make one final point. I believe that the public would not be offended or believe the media less by seeing newspapers and television address their errors more openly and more freely, but rather that they would have precisely the opposite reaction. First of all, they're extremely interested in the process, in how news gets gathered. It gets gathered imperfectly, usually under terrific deadlines. They are sympathetic to the idea that mistakes are made, and they are hostile to the arrogance which I believe exists equally in television and in newspapers.

In this conference, what we have to gain is the idea that there can be a dialogue, not a finger-pointing but a dialogue, towards bringing about the kind of willingness to admit errors that I believe ultimately will increase credibility.

MARILYN BERGER: We've all finally hit on one of the real problems, and I'll call it by its name, and that is "jealousy." Having made the crossover, having been in print and been stepped on, kicked by camera-

men, and upset by television reporters, and then having gone into television and been stepped on the print
reporters, I know what goes on from the lowly perception of a reporter, which is a long way from what a lot
of you have been doing for some time.

I was just thinking of something the major editor
of a major New York newspaper said to me during the
newspaper strike. I was in the position of putting on
a little show on public television to replace the
newspapers for the duration of the strike, to inform the
public of what was going on while the newspapers were
black. This editor of a major newspaper had, I'm sure,
a mission to inform. It's been his life; he loves to inform the public. His reporters would come onto my
little show, and they would report the little things they
knew about New York, about culture, about various
things. And suddenly they were no longer allowed to
appear during the strike; they could not come on my
show. And this major editor, whose mission to inform
is legendary, said to me, "I don't like your show." And
I said, "Why?" And he said, "You make them miss us
less." He didn't care about informing at that point. He
cared about getting his newspaper back.

Well, I understand that he wanted to have his
newspaper back on the stands. But I also think that
he did have a certain mission, that he might have
allowed us to be informed. Well, several years later,
I ran into him. He was sitting in Twenty One, watching
the television set with all his other editors around him,
and the MacNeil-Lehrer-Woodruff show was on. And
I went over to him, and I said, "If it had been one of
your reporters, would you have allowed him to be on
this show?" And he said, "Get away from me."

Well, it's funny. We laugh about it together, but
there is so much jealousy between the two. It is so unnecessary because both sides have so much to add. Now,
having said that, I'd like to get to David's question of
credibility on both sides, then we can be statesmanlike.

LARRY JINKS: I was struck by how far Van
Sauter and Don Hewitt came to tell Creed Black that
they really didn't care what he thought of them. With

the passion and effort that they put into it, I tremble to think how they would react if they truly cared.

The fact is that they care very, very much, as they showed us. The fact is that all of us care very, very much what people think about what we do, the standards of what we do, the effect of what we do. I agree with Marilyn Berger and David Laventhol and the thrust of what you're doing: we're headed toward talking about credibility as a problem for all of us.

There are some serious ways in which television affects the credibility problems for all of us, ways that have more to do with the nature of television than with the character and quality of the people who run it. The ante has been upped a great deal from 1968 on, partly because of what's happening in the world, but partly also because of the immediacy of how television shows events of that sort. I hope that as we lob grenades back and forth, and as we recognize the jealousy that Marilyn Berger was talking about, that we're able to get beyond that contention and talk about the serious issues that grow out of Creed's speech. Those issues don't have anything to do with our pettiness or the pettiness of television people, but with the nature of how people get their news and the inevitably of certain things. We cannot put the milk back in the bottle, even if some of us who are basically newspaper people, look back with some joy to the day when almost everybody got their news from newspapers. That's not going to happen.

BARBER: I want to keep calling on different people, but I'm going to ask David Broder and John Chancellor to be thinking while the rest of us are talking.

CHANCELLOR: We can't think and talk at the same time?

DAVID BRODER: Can we do it alternately please?

BARBER: No, I hope to get some definition of our problem here and its emerging dimensions. Perhaps from your different experiences, you could do that, perhaps others too. Mike Gartner, perhaps that's what you were going to do.

MICHAEL GARTNER: First of all, I'd like to say, if you took all the money spent on this conference and preparation of special newspapers and tapes and surveys and everything, we could have put it all together and bought the *Des Moines Register* and *Tribune* companies.

Second, I'd like to ask Creed a simple question: do you believe that the First Amendment applies to television?

BLACK: Yes.

GARTNER: Then your speech is not constructive, and your thesis is not constructive. As I told you at the time, I basically disagree with much of what you say. By going around as the president of the American Society of Newspaper Editors and a respected figure in the industry, and repeatedly attacking television, you are feeding thoughts that the public might have, and lending credence to things that probably aren't true, and therefore undermining the whole First Amendment for television and for the press. I didn't see you or anyone else speak out 10 or 12 years ago when cigarette ads were banned on television, one of the worst things that ever happened to the First Amendment. Now there's a movement to ban cigarette ads in newspapers; there's a movement to ban liquor and beer ads on television. And David mentioned other issues in the Reagan Administration. You're just spending all your time, and we're all spending all our time on the wrong issue. We're tending to undermine our own credibility by going around saying, "The sky is falling, the sky is falling," when there's a bigger problem out there that nobody seems to be paying any attention to.

MARTIN NOLAN: We've had two terrific props, neither one of which would qualify to get into print or on the air. I don't think you could put a story like that

on *60 Minutes;* I don't think we'd print this mockup.
I feel like a hockey referee, and I like television. I rely
on television to keep newspapers honest. And of course
I love newspapers. As I said to Dave Burgin, you get
two minutes high-sticking on this caper, and no Lady
Byng trophy for you, Hewitt.*

HEWITT: Those were his people you were looking
at, not mine.

NOLAN: I heard a couple of things said that do call
for a whistle. I heard Creed Black say that television
news weakened political parties, which had already
been weakened; I think that is a crock. Suburbia
weakened political parties. Suburbia, the greatest mass
migration in history, was not covered by American
newspapers, by and large. It happened in the 1950s,
and John Cameron Swayze was there. I don't think
television had anything to do with weakening political
parties generally.

The real problem with television news is that it
leads off with a story from an unnamed source. But
we're responsible for the heavy use of unnamed sources.
If television weren't around to keep the print medium
honest, we would have just more and more unnamed
source stories. Our State Department guys and White
House people would just give you more. You wouldn't
know the name of anyone in the government. We've
got a President who loves to have all these anonymous
aides going around giving dope stories, and we all know
every reporter falls for it. They say, "Well, gee, if I can't
use the unnamed source in the county commissioner's
office, we can't get the story in." We say, "Oh, sure
Roscoe. We'll let it go this time."

I do think that there's a positive aspect of the print
medium. Despite all our faults, the Janet Cookes and
the R. Foster Winans, I do think there's a trend towards
improvement. Mr. Sauter quoted *The Front Page,* but

---

* *A trophy given by the National Hockey League to "the player
adjudged to have exhibited the best type of sportsmanship and
gentlemanly conduct combined with a high standard of playing
ability."*

I think there's a world of difference between David Broder and Hildy Johnson. But in the television business, I shudder a bit when I look at the progression, if you can call it that, from Edward R. Murrow to Phyllis George. I wonder what is happening there; I'm not entirely comfortable with it as a TV consumer. But I must say, there's nothing on television as bad as the *National Enquirer*, and I hope nobody calls on me to defend Rupert Murdoch.

JACK NELSON: I agree with the comment that Don Hewitt and Van Sauter both came an awful long way to say that they weren't concerned; it's kind of like saying, "I am not mad!" But there's a tremendous amount of sensitivity on both sides, newspapers and television. Van Sauter really put his finger on a good point when he talked about the big media, because it is the big media that's mostly involved.

It reminded me of a few years ago when I was at a Gridiron meeting, and I was sitting there with Otis Chandler and Jerry Ter Horst, who was the outgoing president of Gridiron. The incoming president was Al Cromley, whose boss was sitting at the table there, head of the Oklahoma City Times Publishing Company. And Cromley asked Ter Horst, "When you introduce him, if you could mention, without it being too embarrassing, that he is head of the Oklahoma City Times Publishing Company, which also includes two television stations, three radio stations and an oil company, I'd appreciate it." And so Jerry gets up and introduces him, and he said, "Head of the Oklahoma City Times Publishing Company, which is not only the two newspapers, but also three television stations, two radio stations, and last, but not least, an oil company." And Otis Chandler turned to me and said, "It still isn't very big."

I do think that most of the public's animosity is aimed not just at the networks but also at the big media. They feel distanced from the media. The real problem here is one of credibility for us all, and we are all in the same boat. I disagree that television doesn't have the same First Amendment rights; I think they do have them. We ought to talk about that as this conference goes on.

CHANCELLOR: I have a parenthetical remark I'd like to put in here: on many weeks, Jack Nelson is on television more than I am.

HEWITT: Creed's big point is that broadcasters give the word "journalism" a bad name, that you can lay all your problems at our feet. But you guys are as much in the broadcast business as you're in the newspaper business. There are very few big news organizations or newspapers in this country that don't also own television stations. They're all in the same business. I would like to ask Larry Jinks, when you heard Creed making that speech about all of this terrible stuff on television, did you realize he was talking about you and your company?

JINKS: I didn't think in those terms. I'm essentially a newspaper man, and our company is over 90 percent a newspaper company. I'm not surprised that you're able to use our television stations in the film clip, but I certainly don't think they are an argument against Creed's speech.

HEWITT: At no point in that speech did he ever say, "I work for a company that owns five television stations."

JINKS: Why should he have said that? What is the point in his saying that?

HEWITT: Well, maybe the whole point's missed. It's a very important part of the problem that newspapers today have all gone into broadcasting.

JINKS: He was speaking in his capacity as president of the American Society of Newspaper Editors. It would have been remarkable if he had stopped to say, "And parenthetically I work for a company which also owns five television stations." Barbara Matusow's earlier point, that a lot of the hostility is economically motivated, is largely not true today. If Creed or I or somebody from Knight-Ridder is critical of television, obviously we're not that way out of economic motivation. I don't think there are very many people who sit there and develop their opinions about television because they perceive it primarily as an economic threat to the newspapers.

BARBER: Larry, as a practical matter, suppose that Knight-Ridder really wanted to reform those stations and have them do things very differently, could that happen?

JINKS: It absolutely could happen. My own responsibilities are with the newspaper division of Knight-Ridder, but we make decisions about the kind of people we want running our institutions. We set standards. I certainly would not argue that we are not ultimately responsible for the quality and content of those stations. I think we are.

HEWITT: It may be right someday for all the great journalistic minds in Knight-Ridder to get together and say, "How can we make our broadcast product better than this junk that Creed talked to the newspaper editors about?" But that just seems to go right over everybody's head. It's got nothing to do with it.

JINKS: Don, do you think their junk is any different?

HEWITT: No, no, no. I could have taken 300 television stations. I took five from Knight-Ridder to make a point: it all looks the same. I don't think it's so bad, incidentally. I know you guys do, but I don't really think it's all that bad.

SAUTER: I'm not convinced those Knight-Ridder television stations are bad performers. In terms of their function, they might be quite good. This may be one of the most repellent thoughts that you've experienced in many years: if you, Creed, suddenly found yourself running the television side of Knight-Ridder, I suspect that you would be turning out television news products fairly close to what these people are doing. And this may be equally repugnant to you and to Don: I tend to think that if Don ended up running the paper in Lexington, which is a fine newspaper, he would probably attempt to run it exactly as you do.

Another point, we are not in economic competition with newspapers. If you go from market to market, you'll find that there's been very little fluctuation in terms of the share of market that broadcasters and print people have. It's fairly static and has been static for the last several years. There's a lot of movement now within the print side because of new forms of publications. And there's some movement within our business because of competition from independent television stations. But we're really not competing fundamentally for those same dollars.

And finally, it's fun to come down here and beat up on Creed Black. When I was a reporter for him at the *Chicago Daily News*, he used to beat up on me, and this is the one moment of retribution I've had in 20 years.

There are a lot of major problems out there for both of us, and I'm not personally convinced that the credibility problem is as large as it's made out to be. I am far more concerned about the long-term ramifications of losing First Amendment coverage for advertising. If we lose in the networks on the beer and wine, you guys are going to lose on cigarettes, and cigarettes are going to be out of your newspapers. If they get the cigarettes out, then they're going to get the beer and the wine out. Now I don't know what that means to newspapers, but I know it means a lot in our business.

There are forces at work out there that are far more dangerous to our long-term effectiveness and survival than the issue of credibility. We don't do any research for the network news organization outside of some research on the effectiveness of advertising and promotion, so we have no network research base. But we do a tremendous amount of research for our five company-owned television stations, and credibility is not a problem.

The problem that television has is arrogance, not the arrogance that we normally think of, that anchor people are arrogant or have too much power. The

arrogance is manifested on our viewers' parts that they
don't have access to talk back to the media. "Arrogance" is a word that the pollsters lay on it, but that's
really the feeling. In terms of credibility, the credibility
is really quite high.

NELSON: Do you really think that the credibility of the media is high in this country?

SAUTER: I think it's far higher than it's made out
to be.

NELSON: As far as arrogance is concerned, TV
news comes across as arrogant. This morning, for example, the news programs had *TIME* magazine editors
Henry Grunwald and Ray Cave on, reacting to the
Sharon trial verdict, and I thought both of those guys
came across as very arrogant. Both of them were saying, "We really haven't made any mistakes. We're going to try to be correct and accurate, and we always
have been and will continue to be. We're going to keep
this same newspaper reporter, this magazine reporter
the jury found had been guilty of negligence." I can
say the same about things I've seen concerning CBS
and the Westmoreland trial. And CBS never seems to
concede that they did anything wrong on *60 Minutes,*
in some of their ambush interviews and so forth. I have
seen very little in the way of recognition on the part
of television, CBS or the other networks, that they have
made mistakes; and they have. It's true that
newspapers frequently don't make concessions about
their own mistakes. I also think, if you've got a
credibility problem with the public, it's going to hurt
you on the First Amendment question.

SAUTER: The vast majority of people, when they
discuss the media, discuss their own personal universe.
And that's their daily relationship with it, and they
feel very well served by it.

NELSON: Just as they like their individual con-
gressman, but they don't like Congress as whole, and
they don't trust Congress as a whole.

BERGER: If Jesse Helms takes over CBS, I wonder if you'll get cigarette ads back on television.

HEWITT: You've brought up Ray Cave and Henry Grunwald. Remember the famous *TIME* magazine story of "Journalism under Fire?" [See Appendix, Essay 3.] Remember the picture of Mike Wallace and Westmoreland and all the things we did wrong? Caption: "Fairness can be sacrificed when reporters go into a story with a preconceived thesis. CBS's Mike Wallace confronted General Westmoreland about allegedly misleading military reports for the Vietnam War." Big part of their story. I defy anybody to find one word in there about *TIME*'s lawsuit with Ariel Sharon. I called Henry Grunwald. I said, "You've done a whole thing on journalism under fire, and you have never mentioned your own lawsuit." And he said, "Well, I didn't think we should go into our things in this piece." You talk about a vendetta between the print and television, there it is, right there.

LOUIS BOCCARDI: I know the schedule calls for a certain period of mogul-bashing, but if there were any members of the public here, and we hadn't locked the doors, most of them would have walked out by now. There is a serious credibility problem; different aspects of it exist in different degrees for television and for print. But anonymity is a serious issue that affects both sides. And Marty, I don't think television is keeping print honest on that. It's a problem for both of them, a problem with public perception of unfairness, of privacy.

If you show the least little bit of concern or humanity as an editor, you have to put up with untold grief from your peers for trying to be a little bit, I won't say "kind," but just to show some understanding for the privacy issue. Television has exposed the way reporters operate, and that's a huge piece of the problem. Putting the newsgathering process on television is an inevitable part of what we do now. You can make Creed's case, and, as Don and Van have done, you can make television's case. I don't think we're going to solve the credibility issue by continuing to bludgeon each other.

The problems are common in different degrees because of the different media. That press crowd on the lawn digging up Allen's rosebushes is more of a problem now, and it's seen now by the public because of the mass that's involved in television. When there were nine reporters there with a pad and pencil, it was different. So the problems have changed because of the two media.

BLACK: I don't want to appear as simple-minded as I think I'm being presented. Don said a minute ago that he understood my point to be: if it weren't for TV, we wouldn't have a credibility problem. I don't believe that at all. I quoted somebody in my speech as saying that "news people are...fallible at their worst, some can be careless, stupid, insensitive, lazy, arrogant, biased, and vindictive. Most galling of all, they can be obdurately unrepentant."

But I agree fully that we've got some credibility problems of our own. We've got image problems, and I have some suggestions later on to make that apply to newspapers and television. The media are different in some respects, but I don't presume that our problems would disappear if there were no such thing as television.

Because I think historically newspapers are so much better, it puzzled me as I went around the country and read all of these surveys and listened to people. I wondered why, if we have done it so much better, has our image suddenly gone down?

I also mentioned the loss of confidence in all of our institutions, and I think some of that is rubbing off on the newspapers. But there's one new element in the whole picture with respect to newspapers, and that is television. I don't mean to say that we don't have any problems of our own.

PATTERSON: We've all pranced out upon the stage and dazzled each other with predictable adagios and arabesques that we've all seen and heard before. What I hear from Lou Boccardi is a quiet invitation to speak the unspeakable, to suggest that perhaps one of our credibility problems rests right here, that the enemy may in fact be us. I haven't heard anybody really rushing forward to volunteer that idea yet.

But I think Sandy Vanocur is right. At some point across this 35 years, newspapers learned that television is not going to kill them economically. Somewhere in that time, the public got a look at us, and they didn't like what they saw. Television put us into the living rooms of America, we who had previously been anonymous bylines. It worked a particular magic in the breasts of all of us, down where the ego resides. We like to be recognized; we like to be known. Television has that fatal attraction: it can make you famous, in your hometown, or in the nation. Every one of us around the table at one time or another has been seduced by that because we like to be famous. In the process of getting famous, we get our faces known. Once those faces get known, we begin listening to what Lou Boccardi just called "the rules as laid down by our peers."

Don Hewitt, God bless him, early on laid some of those ground rules aside, used not simply adversary journalism, but attack journalism. Let the public see how big and strong we are, and how we can shove people around. It carried right over into the print media. Maybe it came from the print media into television; I don't care about placing the blame. I'm saying that television has the instrument that magnified it and amplified it, and created in the breasts of all of us, television and print alike, this demon who says, "I've got to be tougher and throw harder balls than Joe over here at the next desk to really get ahead."

We lost our way when we lost the civility and the humanity, the fun-ness and the fairness that goes with a good cop. On the police beat we all learned early that you've got good cops and you've got mean cops. Around the city rooms, one of the earliest detestations that a young newspaper man or woman gained was the mean cop, the guy that you hang a badge and a gun on, and he loves to push people around. The public sees us that way, I'll bet. They give us a pencil and a press card, and it's our license to shove people around.

I think this credibility problem is a little worse than Van Sauter said. It may not be a grizzly bear out there in the brush, but if it's a moose, he's mad, and I think it's because he doesn't like the way we operate. He doesn't like to see Ray Cave and Henry Grunwald saying, "We did no wrong." They *did* do wrong. CBS made a hash of the Westmoreland thing. The public sees that. Thank God that we've got a jury in the *TIME* case who recognized what the law said. But I don't think people, having seen us, like us. I wonder how much of that is our fault, and what can we do about it?

VANOCUR: I started on a very high note in journalism, thanks to Gene Patterson. I was working for nothing at the United Press in London while I was in trouble with my labor printer at the *Manchester Guardian*. The arrangement was that I could go to Spain after six months if I learned Spanish, and Patterson didn't like me because I didn't type well.

PATTERSON: He couldn't type.

VANOCUR: Then one day, when I was rewriting the rags, I wrote that Western astronomers would get a better angle on today's eclipse of the sun than their counterparts in the Soviet Union. Patterson came over and hugged me and said, "You're going to be just wonderful at UP, Vanocur. You've got the anti-Communist lead and the total eclipse of the sun into the first paragraph." That's the high-class level I started on in journalism.

But the reason I raise '68 is that somewhere something happened. Papers then were terrible. *TIME* was never fair in the past, and everybody read it. The day that Castro marched into Havana, *The Chicago Tribune*, the world's greatest newspaper, printed the headline, "98 Chicagoans Stranded in Havana." Remember Pulitzer, Hearst, the tabloids, people like Jimmy Fidler and Walter Winchell. Newspapers are better today; television is better today. Something happened, and I think it happened because we got to be stars. Not just on television, but when Swifty Lazar started to come to Washington after Watergate, I knew we were in big trouble. This arrogance came out of that period, '68 plus Watergate. You'd ask young people what they wanted to do, and they'd say, "Communications." There is a lot of arrogance.

I agree that we don't have a basic credibility problem. *The Boston Globe* is better. The *Los Angeles Times* is better. *The Philadelphia Inquirer* is better. *The Washington Post* and *The New York Times*, they're all better. The networks are better. But something is out there, and they do not like us, and they fear us, and it's more than just size. It's got a lot to do with the people who don't have the credentials strutting.

BERGER: I think the process that Gene was talking about may be one of the keys, that television brings the process into the home, and it's not a pretty process. To make an omelette you have to break an egg, and to get news sometimes you have to be not very pretty about it. The least pretty people in one of the biggest stories in America (Gene was there, and I was there at *The Washington Post*) were the boys who broke Watergate, and they didn't do it by being gentle. Carl Bernstein and Bob Woodward interviewed me, and they weren't gentle, I can assure you. That process was never really seen because they were not television reporters. It is the same process.

JUDY WOODRUFF: I came here thinking I was going to be sitting on the fence. Being in public television, you think, "Well, I can really understand both sides." Maybe it's because I'm perhaps the only one around this table who's never worked for a newspaper, I'm coming more and more down on the side of television, although I hate to see us split that way.

I'd like to see us talk about two things, and they've both already come up. One is this question of the star system, and how the personality of the reporter or the newscaster has become more important in some instances than the story that's being told, than the substance of the reporting.

The second thing is this question of bias. I was looking at Creed Black's mockup. The stories here from Chris Wallace, from Bob Kur and John Severson are exactly what we read in the newspapers on those days. Just because there's some analysis or opinion or whatever you want to call it, doesn't make it any different from what the people who were traveling with those candidates or with the President were saying at the same time. It's time for us to look at ourselves and ask, "What *is* our role as journalists?"

We all know by now we can't just report the facts as we see them; there's more to journalism than that. It's just too easy to sit back and say, "Well, you shouldn't be doing analyis. You shouldn't be doing opinion." That's what it's all about. We in the television business are doing it, you in the newspaper business are doing it, and let's get it out on the table. Let's talk about why we're doing it, and be a little more honest about it, because I think it exists. Surveys done on both sides have said, "Yes, journalists are biased," and "No, they're not biased." We're all human beings. But the quality of journalism has changed: we are not in the business of putting out press releases from the White House anymore.

BARBER: Now, can we impose on John Chancellor and David Broder to clarify where we are?

CHANCELLOR: David?

BRODER: John? (Laughter)

CHANCELLOR: Well, having been ordered to think, I have a couple of things we ought to be talking about. I would like everybody to consider here the fact that the society in which we practice journalism has changed considerably in the last 35 to 40 years. When I was a young reporter, I would get assigned to cover sermons on Sunday and write the story for the Monday morning newspaper. Important clergymen would call the *Sun-Times* and say, "I'm going to make an important sermon," and we would send out young reporters and cover that. A lot of those powerful voices have gone, or been subdued in some way, and I'm not quite sure why.

Now we practice journalism in a world where the voices of clergymen, of educators, of the senior members of the business community, are not as prominent as they used to be. And in some way, the press has been asked to do something the press is not very good at, and shouldn't probably do, to represent this kind of chorus of the important people in the society. These voices that were very important in the 1930s and the 1940s, and in the 1950s, began to disappear along about the 1960s and 1970s. We don't seem to have that resource, because we were just passing these opinions and these ideas through journalism to the public. Now the public, and a lot of young people especially, are asking us to be the voice, and I don't think we're qualified to do that.

In terms of the charges about arrogance, I think that television is a mindless instrument that has helped create the problem of credibility. I don't say that television journalists did it; I just say electronics has done it. The main culprit is the televised press conference. Before television, reporters asked tough questions of people in the news and then went back to the office and wrote the story and smoothed it over. All press conferences before television must have seemed to the readers like very civilized encounters. And when television came along, especially with Jack Kennedy's press conferences and Sarah McClendon and others, the public suddenly saw people asking nasty questions of the President of the United States. It helped start the credibility problem or the arrogance problem, and that is simply technological change.

I'm not blaming the television journalists; Sarah McClendon didn't work for us. But this process is repeated in communities all over the country, where rude questions are being put, and on courthouse steps in the Sharon and Westmoreland trials. The public sees that part of the process, and they don't like what they see, because they are not journalists, and they don't know that these sometimes very, very hard questions have to be asked.

I remember how my father read the *Chicago Tribune* at the breakfast table. The *Tribune* had an editor, but my father was *the* editor as far as he was concerned. My father would read the business news first, then read the sports news, then read the editorials, part of the front page (never read a story about an ax murderer in his life), and put the paper away. He had had the news he wanted in that paper.

Half-hour television programs presented the people of the United States with an entirely different situation about getting the news. You can either turn it off or leave it on. There's no editing within that half hour. When we showed people the civil rights stories in the South and the Vietnam War and Watergate, a lot of them didn't like what they saw. But they could either leave it on or turn it off, and they were hypnotized by television and left it on.

And finally, on the star system, I just have one observation. I used to be an anchorman. I have borrowed a phrase from Alcoholics Anonymous to describe my present status: I am a recovering celebrity. We ought to examine the star system, because I think it's terrible when an anchorperson's agent says, "I have signed a million-dollar contract." That really kills us in this business.

On the other hand, most of us around here know that the editors and many of the journalists on newspapers in medium-size communities are as well-known within those communities as the people on television. I look at a bunch of you around this table, and I know you're very well-known in your own communities. On television, we happen to be very well-known in a lot of communities, but I wonder if there's all that much difference. And that was all I was able to think.

BRODER: Just a couple of points, not nearly as well organized as what Jack has just said. When I read Creed Black's speech, my initial reaction was to think that I was going to be a traitor to my class and express some dissent from his view. And today, I was so put off by the extraordinarily defensive tone of the two television spokesmen here that I thought I'd just keep my mouth shut. Their reaction struck me as characteristic of what I see in my own business: whenever there is any criticism, put up a protective shell and then in the style of my boss, Ben Bradlee, say, "Don't just stay in the shell; smash the bastards before they smash you." That reflex, which we all share to some degree, is part of this credibility problem we're talking about.

Creed, the relevant distinctions are not between print and television, but between good journalism and bad journalism, and there are plenty of examples of both on both sides. As Marty Nolan said, none of us would want to be put in a position of arguing that the *MacNeil/Lehrer NewsHour* and Judy Woodruff's work are less responsible in terms of journalism, or more or less informative than the typical edition of the *New York Post*.

Creed, I've shared your experience that when you ask for examples, people tend to respond in terms of television correspondents or programs. But that reaction is simply a reflection of the reality that they are much more visible than we are. They see Sam Donaldson at work. They do not see Lou Cannon at work. If they saw Lou Cannon or Seymour Hersh working on the phone, cajoling, berating, threatening, intimidating, bluffing somebody to try to get one more piece of information out of them, they might cite that example, but they don't see that. They see Sam Donaldson trying to holler over the helicopter noise, and they say, "Who is that person interrupting the President on the way to his weekend vacation?"

I don't want to embarrass Jack Chancellor, but here is one of the most visible people in America through television, and yet the adjective that leaps to mind is not "arrogant," nor would I assume that that characterization is a particular problem for him in his professional work.

There is plenty of arrogance. You do have a problem on the television side in the way in which you have structured your news programs. If out front every day in *The Washington Post* or in *The New York Times*, the biggest bylines were those of Abe Rosenthal or Ben Bradlee, they would, in a personal sense, be taking the heat for everything that goes on in those papers. And as two not very small egos, not entirely lacking in arrogance themselves, they would probably handle it less well than Dan Rather or Tom Brokaw handle that kind of a problem. Ours is a more depersonalized and more diffused kind of a delivery system, and so the heat gets spread out among more people.

There is no more arrogant slogan than the slogan of the flagship of our business, *The New York Times*, which promises its readers every day to deliver "all the news that's fit to print." Many have said here that our problem is that the news process is becoming more visible. I would argue exactly the opposite. Whatever we decide is the nature of the credibility problem and the specific remedies, we have to make that news process *more* visible, not less visible to the public. Take the presidential press conference. Clearly people react negatively when they see reporters at work. Why do they react negatively? Because we have never explained to them what those reporters think they are doing.

I'll give you an example. Every time the President is on, the television anchors come on and give us 45 seconds or a minute and 15 seconds about what they anticipate the President will do at that press conference. It might be useful for once if they took that minute or minute and 15 seconds to explain what the reporters are going to do and why they are going to do it. We never say to our readers what it is that we deliver. In the case of the flagship paper, we are making a patently false claim. If we were honest with our readers, we would say to them something like, "What we are dropping on the doorstep is a brief, hasty, incomplete, necessarily distorted version of some of the things that are fit to print." And then we might be in a better posture to come back the next day and say to them, "We've learned some things since we've last come into your home. Here's what we've learned; here's how we'd like to revise and update and correct what we told you yesterday." Our audience might welcome that kind of an approach. But in any case, the more visible we make the news process, the better off I would think we're going to be.

SCHWARTZ: Television news and daily newspapers have a much greater problem than *60 Minutes* or a magazine with a longer deadline. As a newspaper reporter, you're working against a terrible deadline with no fact-checkers to stand behind you, as you would have at *TIME* or *Newsweek*; so to get things right, really right, is a virtual miracle. To get them right in the factual sense is something you want to be doing most of the time; to get them interpretatively right under deadline is virtually impossible, particularly on any complex story. Doctors are now accountable in a way that they never were before, because of the growth of malpractice suits; politicians are accountable by reelection. Newspapers are not accountable, so far as I'm aware, in any comparable way, and, therefore, the self-policing becomes that much more important. It's not that the process is too open; it's that the process is too closed. People would genuinely enjoy and be interested in buying a newspaper or watching a newscast for an interesting presentation of the complexities of what happened in the newsgathering process.

BOCCARDI: Whether the process is opened or closed, there may be something wrong with the process.

SCHWARTZ: Let those issues be discussed with the public. Break down the barriers. In other words, they don't only have to be discussed at this table. Let us be accountable to the public.

CHANCELLOR: When I was on *CBS Nightly News,* we had something I devised called "Editor's Notebook," which we would use whenever it was necessary. We always made factual corrections the next night if the numbers were wrong. You'd read the mail carefully, and you could come on with this thing behind you that said "Editor's Notebook," and you could talk a little bit about the program and about problems in covering stories. It was a way for this institution to reach out and actually have the viewers think that you care about them, rather than being priests of the news, which is so often the case in television. I wish we had more of that.

NELSON: Did the viewers react to it?

CHANCELLOR: They loved it.

NELSON: There always has been a tendency on the part of editors to say: "Readers don't care about the problems you had getting the story, just get us the story. Don't tell about the lengths to which you had to go to get the story, or the kind of sources you had to depend on. Just get it on the news." I agree with Tony 100 percent. I think that the reader would be interested in explanations, and it would be an important part of the story if we did more explaining, the problems we had to go through to get the story, the kind of sources we had to use, and the reasons we couldn't name sources.

HEWITT: Jack, ABC does that very thing every once in a while, not very often, late at night. Nobody watches it. They put it on to make all you guys happy. The viewers could care less about it. They shove it in sometimes in place of *Nightline*. It's just not something the country is out there panting for.

NELSON: I'm not saying that they're out there panting for it, but you don't always give them what they're panting for anyway. You give them what's important. I think it's important to put it out there, and I think people would listen to it.

SCHWARTZ: Don, your argument that because ABC has tried it at 11:30 at night, with very little promotion, in a very limited capacity, on a totally infrequent basis, does not suggest proof that this does not interest viewers.

LAVENTHOL: There's another distinction here, the national media versus the regional and local media. Most of the people here represent the national media, but in both television and newspapers, there are different kinds of things happening in the regional and local media as opposed to the national media.

I can't speak for television because I don't know what's going on in local television around the country. But there are dozens and dozens of newspapers doing precisely the kind of thing suggested here, whether it's an editor's column, or an ombudsman, or focus groups with readers, or sending forms out to people who have been interviewed so they can evaluate how what they actually said contrasted with what appeared in the paper.

Van mentioned that there is a local universe for most people who receive information, and the local universe is what is in their area. But this local/national opposition really plays itself out in terms of Washington and Washington journalism. The reporters in the newspaper business in Washington are not responsive to the readers of the newspapers they write for. Except for *The Washington Post*, they don't live in the place where the newspaper is published; they almost never have any contact with the readers of their newspapers. They are very remote from what people really feel about their newspaper and about the kind of information they're receiving.

WOODRUFF: How would that make a difference in what they write about or report?

LAVENTHOL: They don't have a sense of what really concerns people who read their newspaper. Furthermore, these people in Washington are usually the best people in our business, and many of them come back to their newspapers and become the editors of those newspapers. Then they begin to direct those newspapers based on the kind of experience they had in Washington, where they were dealing with their peers and not with the people who read the paper. Somebody mentioned that the *Los Angeles Times* is a great newspaper, and *The New York Times* is better, and so on. They all are better, but those are peer judgments, not reader judgments.

Watergate had a lot to do with it. Watergate was the finest moment for print journalism, maybe in the history of this country. But it has also led to a new role model for a journalist. A journalist is somebody who goes out and finds out what these guys in office or in any other form of life have done wrong. John Chancellor mentioned that many people want from their media what people are actually saying. You can't find the sermon that was given on Sunday in a newspaper anymore, and people who read the paper, who are seeking information, want that information.

They want a way to receive uninterpreted information, if you want to call it that, in a way that we in the newspaper profession consider as something negative. If we take uninterpreted information and put it in our publications or on our television stations, we haven't done a very good job.

By the way, I think that television does a better job of that than newspapers do. Television does permit you to see the President for 30 minutes without forcing an interpretation on the event while it's happening. The *MacNeil/Lehrer NewsHour* is one of the best examples of that technique, where you permit the people to get on and talk.

DAVID BURGIN: There's such heavy stuff being talked about here, I feel that after this is over, Gene Patterson and Bob Haiman will crank up a stove and out will come either white smoke or black smoke. (Laughter)

If I could return to grassroots for a second from platitudes, from the higher ground, I represent what some of you might call a small newspaper, *The Orlando Sentinel*, which, I might add, is part of the Tribune Company which owns the *Chicago Tribune*, much alluded to, and *The New York Daily News* and television stations in major markets and, before Marty Nolan jumps in, the Chicago Cubs...(Laughter)

NOLAN: Choke. Choke. Choke. (Laughter)

BURGIN: ...an acquisition I had no say in. I'd like to fire a shot across the bow of local television, which I think is the lower turf. On a credibility scale of, say, one to 10, if *The New York Times* and CBS are nine, local television is one or zero. *The Orlando Sentinel's* masthead implies an obligation to cover local news first, the same thing with Channel Nine, Channel Four, Channel Six in Orlando. There is a relationship there that the reader, the listener, or the viewer, all are aware of. I don't think that relationship is as big or as important on the grand national scale as it is at the local level.

On that grassroots level (and here's my shot across the bow), local television is an absolute joke. There is no semblance of credibility. I'll give you an example, if I can generalize from a personal anecdote. I was in a discussion like this not too long ago, where, like Creed Black, I was fortunate enough to go first and deliver 20 minutes of my best thinking, ripping away at local television, when the guy I was debating came back and said, "I don't know what you're bitching about. Most of our local news comes from out of *The Orlando Sentinel*." (Laughter) Local television has abdicated, if it in fact ever had anything to do with, any notion of watchdogging local government. If they can't shoot it (and local government is arcane and slippery; you can't really get a fix on it), they're not going to cover it. Local government on local television is restricted to ambulance chasing.

I have a hard time finding any credibility on any local television all over the country, wherever you go, even in Washington, D.C. I just got back from San Francisco. Local TV there was disgustingly bad. They were covering all the wrong things. There was no relevance. It was strictly show biz.

So, if there is a credibility problem and if it washes over onto newspapers, it starts at the grassroots with local television.

JOHN SEIGENTHALER: I was going to make a footnote on that local newspaper/ television relationship earlier, but the flow was going on that higher plane, and I passed it by. I don't agree completely with David Burgin. When three local stations focus on the same story, they are tough and competitive with each other. When they focus on the big local story, they are competitive with the local newspapers. But they leave the burden for most local coverage and most of the government watchdogging to the local newspaper.

As a local publisher, I have the most concern about conflicts with other institutions in the local community. When there is a conflict with another institution, and there's a need to go to court or even to go to the public, too often the local television station, particularly if it's independently owned, will run away from the fight. Often they get bad legal advice or no legal advice. It's a matter of grave concern to all of us, because some of those local fights go up through the courts and ultimately result in legal decisions that can rule us all.

From my point of view, the greatest threat that will flow from the Westmoreland and Sharon trials is the chilling effect on that local television owner, news director, or station manager who doesn't have the guts to get in the fight to begin with, and who's going to be threatened by a legal bill that he can't afford.

RALPH RENICK: I am the only local television guy here. So you saved the best for last, I guess. (Laughter) The menu keeps growing longer and longer, and it's a little hard to respond to a blanket indictment. Some news operations are putting out a consultant-directed product across America. The sets look the same, and the people generally look the same. The content does steer clear of government reporting and things that are not illustrative; they get a little too simplistic.

I'm glad this meeting was called, because I think that we're engaged in some sort of internecine warfare, and we're all going to get hurt by it. We operate in different spheres, those in broadcast news and in newspapers. One example is Creed's speech to the ASNE. I was involved with the Associated Press for some years on the broadcast board. There was no crossover between the editors and the broadcast people. We couldn't even get committee reports to the APME. But I think getting together like this is going to do some good.

BARBER: I'm thinking of Jack Nelson's passing comment that you don't always give them what they want. You may have to give them some things that they don't want. There's a good deal of evidence on certain questions of public sentiment about journalists, that is, whether they like you or not, or say they trust you or not. If Michael Robinson is correct, there's been a change from a feeling that you have a liberal bias to a sense that the bias is negative, or simply too critical.

But would you consider yourselves credible if everybody liked you? Is that what you're after in the search for credibility? I spent a day about a week ago at a publication that outshines all of you, at home and around the world. It is filled with civility and humanity, and indeed with the sermons that John Chancellor used to report. It is entertaining and attractive and they would say informative. It's a little like television, and it's a little like a good newspaper. It would be more like the original motto of *The New York Times:* "It will not soil the breakfast cloth." Its name is *The Reader's Digest.* And I wonder if that's a model of what you'd like to be in this world?

But the more basic question is: what are we struggling with here? We have criticism from the public, criticism from peers, and aspirations to do better. What is the operative meaning of credibility in this context?

BERGER: One of the credibility problems has nothing to do with television or the printed press as such. It has much more to do with the New Journalism and the old. Most of us around this table are practitioners of what I call the "old" journalism. We all have prejudices; we all have biases. But when we're reporting a story, we try to report the story as best we see it. Certainly we make value judgments. We try to find sources we can believe. We try to put out the best first rough draft of history, as Chalmers Roberts used to call it.

In the New Journalism, as I understand it, reporters reported their point of view and often sought their information to support their point of view. From the '70s, maybe it was the '60s, credibility problems came in, and that's when the arrogance came in, and that's where the question of doubting your messenger came in.

MATUSOW: I'd like to second that notion. The criticism that everyone hears all the time is: "Who elected you?" The public is putting its finger on something not necessarily made by the media, the collapse of so many other strong voices in our society, and in particular, the collapse of the political parties. We don't have any effective opposition today in this country. So when a Watergate comes up, it's up to the press to prosecute the problem initially. The press almost too gleefully jumped into its role as the opposition, and this role offends people very deeply. Fundamentally, the press should report what's happened. It has these additional duties to put matters into perspective, and it has a reformist role too. But for the press to take itself so seriously as to see itself as the only check on government and to operate on that assumption is very poor service to the public. When they stand up in a press conference, newspaper or television reporters ought to realize that they are not appointed to be the one and only check on the President's policy.

HEWITT: You can't divorce the way we operate from the medium in which we operate. The television set is the little stage in everybody's living room. On that stage they watch Michael Jackson, Joe Montana, Ronald Reagan, John Chancellor, Ralph Renick, Mike Wallace, and back to Meryl Streep. It is so different from what you print guys do, that to try to have some sort of blanket rules for the way print reporters work and the way television journalists work is ridiculous.

A guy picks up a newspaper. It *is* a newspaper. A guy turns on a television set, and it's *The Jewel in the Crown* or it's *Face the Nation* or it's *Meet the Press* or it's the Super Bowl. We have problems that have nothing to do with our good intentions. The very fact that we have made broadcast journalism as good as it is is a miracle to me. It is a miracle that ABC, NBC, and CBS didn't start years ago to go the tabloid route, to go The *Enquirer* route.

There's another thing that everybody is forgetting here. When television first came into being, it was pictures, pictures in your living room. By all odds, television should have gone to MGM and 20th Century Fox and Warner Brothers; they were in the picture business. It is a very lucky thing in America that ABC, NBC, and CBS had a history of responsible news reporting, the moral tradition of the guys that took over television. I know this sounds defensive. We may be bad, but I think it's a miracle that we do as well as we do. People bought that set to be entertained; they bought the newspaper to be informed. They did not buy their television set to be informed; that's a bonus. You may entertain them along the way, because that's the only way you can make sure more people read your newspaper than another.

BURGIN: What's the miracle? What forces would be at work to counter what you say?

HEWITT: We're essentially part of an entertainment medium. When the board of directors of your company sits down, they talk about newspapers, about putting out a newspaper. When the board of directors at CBS meets, what we do is a small part of their concern. We're part of this big entertainment thing, and I think it's amazing that, because of people like William Paley and Frank Stanton and David Sarnoff, they took this thing seriously and didn't let it become *Beverly Hillbillies*.

BURGIN: But are you under pressure time after time or over the years from some corporate person to juice it up?

HEWITT: Never. Nobody believes this, about the pressure to keep *60 Minutes* in the top 10; they'd be happy if we were in the top 50. It is not a consideration. Of course you want ratings. Tell me any publisher around this table doesn't want circulation. Gene, you care about the circulation of your paper, don't you?

PATTERSON: Yes.

HEWITT: All right. Van Sauter cares about the circulation of his newscast.

BURGIN: I still don't see where the miracle is. That was a pretty harsh characterization of how you got to where you got.

HEWITT: I'm saying there's a big entertainment business, which is full of Ed Sullivans and Jackie

Gleasons. Out of this also came a John Chancellor, a David Brinkley, an Edward R. Morrow, a Dan Rather, a Walter Cronkite. That's a big bonus for America. We would expect newspapers to come up with the Scotty Restons, the Gene Pattersons; that's the business they were in. But that wasn't the business these television guys were in; they made that their business, which is pretty responsible.

BURGIN: It could just as well have been the *Gong Show*?

SEIGENTHALER: Does it bother you at all that the presidential press conference is a 30-minute show? And I say that advisedly, "a 30-minute show." It's never more or less.

HEWITT: Can I stop it? Would you guys opt tomorrow that we didn't carry the presidential news conference?

SEIGENTHALER: No, but it seems strange to me that that press conference starts at one moment and ends at another moment, and fits right in between those commercials beautifully.

HEWITT: That's a Pierre Salinger, Ron Ziegler decision.

BRODER: Historically, John, that set time period preceded the televising of them, and it was a matter of convenience when we had frequent press conferences.

NELSON: For all of its faults, though, you have to say that that press conferences still serve a purpose. Even as few as Reagan holds, it serves a purpose, because the people do get to see him. Had it not been for those press conferences during Watergate, it would have been much harder to have had Richard Nixon brought to a conclusion.

62

SEIGENTHALER: I certainly concur on that. I don't want to change the presidential press conference. I don't want to do away with it or end it. It does strike me as strange. When I turn on the news conference, I know that the three networks are going to get three questions, and that is pre-arranged, and that's part of that show, and they're going to get started on the hour. The President is going to walk in on the assigned hour.

HEWITT: Everything on television is a show. The news is a show. *Beverly Hillbillies* is a show. The Super Bowl is a show. The coverage of the assassination of Sadat was a show. That's the nature of the business.

SCHWARTZ: I want to correct one of the misunderstandings of newspaper people, and I was guilty of this myself and learned a very harsh lesson. One of the things I learned on television, watching my own tapes as I was failing, was that people will not watch something long on television. They will not watch for a long time something that is not dramatic, that does not include conflict. I started to fall asleep watching my own tapes, literally started to fall asleep. I would be going only two-and-a-half minutes, and I had nothing behind me, and all you were watching was my voice. They will not watch something static. People won't watch old and bald people when they have the opportunity to watch somebody young and pretty. They will not watch someone who lacks performance skills.

One of the important things is to recognize the inherent limitations of the medium, to recognize what people will not watch, and then to make your responsible gestures in the context of what is possible, which is why *60 Minutes* has been so successful. *Nightline* has been successful, not because it deals with ideas, not because Ted Koppel is smarter than anybody else (although that is a part of it), but because Ted Koppel, both personally and in the way he structures the program, has managed to sneak ideas in through what works on television, that is, conflict.

If somebody were to put on television the best examples of David Broder's work, or the best examples of Howell Raines's work, 10, 20, 30 paragraphs, and just have them read it, you and I would all fall asleep. There are limitations that are important to understand within the context of television, without sacrificing the need for a responsible way of addressing them.

BOCCARDI: When we talk about credibility, we want four or five things. We want a greater public acceptance of our role in society, and an acceptance of the fact that a lot of the time we're going to bring them bad news. We want them to trust and believe what we say. We want them to believe that we try to do what we do fairly. We want them to feel that we are responsive, to *their* news and information needs, rather than arrogantly pursuing an agenda that we or our peers set. We want them to feel that we direct our investigative efforts more toward issues that really are important to them, rather than toward some petty skullduggery that makes us look good among our peers. We want the public to feel that our news reports, broadly speaking, reflect that mix of good and bad that really matches their experience.

Most of this credibility fuss is over a lack of public acceptance of one or maybe all of those notions about what we do, whether we do it with a camera or a pencil or one of those portable computers that Van Sauter has in front of him. The challenge that leaders of our business face is what can we do about our performance that advances us in those broad categories; that's what credibility is about. These are the areas where we're hurting, and there's what the best minds in the business ought to be looking at and trying to improve.

WOODRUFF: I just had a quick comment about John Seigenthaler's question. You know why the news conferences are only 30 minutes? It's because the Reagan White House doesn't want the President out there for more than 30 minutes.

CHANCELLOR: But they've always been about 30 minutes. They were 30 minutes when Roosevelt was holding them.

HEWITT: When they were having afternoon news conferences, before they went into prime time, they used to run almost open-ended. Nobody cared.

CHANCELLOR: The senior wire service person is asked by the White House to say, "Thank you, Mr. President." Merriman Smith wrote a book with that title. That's how that form got established.

BRODER: Before it was on television, reporters wanted to get the hell out of that room and file. That's why they were cut off at that point.

NOLAN: There were more afternoon papers then that hadn't been killed by local TV.

BURGIN: Here we go again.

HEWITT: P.M. papers were killed by traffic.

CHANCELLOR: There you go again.

BARBER: As a civics teacher, I have to throw in a footnote, which is that the presidential press conference is an instructional disaster. It is the impolite delivery of cream puffs to the President of the United States. The President held a press conference last summer in which 34 questions were asked; only four of them, by any stretch of the imagination, had to do with the facts. The rest were subjunctive, expectational, participatory, philosophical, or emotional, which presupposes that the President's sentiments are related to his policies, a hypothesis worth considering.

HEWITT: It's not even a great show. It's a lousy show.

VANOCUR: I'd like to return to what Lou Boccardi has brought up and add one other word to account for this feeling about us. Starting before the death of John F. Kennedy in the summer of '63, there had been, for a lot of obvious reasons, a toxic strain in the bloodstream of this country. We lost what we had during the Eisenhower years, the politics of civility in this country. After the hostages were released, Ronald Reagan (and Tip O'Neill in a funny kind of way), reintroduced the idea of civility into our political discourse. We have people like Bob Dole exemplifying this, a completely different kind of a person than when he came into the Senate in the early '70s. We have civility almost everywhere, except the public perceives rightly or wrongly a lot of journalism as they see it on television as not being civil, when the rest of the country has gone civil. We weren't all that civil, but nobody saw us. But television people are now being seen. I think that is our greatest problem; we are not seen to be civil. I don't think it helps, for example, for whoever organized the New Hampshire-Dartmouth presidential debate to link Ted Koppel with Phil Donahue. Donahue walked around, doing a kind of Kabuki dance with a wireless mike, being equated with Ted Koppel, a qualified journalist. Remember that case of the child who disappeared and the father appeared on Donahue; Donahue said, "That's not my problem. I'm just a journalist." He is not a journalist. In this country, we have armed with microphones a lot of fetuses in Gucci loafers. (Laughter) They are Sony shepherds, and they go around sticking mikes up people's nostrils, and that doesn't do much for our image.

CHANCELLOR: We've left one thing out here that's quite important. We've been beating up on ourselves when we should devote a little bit of time to beating up on the U.S. government. This administration has done more to make us look bad, and we have walked into more traps as journalists than I have ever seen before in covering news. This administration is hiding more things from the public than any administration I can remember. And when good journalists uncover these things, they are made to look intrusive. When the *L.A. Times* or *The Washington Post* or one of the big papers comes out with a hell of an exclusive story, an awful lot of Americans get angry because we are prying into the secrets of government.

We had the shuttle launch yesterday, one of the greatest comic operas of press relations I have ever seen, with all the secrecy, and asking the AP and the networks not to run things, and Weinberger getting into the act. I don't think we won on that one.

Let's talk about what I call "Ronald Reagan's cupped ear gambit" around the White House: the press is deliberately and systematically kept away from him, so that when the President walks across the columned walkway near the Rose Garden, all you hear are a lot of monkeys screaming at him, when they easily could have been brought right up, and the President could stand and talk in a conversational tone. That's killing us, and it isn't hurting Ronald Reagan one bit, and they know it.

BOCCARDI: Why do we do it then?

CHANCELLOR: I know why we do it: because a) we're saps, but b) we're trying to do our jobs. And when Sam Donaldson or Chris Wallace or those people say, "How are you going to do it, Mr. President," the country says, "Who the hell cares about them?" But they're trying to cover the news.

VANOCUR: Suppose they don't do it for 10 times in a row? I guarantee Ronald Reagan will start walking on.

CHANCELLOR: Sandy, that's why we're all gathered here. Let me give my final example about how these guys get away with it. The President said, "We bomb in five minutes," and the press reported that. Then the Reagans said, "That was a private remark," which of course makes no sense at all. From personal experience in the U.S. government, I can tell you if it hadn't been reported, the Russians would have heard about it in a half hour, taken it very, very seriously, and probably gone on some modest kind of alert. The President was saved by the fact that the country learned about that through the American press. But where did we come out in the end? I have heard over and over again, "Why don't you guys let the President have a little privacy?"

So I don't think you can go through this conference without acknowledging that, as an institution, we are being shafted by this government.

BOCCARDI: John, I think they may be getting away with some of that because of some of the problems I have enumerated. The public is not with us because of some of these other things.

CHANCELLOR: But the Reagan Administration is making it worse.

NELSON: He's exactly right. The Reagan Administration is helping shape public opinion, and it's not just reflecting it. There's no question about that in my mind.

SCHWARTZ: There's nothing the matter with Sam Donaldson's yelling at the President, but then why do you show it? Why don't you just report what the President said? Why do you show yourselves looking like jerks? (Laughter)

CHANCELLOR: That's a good question, a perfectly valid question. But, as I said, we are saps. I don't think we should be doing it, and, in that sense, I agree with you. But it is impossible to take the Donaldson voice out of it if you're going to see the reality of the exchange.

SCHWARTZ: Well, why do you show it? Why can't you have Dan Rather say it?

HEWITT: No. We're in the reality business. If somewhere in all that yelling and screaming, the President says something newsworthy, and you can't extract it from all the shouting, you go ahead and figure it's your responsibility to put on what he said; and we're going to look bad because a couple of guys are screaming around him.

MATUSOW: I am going to suggest one reason why Dan Rather doesn't do it, and why the White House correspondent does it. There is altogether too much White House news on the evening news every night. One reason there is so much White House news is an effort to get the premier correspondents, the Bill Plantes, the Leslie Stahls, the Sam Donaldsons, and the other starring members of the cast onto the evening news. One of the things that enhances a report is to have footage of the President, whether or not he's making us look like monkeys, at least it's the body, and it's there, and it in some measure enhances the report. I think the evening news producers should resist that temptation.

SAUTER: I'm just speaking for CBS. There is no such motivation to have the White House correspondents on the air every night or with a set regularity. The President is not there because of some external demand.

BERGER: We've just gone through a presidential election year where I was not at the White House. But when I was, very often the opposing candidate got on the air with a story. At that time, it was Carter getting on the air with a news story, and they wanted Ford on the air to balance it out. So you might have the President's body on the air, and, therefore, you had to have the White House correspondent. But that happened for reasons of supposed fairness politically.

NELSON: Don't you think that makes pretty good TV (and I'm just talking about TV) to have Sam Donaldson running out there hollering, "Mr. President," and the President turning around and answering his question?

CHANCELLOR: We never did it before.

HEWITT: Lousy TV.

NELSON: Do you think it's terrible TV?

HEWITT: Yes.

NELSON: Why do you use it all the time then?

CHANCELLOR: The President is on television a lot because, beginning with the Eisenhower administration, all the lines of public information in the federal establishment were drawn closer and closer to the White House. Jim Haggerty instituted a policy that said in effect, "The good news comes from here. Let the agencies handle whatever bad news there is." The White House press corps expanded in number both in print and broadcasting. The White House Press Office grew. We now get all kinds of information out of the White House, such as on the condition of the Pope after he was shot; that news came from the White House. There's no reason in the world why it should come from the White House. But it reinforces this policy of many administrations to make the White House more and more important. At one point, you had to have reporters all over Washington and in the great departments of government covering the news that the federal government made. You can do it now with a handful of people at State and Defense, and especially at the White House. So the nature of government information has changed enormously, and the focus is at 1600 Pennsylvania Avenue, and that's one of the reasons, boring or not, why the President is on television almost every night.

WOODRUFF: But a lot of information isn't getting reported that is happening around and about Washington, that goes beyond the announcements that are made at the White House, particularly the background behind why those decisions were reached.

CHANCELLOR: I don't disagree with that. The upfront news comes from the White House, the stuff that gets on the Associated Press and on the nightly news.

WOODRUFF: That's right, and that happens not just at television networks, but also at the wire services and in the newspapers.

NOLAN: I predict that if Van Sauter and Roone Arledge or, go to a lower level, Sam Donaldson and

Chris Wallace and Leslie Stahl and Bill Plante would go to Larry Speakes and say, "Larry, isn't this really undignified for the President and for us? Why don't you set it up, and let's try it this way." And Larry will say the usual, "Mumble. Mumble. I don't know nothing." And if the networks somehow colluded and decided to impose their own standards of dignity on the presidency, and if you stop filming the shouting over the helicopter roar, then the next Mike Deaver, whoever he is, would find a way to plant news stories. Captain Airwaves would have something about how the White House feels that the networks are ganging up on our poor, beloved President, and the wicked, evil *meisters* of doom are at it again, and isn't it too bad because the President is such a nice guy, and here they're hounding him. They want more of him. So if two networks acted in concert, there would be a conspiracy theory overnight.

HEWITT: The one word I've heard here the most besides "credibility" is "arrogance." I think it's pretty arrogant for all of us to sit around here and decide what the public likes and doesn't like and wants and doesn't want. Gene, what would you think about this? During lunch break call downtown and tell some guy at the desk to go find six people on the street and bring them back this afternoon. I'm so sick of hearing that the public thinks this, and the public doesn't like that, and they don't want to hear them shout. *You* don't want to hear them shout. I'm not sure there isn't some guy at home who doesn't like hearing them shout.

You want to know about arrogance? Arrogance is this college of cardinals deciding what the parishioners out there want and don't want. Why don't we bring some people in here this afternoon?

BARBER: Does that stand as an illustration of research methods at *60 Minutes*? (Laughter)

HEWITT: No. It stands as an illustration of a bunch of news guys all playing with themselves, and saying, "The public doesn't like this; the public doesn't like that."

SCHWARTZ: What do you expect?

HEWITT: I expected it. But why don't you bring somebody in here and say, "Hey, do you feel that way?"

NELSON: You misinterpreted what I said. You put it on the air because you think the public does like to see Sam Donaldson holler over and the President holler back, because you think it's good television. I don't understand why all three networks put it on the air, if you don't think it serves a purpose. What purpose does it serve?

BERGER: It shows he doesn't want to talk to the press.

NELSON: Well, all right. That may not be a bad reason for putting it on, but you put it on repeatedly. I guarantee you, there's never been a case where a network reporter at the White House has hollered over to the President and gotten a response from the President, and the networks didn't run it. I don't care what the question was or what the answer was.

NOLAN: A short definition of credibility. We're trying to determine whether we are believed and therefore respected, not whether we're liked. God help us, who would like us? There's no reason to. H. L. Mencken said in the 1920s, "Nobody likes the press. They have all the best seats, right up front." Nobody is going to like us and love us, but it's a matter of whether they believe us or not that's important. If they stop believing us, we've got troubles. If they don't like us, who cares?

SAUTER: Responding to what Marty Nolan said, if we are talking credibility in the context of whether our product is believed by the viewers or readers, we have a tremendous amount of credibility. If we are talking credibility in the terms of whether they think the product is fair, we have a tremendous amount of credibility. I can't talk to the newspapers in this context, but the people on televisio 1, the people who are doing television news and television reporting, are liked, and they're liked a lot. There's just not a question about that. They're liked a great deal, and you can chart it for years. When you talk about credibility, we're not talking about a product- or performance-related difficulty with the readers or the viewers. It's not perceived by them in that fashion. It's very amusing here that we talk as though the people are really watching television and reading newspapers for one reason only, and that's to get news. That's not the case. They buy these products, view these products for a whole range of reasons, many of them totally unrelated to what we do or don't do at the White House, or how we portray the President, or how we cover Washington. A lot of that material is not nearly as significant to them as it is to us in our professions.

But the problem we have with our viewers in the context of credibility is not performance- or product-related. It is the sense of separation from the institutions that the community feels, and the inability to talk to those institutions, and the inability to make their points heard. That's where our problem exists. I don't think it's quite as large as we make it, but that's why there's a gulf between us and them. How you close that gulf is very, very complex, and there's been a tremendous amount of talk about how one does that without compromising the inherent virtues of the journalistic institutions.

BARBER: I phased out there on one thing. What do you mean by "not product-related?"

SAUTER: It's not product-related in the sense that what we're publishing or broadcasting carries some fraility, which causes them to have some lack of confidence in it. Our products (and I can't speak to newspapers nearly as well as I can to television) in their opinion, are not in some way flawed. There's not a product problem, nor is there a performance problem. Are the people on TV who deliver the news in some way arrogant or insulting or disinterested or callous? That's not a problem. It's an institutional problem, because the people have personal relationships with the people on television, and I presume to some degree with their newspapers, though not people within the newspaper as an entity. They want to communicate with that institution. They want to talk back to it. They want to respond to it. They really want some assurance that this thing is really paying attention to them, and they have no confidence in that.

LAVENTHOL: Certainly Ronald Reagan is one of the people that we need to be concerned about here. It seems to me, beyond everything else on the credibility question, there's the possibility of legislation occurring that will threaten our ability or limit our ability to do what we want to do. But beyond that, it would be a terrible mistake to blame our problems on President Reagan and go home and not deal with a lot of the issues that Lou Boccardi raised. Another part of credibility is related to the kind of things that we cover and the way that we cover them, not in the sense of process but in terms of subject matter.

Five or six years ago or even a little longer, very few people in the media thought that Ronald Reagan would ever be President. We were surprised by the fact that he was elected. The overwhelming way that he was re-elected was probably not a surprise in the short term, but it certainly indicated that a vast majority of the people do like him and do like the way he operates. He has a great sense of taste in popular issues. I don't think he's the one who's creating it; I think he's riding it.

In our coverage of the abortion issue, particularly in the first few years after the Supreme Court ruling, we failed to pick up a lot of feelings that a lot of people have. We failed to represent the point of view of those who thought abortion was wrong.

One of the major issues is whether the things we're writing about or reporting on television are really the subjects that interest people, that concern them, and are important to them. For example, in China, *People's Daily* covers disasters by writing about the hero. They write about the guy who went down in the coal mine, dragged the body out, and helped improve the situation. They never write about the mangled bodies or show the blood or go into the details of the disaster for itself. They use the story as a lesson to point out how society can be better. They're looking for some meaning in the kind of events they're reporting. A lot of the American people are horrified to watch on television or read in the newspaper the endless details of aberration, of torment, of disaster, of crime, all of which, a lot of which, we have to report. They're looking for a perspective that we don't always achieve for them. By the way, I think the network news does a lot better at this than local news and probably newspapers.

JINKS: I wanted to make a point about the coverage of the President on television, with special emphasis on the shouted questions, and so on. All of this conversation started with Don Hewitt's reference to the special qualities of television as a medium, the fact that it is first of all entertainment.

We began by talking about differences between newspapers and television. Nowhere are the differences more fundamentally portrayed than in the coverage of the White House. I am far more likely to understand what is really going on in the White House, what is likely to affect American government, by reading David Broder or Jack Nelson than by listening to Sam Donaldson shout questions at the President, or hearing Sam talk for a minute and a half on the evening news. When Reagan himself wants to go to the public, he's going to do it through television. But in terms of learning what's going on in the White House that affects my life, I am far likelier to learn that from good newspaper reporters. I'm somewhat troubled when I hear Van Sauter talk about the research evidence that people like television reporters.

BARBER: John Chancellor, would you be willing to chime in on the history of the development of television news?

CHANCELLOR: Let me try to answer Larry Jinks. NBC had a meeting after the Second World War ended, perhaps in 1946. I guess CBS had a similar meeting about the same time, but ABC was out of it at that point. They addressed the following question: when we go on television with network news, are we going to have an announcer read it the way the BBC does even now, or are we going to have working journalists read the news on television? I think perhaps the phrase "working journalists" was stretching it a little bit with John Cameron Swayze, but at least he wasn't just an announcer. The American networks decided to go for newspeople doing the news on television, which is why some of us are here today.

The Paleys and the Sarnoffs and later Mr. Goldenson were really people who owned the company and lived above the store. They took personal interest in the broadcasts. Paley would go to parties all over New York City, and people would say, "How are you doing in the news, Bill?" Or, "How's Murrow doing?" It made him feel good. General Sarnoff used to have an editor on our news desk who was prepared for his telephone call at any hour of the day or night, prepared to give him a five-minute newscast on the telephone. He owned the place. That gave us an awful lot of strength, and it gave us an awful lot of pride in the place we worked. When I went to work at NBC, it had its own opera company, its own symphony orchestra with Toscanini conducting it. It regarded itself as a great American institution.

The change that's taken place has a newspaper parallel: bottom line managers are now about to move into the networks. It scares me from my generational point of view, as it ought to scare people who are being taken over by big and faceless newspaper chains. I cannot give you much hope that the standards that Paley and Sarnoff brought to their news organizations because of their pride in ownership are likely to continue very much longer. We just have to admit that.

BARBER: We're getting ready for lunch. I would like to ask Creed Black how he feels about the response his stimulus has created so far this morning.

SCHWARTZ: Cornered.

BLACK: A little bit hot there for a while. No, I think it's very stimulating. I guess I could say, "I was only kidding, fellows."

BARBER: Let's have lunch.

Friday Afternoon

BARBER: Can we begin, if you please? You have in front of you another piece of paper from Creed Black [see Appended Essay 2].

BLACK: I thought this might be a partial answer to Don's request before lunch that we go out and get some people off the street. We can see here what the Kansas City milkman is thinking. This is a piece out of *Editor & Publisher* based on a speech made by the ombudsman for the Kansas City paper. He compiled a list of the most common complaints that he heard day after day from the public. When we start looking at our problems and looking for solutions, there are some things in here for both television and newspapers to take to heart. You'll notice that arrogance is one of these. The others are all pretty basic.

BARBER: We're shifting gears to some degree from diagnostic to prescription. That gives me an opportunity to follow in the footsteps of Van Sauter with a bear story which is very brief but quite to the point, that is, that you can't get the right answer unless you ask the right question. A minister went up to the Maine woods to hunt the grizzly bear. His guide said, "Give us three days, and we'll teach you how to do it." "I'm too impatient," he said. He grabbed his gun and went out in the woods. Suddenly, there's a grizzly bear against the sky. He lifts the gun up and pulls the trigger, but it just clicks because he forgot to put the cartridge in. The bear hears it, turns, and runs towards the minister. The minister flees down the trail. He races over to a cliff and looks 3,000 feet to the rocks below. The bear is closing on him. The minister falls to his knees and pleads, "God, I've never asked anything personal before, but please let that bear get religion." Suddenly, there's a bolt of lightning across the sky. The bear stops in his tracks and looks up and then looks down again, and rushes over to the minister. The bear falls to his knees. Clapping his paws together, he bows his head and prays, "Dear Lord, for what we are about to receive, we give you thanks." (Laughter)

Okay, that's bear story number two. In terms of alternatives, Judy Woodruff has had a variety of experiences, including the regular network news and the *MacNeil/Lehrer NewsHour* and *Frontline*. I'm going to ask her to lead off with whatever she wants to say with respect to conceivable alternatives, emphases, or dimensions of television news. And then we'll go immediately to John Seigenthaler for the same kind of thing regarding print.

WOODRUFF: I don't have a bear story, sorry. I refuse to start out with the premise that everything we are doing in television is wrong. There are many things that we do extremely well, and Don Hewitt is responsible for one of them. In *60 Minutes* we have journalism that succeeds. It's interesting to watch. It's relevant. It's human. And we learn from it. Sometimes it's criticized for being too sensational. Usually it produces the kind of piece that won a DuPont Columbia University award a couple of nights ago, the story of Lenel Jeeter, the man who was sent to prison for life for a robbery that he didn't commit. Thanks to Morley Safer and the work that his team did, Lenel Jeeter was released from prison. *Nightline* is another example. What is unprofessional about the way Ted Koppel goes after a story? What is wrong with the idea of spending a whole half an hour on a subject, not "a minute-thirty," and keeping it interesting? Nobody's perfect. But *Nightline* proves that they can do it well consistently.

What about the special series of reports that some of the morning network shows have been doing, the *Today Show*, as an example? They spent a week in Moscow. Bryant Gumbel interviewed a number of Soviet officials who've probably never been interviewed by an American reporter before. We came away with a little better understanding of what's going on, which is all we can ever expect to get from one brief contact.

Take CBS's *Sunday Morning*. What is more civilized than waking up and listening to Charles Kuralt? Documentaries. The work that NBC's Marvin Kalb did on the Pope and the Bulgarian connection. The type of interviews that are done on the Sunday shows, *Meet the Press, Face the Nation.*

And last but not least, the day in, day out, long hours and hard work the networks are putting in doing the most comprehensive job they've ever done covering the daily story. I could go on and on. We in television are doing some things right already, and we ought to keep doing them that way. The problem is that we are not doing enough of them.

There still are too many "minute-fifteen" quick reports on issues that deserve 10 times that much attention, but lack the visuals to make interesting television. We need to do more background reporting of the type that newspapers do; we certainly have the resources to do it. And we are covering too many stories that don't deserve to be covered, just because they do have visuals, or because we can create fancy graphics to go along with them, or because we want to establish a presence.

How else do you explain the overkill coverage in Geneva? Yes, it was an important meeting. Yes, it should have been covered. But did it deserve the extent of coverage that it received?

Inauguration day. The networks spent hours and hours on some events that would have been better left uncovered. But what should have been covered was the main event, the inauguration and maybe the President's speech at the lunch.

It's not that there's anything wrong with covering these things. It just makes me wish that we paid as much attention to uncovering waste in the Pentagon or detailing what's right or what's wrong with the public schools in this country.

The Reagan White House, or any White House for that matter, is another case in point. The commercial networks put the President on, frequently whether he makes news or not. How can the press complain that they are being manipulated, that we are being manipulated, when we have made the decision to air whatever the vignette of the day is?

Here's a good example. In 1983, the President's pollsters found that by a 2-to-1 margin, the American people were opposed to the President's educational policies. Without changing a single item of policy, the White House launched a blitz of education-related activities. They had educational bigwigs in to visit with the President in the Oval Office. They had him photographed at a few schools. There were speeches. The networks put these stories on. After a short time, an amazing thing happened. The polls showed that the public opinion had flip-flopped. Instead of being 2-to-1 *against,* it was 2-to-1 *for* the President's policy, largely because so many stories were on the air.

The people in the White House went around boasting that all they had to do was put the President in front of some interesting backdrop, and they could count on their point getting across, if the networks would carry their story. They made no secret of this, and they still don't, that it doesn't make any difference what the correspondent says. It can be Leslie Stahl or Chris Wallace or Sam Donaldson. They can point out the contradictions. They can tell you what in-fighting in the White House led to a policy decision, a mistake, or whatever. But if they show the pictures of the President standing there in front of the balloons, or standing there at the school, or whatever, the point that the White House wants to get across gets across.

The re-election campaign last year was at some times an embarrassment for us in television because we found ourselves putting on cheering rallies night after night, even though the President wasn't making any news, not even campaign news. He was talking about the Olympic athletes, about how wonderful it is to be patriotic. The correspondents were trying. They were asking him questions about the deficit, about Mondale's budget reduction plan, but he stuck to his script. Many of the newspapers made the same mistake, but they've got the space to tell us more about the Reagan administration and about the Reagan campaign than just what happened that day.

The only way to beat that is not to put the President on every day. Show him for a few seconds if you have to, just as you show Mondale on a campaign; the American people want to know that the two candidates are alive and well. But use our precious air time to inform the public about this President's policies and their effects.

Let me talk a little about *MacNeil/Lehrer.* On occasion last fall, we tried to talk to our audience about the choices that were facing them. Jim Lehrer and Robin MacNeil had what we call "issue debates," where we would bring in three or four people from different sides of an issue like arms control, and we'd discuss it at length for 30 or 40 minutes. We tried another thing. I was lucky enough to be able to go out for a week with a candidate, and come back and do a 12- or 15-minute report on the candidate, how the campaign was organized, how he was responding to the pressures from the press, from the public, and so forth.

I just finished a piece similar to the other kinds of pieces that our correspondents have done. It ran the night of the inaugural, 12 minutes and 40 seconds on what Ronald Reagan wants from a second term. But more than that, what's motivating this man, how he runs his administration. We've all heard all this before; we've heard about it for the last four years. But it helped on that particular night to focus all of our attention again on what makes this man tick, what we ought to be on alert about, as he goes into a second term.

During the rest of the year, when there's no campaign, we take issue after issue. We take important personalities. We try to give them the same sort of treatment. We don't do it enough. We don't have the budget. We don't have the large number of people. But we are committed to taking the longer look, to going behind the scenes, to not worrying about the daily development, except for a big news story. We do it with the idea of explaining to people why they should care, and then going on at length to help them understand what happened, why it happened, and the issues involved.

The reason we're able to get such good guests, occasionally experts that nobody else has been able to find, is that we are organized into a beat system more like what the newspapers have than what the commercial networks have. There are four or five reporters who cover just politics, others who cover just foreign policy, economics, science, and medicine, or whatever. These people do not appear on the air. But they make it their business to know everything there is to know, within reason, about an issue, so that they've cultivated sources, so that when there's political turmoil in India or whatever, we've got somebody we can call on the spur of the moment and say, "Can you spend 10 or 15 minutes with us on the air tonight?"

Our own organization does not lack critics of public television. A lot of the stations in public television think we either shouldn't be in the news business at all, or we should be doing glitzier news, or we should go back to half an hour. We make a lot of mistakes. We are dull sometimes, as my friends remind me. We don't ever want to be dull, but we have decided to run that risk in the interest of showing that television can sustain itself for more than a "minute-thirty," or a "minute-forty-five" or two minutes.

A word about *Frontline,* obviously a different experience because it's a documentary. But at the very least it makes a statement because of what it sets out to do: to put an hour-long documentary on the air, once a week, three-fourths of the year. I'm proud to say we won a DuPont Award this week; I'm still boasting about that. *Frontline* does investigative reporting, such as looking at the Reagan administration's cutbacks in Social Security disability benefits. We got a recent look at Vietnam from a local station in Minneapolis, a CBS affiliate, WCCO, who sent a crew over there. They spent a month shooting in Vietnam, and the material they sent back was just extraordinary. This winter two print people, Bill Greider and Sy Hersh, have done some brilliant reporting, two different stories you're going to see in the next month or so. With smaller budgets than some of the commercial networks, *Frontline* has been able to do some pretty decent work.

The bottom line in all of this? With more time, we in television don't have to let print set the agenda, as my friend Mark Shields likes to say. We can set our own agenda when it's called for. We don't have to feel insecure, to wait for the newspapers to break ground for us. With the resources they have, the commercial networks and all of us in television are getting better. But we're still not as self-confident as we should be, and I think that's something we all should work on.

BARBER: Thank you very much, Judy. We move right away to John Seigenthaler.

SEIGENTHALER: When David Barber asked me to discuss *USA Today* as an alternative, I agreed, but not because I consider it to be an alternative, if you mean by that a replacement for anything else, and not because most (or all) of its readers buy it as a replacement. Indeed the evidence is pretty clear that most of the readers buy it as a supplement. I agreed because it seemed to me that so many of *USA Today*'s critics (and they include many who are in the print media and many who are critics of television news) have treated it as if it were an alternative to daily newspapers.

I would like to define a little more clearly what it's not, what it doesn't intend to be, and what indeed it can become, an alternative to daily newspapers. Beneath the surface of the cracks about "McPaper" and "freeze-dried journalism," and the joke about the new Pulitzer Prize category for the paragraph of the year, and beyond the dislike for its founder's style and dress, there was a serious concern whether *USA Today* would set some new standard for all of journalism, that its audience would be so magnetized by it that they would require other publications to copy it. Or that editors would be so fascinated by it or frightened by it that they would alter what they do and how they do it.

In some quarters, that criticism became almost shrill. Some local newspapers, anticipating the arrival of *USA Today* in town, began to print full page weather maps, splash color all over the top of page one, and expand the sports section news hole. I spent too much time one evening in Washington arguing with some editors (some of whom are here today) about what *USA Today* is and what it isn't. To quote Don Hewitt, it is what it is. *USA Today* repeatedly says what it is: a quick read. And now 1,300,000 people take it five days a week because they want a quick read.

In the planning period, I predicted it would fail, because it didn't seem to me that there was any need for it. If I had seen the research before I made that judgment, I would have been unsure about it from the outset. That research established that there was an audience of about 5 percent in most newspaper markets in the country, people who said they had a need for another publication, people who could afford to buy it, people who were busy, and who, in response to questions, set out some guides for the planners to follow. That early research indicated that the publication had to be different from the local newspapers, from *The New York Times* or *The Wall Street Journal*, which have national editions, different in design and different in daily content. In retrospect, it's remarkable how closely *USA Today* has followed those guidelines as they were set out in that research, and how, with few exceptions, it has reached just about that targeted audience, in some places a little more and in some a little less, of 5 percent.

It's clear to everybody that it's not a publication that's going to replace local newspapers or newspapers that have national editions. As most of you know, my own role there is limited to the opinion page. I've never attended a daily news planning meeting; I'm not part of the setting of that different daily news agenda. But I do know that there is a calculated effort every day by those editors who are there, to try to the best of their ability to create a different news agenda, so that this paper is not a replica of any local newspaper or newspaper with a national edition.

As Joseph Pulitzer once said, "A newspaper should be proud of the enemies it makes." He said it when his papers were under attack from President Theodore Roosevelt. At times, some of the criticism seemed to suggest there is something wrong with *USA Today* because it has failed to make many enemies so far. Yet much of the mail I receive in response to the opinion pages is not unlike the mail I get in response to editorials in *The Tennessean*. It comes from the National Rifle Association. It comes from the Right to Life Movement. It comes from those who want Jesus in the crib on the public streets and in the parks at

Christmastime. It comes from the people who didn't want the press in Grenada, from those who supported James Watt and Rita Lavelle and Anne Gorsuch.

I really don't think of them or look upon them as enemies. But I don't apologize to them or others for what makes them upset about what they get from those pages. And there is a larger body that responds with positive expressions and favorable comments about what they see as balance and fairness, and what they regard as a pleasurable reading experience.

USA Today is too young, too new, still too uncertain of its future (either its financial future or its journalistic future) to be used as a model for anything. It's still too early to know whether we'll ever earn legitimacy as a real alternative. It is not Van Sauter's bear, nor Gene Patterson's moose, nor even at this point a viable alternative. It hasn't lived long enough to learn to be arrogant, but with time and practice it may succeed.

BARBER: John is talking about shorter news and what he calls a pleasurable reading experience. One could derive from what he says an implicit suggestion that maybe ordinary, regular newspapers might move somewhat in that direction, away from longer pieces and less pleasurable reading, towards perhaps some more of that color in the graphics as well as in the language.

One way of looking at *USA Today* is not necessarily that people would buy it instead of a daily newspaper, but rather does it say something to the daily newspaper about some ways which might make it more credible to its readership? Judy Woodruff's concerns in television can be considered a witness of some things that might be done: more time to break out of the brevity trap; more freedom from routinized coverage of the President every time he appears; less dependence on visuals and more of the kind of digging and investigative work that has been more often traditionally done in print to uncover explanation as well as simply events.

I was hoping that we might take those suggestions as a beginning point for some discussion of what directions change in these two regular news media might take.

BERGER: You're suggesting that newspapers need to be more like television and have shorter things, and television should be more like newspapers and have longer things.

BURGIN: John Chancellor remarked about "bottom line journalism" or "bottom line management." Maybe you're not even mindful of this, but *USA Today* has done American journalism, specifically newspapers, a very great favor. There are probably something like 1,750 daily newspapers remaining in this country. About 97 percent of those are in monopoly markets. Of the 45 or so papers in Florida, all are in monopoly markets, including Miami, which has got a joint operating agreement and doesn't really count.

USA Today got a lot of publishers off the dime, and for that I am thankful and grateful. It made us think anew of ways to compete. It made us re-examine what we have, whether there should be shorter stories, longer stories, more emphasis on graphics, or whatever. It made me wonder again about credibility. We spent $100,000 to find out about the credibility of one newspaper, *The Orlando Sentinel*, and discovered one thing that the public does perceive, the lack of competition. So I hope *USA Today* makes it in every market, if for no other reason, that it's all we've got to compete against.

BRODER: I'd like to suggest a thread that connects these two comments from Judy Woodruff and from John Seigenthaler. Both of them are saying in part that there's a need to recognize a kind of segmentation of the audience, that there is a natural sort of size and bulk of stories, that there is a natural weight and scope to various kinds of stories.

I'm probably in a minority in our newsroom because I admire a lot of what *USA Today* has done. And what I admire most is that it has organized itself as a newspaper in a way that lets you as a reader get a crack at what has happened in one page, and then find out, if you want to read more about that aspect of the news, where to look. That's something that papers like mine have notably refused to do. We just dump ourselves and all of our overwhelming bulk on the doorstep every damn morning and leave it to the readers to find their way through that mess.

I suggest as a possible area of exploration for this group the point that was suggested by Van Sauter's earlier comments about there being a six-track communication system in this country where different needs can be well satisfied by different media. One of the things I think would be helpful is for each medium to become more conscious of what specific need it is trying to focus on. And the second thing, which I think does not exist hardly at all, is if we could somehow loosen up enough so that we could refer our readers or viewers to places where they could go to pursue their own interest in that subject. *USA Today* does that in keying off the lead page in each section. You stop short on a lot of stories where I would like to go further. But you're ahead of us because we never tell the reader where to go to find out more about anything. We assume that what we have delivered on that particular date is all anybody is going to want to know. That's unrealistic.

I don't know why there couldn't be a regular way in which radio or television could refer to magazines and newspapers, where newspapers could refer to magazines, where magazines could refer to books, to give people some guidance for further exploration of a subject they may be interested in.

HEWITT: You are in a unique position; Post-Newsweek is the perfect organism if you want to try that as an experiment, and the Post-Newsweek stations. You have the structure to do that, but we don't. I mean, what are we going to say: "You want to read more about this, read Jack Nelson?" If I owned a newspaper, the very first thing I'd do is hire John Seigenthaler to run the opinion page. I think that's the best opinion page in America, the fairest opinion page in America. There is probably no credibility problem because I don't think anybody can conceive that page as being left, right, anything. That's what is so great about that paper, probably the only thing at this point. They whet people's appetite for news. That's what we should do, and that's where you guys are falling down. We've excited the whole country about seeing news events, going to places, doing things. But if they want to read more about it, it doesn't seem to me that you're picking up from us. Newspapers should rise to the challenge that the American public is now better informed. Their appetites are whetted every night: we take you to the Berlin Wall; we take you to Lebanon. That's a service we've done for newspapers.

NELSON: I'd like to make one point about *USA Today*. As Dave Burgin said, it's had a tremendous impact on other newspapers. Look at weather coverage. Look at sports coverage. Look at television coverage. They've had a tremendous impact on all those areas.

Dave Broder was mentioning the question of bulk. On a recent Sunday, I went out and picked up the *L.A. Times, The New York Times,* and *The Washington Post,* and stepped on the scales. They weighed 16 pounds. We run some of the longest damn stories; I know nobody ever reads them. I just came from an editorial meeting in L.A. where there was a big discussion about the fact that we'll sometimes run a story of 5,000 words. Occasionally there is a story worth that length. Newspapers get involved in writing very long stories, a series of stories, and sometimes the idea is to win an award. One of the reasons for our credibility problems is the great emphasis on winning awards. Whether it's a Pulitzer, or whether it's covering some industry that gives an award, there's a tremendous proliferation of awards: editor of the year, broadcast journalist of the year, this of the year, that of the year. When they criticize newspapers, members of the public say, "He's just out to win an award; that's all he's trying to do." That's something we never talk too much about, but it's there. If newspapers undertake a project just "to win an award," that's the worst way in the world to cover a story. I would like to think that nobody ever gets an award except as a by-product of doing the job, but I don't think that's what happens.

BARBER: Is it true that you don't get awards for short stories?

NELSON: You seldom see an award for a tightly written, very good story. Mike Miller, our national editor, had a meeting of national correspondents and editors out of the Washington bureau recently. He made the point that some people seem to think that quantity is quality in the way they played stories, in the way stories are written; and I think that's true. There are a few reporters who write very long stories, who seem to have some license to write very long stories; and they objected and took great offense. But I think that accusation is accurate, that many people look on the length of the story as some standard of quality.

SCHWARTZ: This should be our worst problem in newspapers, that the stories are too long!

LAVENTHOL: I want to ask John Seigenthaler a question. It's conventional wisdom that *USA Today* is a "good news" newspaper, that it emphasizes things that are more upbeat than downbeat. There is little crime news, little violence news. I was mentioning earlier about the Chinese model, where they write about the hero in a disaster; *USA Today* seems to have that kind of approach. I would like your assessment of both how that is and whether it works.

SEIGENTHALER: As I said, I've never been to one of the news meetings, and don't really plan to go to one. I made up my mind at the outset that I'd like to keep the opinion pages as far away from any other editor in that building as I could, and in order to do that, I'd set an example by not sticking my nose into anybody else's business. I don't mean that I don't have a working relationship with them, and I don't mean that I don't use ideas that they develop, and play off their ball, and will help them in any way that I can.
But in the specific area of whether there is a calculation to be the "good news" bearer, my perception is that there is no calculation there. There is clear-

ly an effort every day to look at the expected news agenda, at those stories that are going to appear on the front page of all of our papers around the country, and to take from that agenda what has to go outside, those one or two stories that are just so compelling that you're going to have to play them out front. I think there is no written or spoken mandate to be the "good news" bearer at *USA Today*.

BARBER: How about Al Neuharth? He goes around making speeches about the evening news.

SEIGENTHALER: Yes, he does talk a lot about the journalism of hope. But he's always careful to juxtapose the journalism of hope with the journalism of despair. And he's always careful to say that when he shouts the good, he whispers the bad. And you read it, and they're both there. I don't think the people who work there come in every day and say, "How can we put the best light on this story?"

The initial judgment on the first day of publication, to put Princess Grace's death outside and Jemayel's in that box and then refer it inside, that set in the minds of an awful lot of people that that's the way it was going to be. And Neuharth defended that decision and has since then defended it. From that day to this, that image, that label has been on the paper. But a day-to-day reading of the paper will find bad news stories outside, played big.

LAVENTHOL: I wasn't criticizing. All newspapers and all television shows are edited by a selective process, both in terms of the material that you use and in terms of the kind of emphasis you give that material. The *New York Post*, for example, will take that material and present it in an entirely different way, and give you a sense of the horror of the world that you're living in. And another paper, for example, *The New York Times*, on the same kind of subject will try to give it a more balanced presentation, a larger perspective of the world where there's good and bad. And *USA Today*, for example, on July 4th will go with a lovely fireworks picture and "Nation Celebrates a Glorious Fourth." Its selective process is upbeat, patriotic, positive, not deceitful. It's "what's happening." But it's how you play it, how you display it, what you emphasize, what you choose to use in terms of your resources, that creates an overall climate and attitude. *USA Today* in that sense is probably more closely attuned to the perceptions of people who read newspapers, to the kind of things they would like to see in newspapers, whether they're right or wrong. If they're wrong, we haven't done the job of trying to explain to them why it is that we're doing what we're doing.

BARBER: Whether or not *USA Today* does it consciously, is it a good idea? That is, will it increase the credibility of the print press in the country to have more upbeat stories?

MATUSOW: A decision to "make people feel better about themselves, their communities and their government" is much more apt to occur at the local television level. The industry believes that people feel very depressed by the overload of bad news, and that a local television station can increase its popularity in the community by emphasizing the public's wishes. The role of cheerleader for the community or the President or whatever, is basically a political decision. I think it's very harmful overall to credibility.

On the other hand, what we didn't talk about this morning was a feeling by the public, quite correct, that newspapers as well as television overemphasize the negative. Michael Robinson's most recent study showed that there really was no political bias in the news, but that, by a ratio of 20-to-1, negative stories outnumbered positive stories in the major media organs that he examined. That really is something to think about. People just can't stand that much bad news; they just can't take it.

I don't think the antidote is to get out there and wave the flag and be patriotic and pump for feeling better about ourselves. Maybe a wider range of stories should be covered, a wider range of trend stories. In other words, more creative thinking needs to be spent on how to overcome what has become a very deep institutional bias in favor of negative news.

SEIGENTHALER: Let me just say a word in response to David and Barbara. There is absolutely no doubt that *USA Today* will take events, for example, the Martin Luther King birthday, the inaugural, the two national conventions, etc., and that those stories do get dramatic positive play outside. There's no question that it is legitimate news. It just seems that the approach is different. And I certainly think that while you might not have meant that as criticism, I think that's fair criticism.

HEWITT: What do you mean by credibility? Somebody explain it to me. Everybody uses the word differently. Would somebody define what credibility is in the context of this meeting? I've heard it used to explain popularity. What is credibility?

NOLAN: It's not what Van Sauter said; it's not likability. Let's start out with that.

HEWITT: All right. What's credibility if it's not likability? Who are we to decide?

NOLAN: I think it's believability.

HEWITT: So you're saying that the public does not believe what you print and what we broadcast?

NELSON: I would say that to some extent they have questions about whether it's fair or not.

HEWITT: You say credibility is believability. Sometimes very unfair things are believable.

BURGIN: Somebody said earlier that you have to ask the right question to get the right answer. So if you're going to find out what credibility is, these are the components: believability, fair and objective reporting, accurate reporting, integrity, professional versus not-professional, and this may be taking issue with what you said, cares about community, careful with grammar and spelling, easy to read, timely, up-to-the-minute reporting, good value for the money, bright and lively as opposed to dull and boring, and helps me understand the time and place we live in versus does not. Of all those factors, the two most important are cares about my community and helps to understand the time and place we live in.

HEWITT: What's that got to do with being credible?

BURGIN: Those are the components of credibility.

HEWITT: No, but I'm saying everybody here has his own definition of credibility.

BURGIN: Well, these are unassailable.

HEWITT: If being fair to the community is credibility, then I see this whole thing in an entirely different light.

BARBER: I shouldn't think that fairness to community is a definition of credibility, but maybe a contributor to it. Technically, etymologically, the word "credibility" comes from the word "belief" or "to believe." The useful ambiguity is the distinction between whether it's believed and whether it's worth believing. Part of it is how is the thing received by others, and part of it is what, in our judgment or in the judgment of worthy readers, ought to be believed about it. In other words, one way of making news more believable is making it worth believing. You've hit on a problem: it is not just the popular reaction we're getting at, but it's also the worthiness of what's put out.

HEWITT: But one man's credibility is not another man's.

CHANCELLOR: We have to go beyond just the old and easy definition of credibility and acceptance of the product. What I find interesting when I begin to think about credibility and hostility (if there is any towards the institution of journalism in America) is that we've had a very interesting exercise in the early projections made by the networks using exit polls on elections. We find ourselves this year in the position where people want to reject truth. They don't question the accuracy of the early calls; they all know they're on the money. What they're saying to us is something else. They're saying, "We want to go beyond accuracy, we want to go beyond truth, we don't want you to tell us this." I haven't figured it out in my own mind, but the rejection of truth on the part of any audience or group is something that ought to make journalists sit up and take notice.

BERGER: I don't think it's a rejection of truth.

JINKS: You're talking about a delay of truth for a reason that has to do with fairness, and you've got to have fairness in that definition.

CHANCELLOR: We're all trying to find out what's going on, as accurately as we can, and getting it to people as quickly as we can. I'm not defending early calls; I hate them. I would love to go back to blackboards and the wait until 7:00 in the morning to find out who is President. But that's beside the point. Journalism has developed a tool to tell people what's happening in the country, and the people are rejecting it. That complicates the mix of our relationship as journalists to the public in that there are certain things that we do that are soundly based. Exit polls, which I hate, are soundly based. And we offer such information to them, and in growing numbers they are saying, "Uh-uh. We don't want that."

BURGIN: I think they're saying, "I don't want your sports reporters to tell me who won the game until the game is over. I don't want your election reporters to tell me who won the election until all the folks have had a chance to vote."

CHANCELLOR: Actually the election, if you want to be really brutal about it, is decided by the time the networks get their second cut on their exit polls at about 6:00 in the evening. It's a nasty truth, but there it is.

JINKS: But there are other factors involved, other West Coast races, for example, that are affected because people know that their vote in the presidential election is irrelevant.

BLACK: This is an unloaded question, and I guess Van Sauter could answer it better than anybody. In discussions like this, we always hear television people talk about the time constraints. What do you have, 22 minutes of time on a 30-minute show? Judy's been telling us what you can do when you have an hour. What is the resistance, Van, to a one-hour network show? In Lexington, until recently, your CBS outlet there was running an hour and a half of local news before they ever got to the network, and there was a lot of fluff in there. As a viewer, I would much rather have seen an hour of network news plus an hour of local news.

SAUTER: Well, our affiliates would say it's a network problem; and the network would say it's an affiliate problem. The basic difficulty is that the affiliates have a time period which they have traditionally used for local news or any other form of programming that time of the day. To facilitate a one-hour network broadcast, they would have to surrender one half-hour of what is now their local time, their editorial option, if you will. Some of them oppose giving it up because they have a territorial imperative. It's always been theirs, and they're not about to give it up. Others refuse to give it up because there's a severe economic disadvantage to them if they take a half-hour of time and turn it over to the network. They lose the eight minutes of commercials or the 16 commercial units that would be in that half-hour period.

BLACK: They don't share in the network revenues?

SAUTER: They do. But they would do far better at that time of the day selling locally rather than taking a payment for giving up their time to the network. So there are two basic problems. One, the affiliates are saying, "It's not economically feasible," and second, "This is our time to do with as we want, whether it's local news or whatever." The proposals that the networks have taken to the affiliates have always been viewed as inequitable by the affiliates; either the networks are not giving enough compensation to justify giving up a half-hour, or whatever. It's at loggerheads, and it'll be that way, I suspect, for years. At some point, one network will do it, and as soon as one does it, the other two will fall quickly into line.

MATUSOW: What time would it be?

SAUTER: It would be at approximately the same time it is now. It would probably be Eastern time, 6:30 to 7:30.

MATUSOW: What about 10:00 to 11:00?

NELSON: Don't you have a large audience from 10:00 to 11:00 at night?

SCHWARTZ: They watch *Dallas*.

SAUTER: From 10:00 to 11:00, they're watching entertainment programming.

NELSON: Has anyone tried to put on a news show at 10:00 at night?

SAUTER: A lot of people do such news shows, in Los Angeles, New York, and Chicago.

NELSON: Suppose all three put it on at 10:00?

SAUTER: Then you would take an audience and fragment it even further. The economic return would be absolutely minuscule, and you would lose a significant amount of revenue. On top of that, the lead-in you would give to your local news at 11:00 would be catastrophic. It is just not practical. The networks, the network-owned stations, and the network affiliates compete generally in the 5:00 to 7:00 period with one form of news or another, and they're very, very successful there, or they traditionally have been successful there, because that's when they do news, because it's news competing with news. Across the country, the independent stations, as they multiply in number, are bringing in entertainment shows of some merit and playing those against the news. Any time news has to play against an effective entertainment show, it's running at a terrible disadvantage. Some of the atrophy in early news numbers over the last few years is a direct result of the entertainment competition against them. But a 10:00 to 11:00 news show would be an economic catastrophe.

CHANCELLOR: There is a station in New York that puts *Dallas* on at 7:00 in the evening. I don't know what that's done to our ratings in New York, but I can guess.

HEWITT: It hasn't done well; the reruns of *Dallas* have been a big disappointment.

BERGER: Because everyone saw it the first time.

VANOCUR: At the risk of wearing a hairshirt on the outside, on the network level we have not yet come up with what the Gannett chain did with *USA Today.* I'm opposed to an hour news show because I don't think we know what to do with an hour news show, unless it's just shoe-horning double what we do right now. Consider what television looks like today. It starts in the morning with the regular news shows from 7:00 to 9:00 and then at 6:00. At CBS, it almost merges because of the late night show with Charlie Rose.

In many areas, local stations (maybe not Orlando) are very good. They've got a lot of money; they put on a noonday show; they start broadcasting news at 4:00. To keep their affiliates, the networks have to feed stuff that they have, which they intend to show later on the evening news, to these affiliates. By the time the network news show comes on, plus Ted Turner, you have about been newsed out.

Now we have to face a very difficult problem, how to redefine network news. I'm a faithful watcher of *Entertainment Tonight* because they do a pretty credible job about things in which I'm interested. If anybody at this table will stand up and say, "No, my eyes don't glaze over when they talk about SALT," I will buy that person five drinks tonight.

Twenty-five years ago Nick Williams redefined the *Los Angeles Times* because he knew what television was doing. We have got to figure out a way to redefine television news. Nobody talks about it more than public broadcasting, about the equipment, and the technology. We have now the capability to be almost everywhere almost at once. And having the capability to go almost everywhere almost at once makes it important. Because if we weren't there, it wouldn't be important. So that makes everything significant. If everything's significant, nothing is significant. So until we redefine what we want to do in the face of these challenges of technology and the growth of local stations, I'm against giving us an hour news show.

BARBER: Sandy, could you just back up a minute for those of us who are not regular viewers of *Entertainment Tonight.* What lesson has that program for the regular news shows?

VANOCUR: It does a lot of things that I'm interested in, like celebrity birthdays. People talk about Edward R. Murrow. Remember in the 1930s Walter Winchell was the most important influence on America's involvement in World War II. Jim Rowe told me that Roosevelt's charge to him was to keep Walter Winchell happy and get him a reserve commission in the Navy, because Roosevelt wanted us to be prepared. Jimmy Fidler, Hedda Hopper, Kaltenborn, all those people. You read Ed Sullivan and Walter Winchell. Who were the others? The so-called "sob sisters," and so forth. *Photoplay, Modern Screen,* and so forth.

Everybody fed upon that. *Life Magazine* was marvelous in that department.

HEWITT: Sandy, you mentioned Ed Murrow. I directed *See It Now.* It went off the air because it could not compete. Murrow never caught on in this country with *See It Now.* It had ratings that were so low that I remember the time they dropped us in Atlanta because we couldn't compete with *Amos 'n' Andy.* And we got dropped somewhere else because we couldn't compete with *The Lone Ranger.* Murrow, of *Person to Person,* who took you to look at Marilyn Monroe's closet, was always the top 10 show. Somewhere there's an unrealistic view of us by you print guys. Jack Chancellor's father "edited" the *Chicago Tribune.* Everybody runs a television network. Everybody knows what we should do, what we shouldn't do. Van does the best possible job to reach the most possible people, to be the most responsible without putting the whole place in the red and going out of business. I'm sorry, but I had to bring the Murrow thing in.

VANOCUR: It's true, and no disrespect to Ed Murrow. We are at a bigger crisis point, beyond the arrogance and the fear of us, which is the boredom factor. The figures indicate that our audiences are diminishing with the evening newscast, and I find it rare to see people who really can learn anything or want to learn anything from what we have by that time of night.

CHANCELLOR: William Allen White said there were three things that every man thinks he can do better than every other man. (The sexist tone of that remark shows you how long ago it was made.) They are: to make love to a woman, to set logs in the fireplace, and to edit a newspaper. I agree with Sandy that the network programs need to be redefined. When we began news broadcasts with John Cameron Swayze a long time ago and with Doug Edwards at CBS, there weren't all that many local stations. There was no alternative competition. The networks felt that they had to put out a credible national news report, and that report arrived in virgin form in most of the markets. The local stations were covering cats in trees and accidents on the superhighways.

Now the mix is entirely different. We are very often preceded by one-, one-and-a-half-, and two-hour local programs that cover not just the community but also the entire world. And the networks in their dimwitted, dinosaur way come along with programs that cover the world and the nation. Aside from occasionally better correspondents, they almost duplicate what the audience has seen on those local programs. This is a great opportunity if the networks could only wake up to it. The networks should acknowledge and recognize the truth that the audiences had that news. I just added it up here. If you live in New York City, and you watch NBC, there's five and a half hours of news a day, starting at 6:30 in the morning, ending up at 11:30 at night, five and a half hours of it. Of that time, we only have one half-hour for the serious stuff, and I think we ought to be far more serious about it.

The networks ought to acknowledge that there are other media and other parts of television, especially local television, covering the news for better or for worse. But we should not think, as I thought for so many years, that we are the program of record, the only serious news that the public would get. We ought to go beyond that now, use the technology that we have, and give the people a genuinely classic network world news service that is not a replication of much of what they've just seen.

BERGER: You can't assume that everyone's seen the 4:00 to 7:00 news.

CHANCELLOR: They're going to see a lot of it.

SAUTER: It's true that the people who watch a network evening news broadcast know the news from any number of sources before they come to the set.

At CBS News three years ago, we began to make a substantial change in our broadcast, and part of that change was directly responsive to the fact that we were no longer the first one with that information.

We need to make substantial changes in the way news is done, but I probably come to it from an entirely different direction than you do. In this context you're very editorially-oriented, while I'm very cost-oriented in this discussion. If you factor out the *20/20*s and the *60 Minutes,* the network news organizations lose zillions of dollars, zillions of dollars, enough money that if it were a newspaper it would be shut down.

We have to make a change in those evening broadcasts. At CBS at least, we've begun to make a change. NBC and ABC have been following our lead on that, although I think many editorial purists would say it's not a good lead. But we have a system that works; it serves the audience. But is it the best form of service we can give with the quality of the employees and the technology available? I don't think it is.

The Sharon case notwithstanding, I've always wanted to do the evening news as a news magazine, where a lot of the people we have in the field would be information gatherers and video gatherers. That material would be sent to New York and collated there. The anchorpeople would fundamentally do all the news, with the exception of probably 15 or 20 correspondents who had some specialty that was very important, that either they did very well, or their expertise could not be duplicated. But in the meantime, we have to keep in mind that, unlike most of the newspapers in this country, we are involved in a cutthroat competition, and we cannot afford to lose audience through program experimentation. Whatever change that's going to be made is going to be made quite gradually, because the financial stakes are just too large.

HEWITT: Van, is it ever possible ABC News, NBC News, and CBS News will be a service to local stations, and we will service them the way Lou Boccardi services newspapers?

SAUTER: No. There are certainly local stations who would prefer that to the current arrangement. There are some local stations who would like to have the networks become in effect electronic wire services.

We are going to go into an electronic wire service business ourselves, but primarily to service foreign clients.

There's going to be no substantial change between now and the end of this decade. The face of television network news or the relationship between the viewer and the set, fundamentally will not change over the next 15 years. But nine or 10 years from now, viewers at home will be capable of having large, wall-size, high-definition television. When that begins to happen, every business that we represent in this room is going to change.

Fundamentally, the only persons not affected by it will be the reporters, because they are really the software generators. But it is highly conceivable and technically feasible that within 15 years, we'll be able to sit at home with the right kind of interactive television control device with us, put up on the screen a large index of video and print stories, and call those up at will, in effect becoming our own editors. Or we can go to the information service to which we subscribe, and they will do it for us, give us all text, all video, or an integration of the two. That will be the most significant change, and it's going to change everything in our business except the basic function of the journalist.

GARTNER: How will you call up the commercials?

NELSON: Yes, who's going to pay for it?

SAUTER: You're really talking about a system which, in effect, is not unlike pay television, where you buy this service from an information service. There'll probably be several competing information services, and they will very probably flow out of some amalgamation between existing broadcast and existing print form in some fashion. That's going to change a lot of things in our business, because that service will be readily available, always current, and available at the viewers' discretion. It's going to change the world.

NOLAN: There was one witness we haven't called; I thought of him during Judy's and John's presentation on different forms. John Keats line: "Oh, thou prisoner of silence and slow time," from "Ode on a Grecian Urn."* I thought of that line with an hour of news and a smaller, shorter newspaper. We, of course, are prisoners of noise and speed. What's the worst thing in television: dead air. What's the worst thing in newspapers: a missed deadline. Notice they both have the word "dead" in them. And that's where we'll all be if we don't move on to these new forms and understand them.

I think the greatest enemy of both of the new forms is gimmickry. I remember when Jim Bellows came to Washington after having edited the *New York Herald Tribune*, the single most influential modern newspaper, I think it's fair to say. He started out every day with a gimmick on page one, "Q&A" every day. And guess why. Because it had credibility. Because the *Playboy* interviews had given the "Q&A" format credibility. And I said, "Jim, you mean to say you're going to have a major news story, you're going to have the Russian Army moving into Poland, and that "Q&A" with the Prince Georges County sewer commissioner is going to stay there all day, all editions?" And he said, "Yep, yep. It's gotta stay that way."

That's what makes me a little itchy about *USA Today*. I can see the headline: "Soviet troops invade Bucharest." And in the meantime that cute little graphic: "How many hot dogs were consumed at the Super Bowl?" You wouldn't want to miss that on page one.

I feel constrained by these gimmicks, and that's what worries me about the shorter form and the longer form too. If you want *Entertainment Tonight,* you're going to get it. Judy has a problem on her show of disdain towards "talking heads." I'm afraid the network will have a different kind of talking heads, the rock group Talking Heads. I'm sure we'd have rock video in an hour-long TV program. I don't think television is ready for the hour-long news show. I don't think I'm ready for the tighter hot dog graphics. So we can't have Grecian urns, but I hope we stay away from gimmicks.

---

* *Keats actually wrote, "Thou foster child of silence and slow time."*

ROY PETER CLARK: We talked about this at a previous seminar when Bill Greider was here discussing some of his work. We talked about a serious distinction that Professor John Robinson made between truly informing the public and simply making information available to the public. At that time, I made the comment that one of my favorite news programs is on Saturday morning CBS, called *In the News*. It's supposed to be a news program for children, but when I watch it I'm always astonished at how much I learn about world events, about issues, about the Palestinians. They show you maps. They slow down the pace of information a little bit. The language is clear and straightforward. I feel informed in ways that I don't quite feel informed on some other kinds of news programs. Another model might be a style of news-telling on the network which is a little bit slower perhaps and more explanatory, but manages somehow to be informative and interesting at the same time.

* * *

[At this point, the conference broke into three unrecorded caucuses: broadcast, print, and management. After a half-hour, the conferees returned, and each group presented its report via a short list and comment by a spokesperson.]

* * *

BARBER: First we'll hear from the rapporteurs, and they can be corrected or supplemented by the members of their group. We'll begin with John Chancellor.

TELEVISION

1. Anchor summarizes news, then longer stories. Variation in length.
2. Quotes should be longer.
3. Identify person in sound, by name.
4. Experiment with local press-TV cooperation
5. Not agreed on: Source problems, editing, ambush interviews.

CHANCELLOR: Our group talked about broadcasting, and we divided into about four categories, Mr. Chairman. One was the compression of the reports on television that the reporters do. Some said they thought that these compressed reports were trying to do too much, that we ought to break up the news on television programs into reports of different length, that some of them could be a lot shorter than they are, and that would allow room for some to be longer. Don Hewitt pointed out that television, especially at the network level, still tends to want to put news on the air just for the record, when it may not be of that much interest to the audience on that particular day.

We talked about people speaking on television in units called "sound bytes" in the television business. Barbara Matusow pointed out that they had now reached the irreducible minimum: they were so short that nobody ever got to finish a sentence. We thought that might be damaging to credibility because people were just speaking in little tiny bursts. Again, Matusow said that when we have people say eight words on a very complicated subject, we're assuming a level of concentration that the audience may not in fact have, given the distractions of being at home.

We also talked about identifying people on television only by what we call "supers," the words, the letters that come on under their faces. There's a tendency in television to depersonalize people who appear on it, and just to identify them in the supers. Hewitt pointed out that they have never done that on *60 Minutes*. Again there is a problem of a lack of comprehension, because if you're in your living room and the kids want to be played with and the dog wants to be taken out and you're trying to make a martini and this thing comes up for eight seconds on television, you're probably going to miss it.

In terms of sources, we did not agree at all. But there was a general feeling that a lot of the things that networks and local stations are given by the police ought to be handled with more care, because the danger exists that people will think that the big media are giving them news that springs from the head of the newscaster and doesn't really exist. We talked about privacy, especially for grieving relatives. Don Hewitt believes that picturing grief is obscene, but he added that the newspapers and magazines very often get the pictures of the same grieving relatives that we put on television. We also noted that in some cases relatives of the Marines who were killed in Beirut called the networks, asked them to come over and take pictures of them grieving in public. The networks did so, which led me to point out that death in America now needs to be validated by being on television.

We talked about ambush interviews. Hewitt said, "This is a phony term made up by newspapers, who have done it for years." We did not come to a satisfactory ethical judgment on *60 Minutes* once having its people pose as cancer patients. But Hewitt pointed out that the newspapers show pictures taken in banks of people robbing banks when they have not been indicted or even caught.

We talked about local television and discussed the idea that more cooperation on a big, important local story between a local newspaper and a local television operation might be a good idea. Somebody said, "Is television copy less carefully edited than newspaper copy?" Barbara Matusow said yes. Ralph Renick said that very often on a local station, somebody will come in and record the copy that the reporter has written, and it gets matched up to the sound mike. All the producer wants is to know how long it is. And that is our report.

BARBER: Thank you. Does any member of that caucus wish to amend the report of your chair or supplement it in a brief way?

RENICK: Just 30 seconds worth about this idea of cooperation. *The Miami Herald* has done several major stories; the Bahamas corruption revelations come to mind. Despite a very detailed and thorough investigative job, I'm afraid everybody didn't read it. It could have been presented in another form in prime time. One medium could complement the other in terms of cross-promotion of the story. As we identify major problems within the community, maybe we could seek out three or four during the year and have various stations participate with *The Herald*, or *The News*. You may find in your community a TV station that would be able to cooperate with the newspaper on something like this, perhaps as a pilot project. We could do it in a way that would not be interpreted as collusive.

WOODRUFF: When John talked about shorter reports, he did not mean shortening them from a minute-fifteen to 50 seconds. He meant having the anchor reading the stories that we assume everybody's already aware of, and then spending more time, two or three or more minutes, on stories that warrant our attention.

BARBER: Thank you. Could we turn to Marty Nolan and the print group?

PRINT

1. Tighter control of use of anonymous sources.
2. Written memo by mistake-maker (Seigenthaler's Caveat).
3. Spend more on salaries and counsel.
4. Outreach to readers explaining the news business.
5. Limit awards, each newspaper awards its own.
6. Fairness, skeptical not cynical.
7. Accuracy over all.

NOLAN: These ideas take the form of recommendations to the management of American newspapers. First is to tighten control over the use of anonymous sources. Although we all acknowledge the value of confidential sources, we realize that this tradition has been abused. As Lou Boccardi said, it shouldn't sail right through the desk. Before an anonymous source is quoted in the paper, a higher level of management (for instance, an assistant managing editor) should be called upon to approve it.

On mistakes, corrections, and clarifications: as an internal management guide and tool, we urge that a written memo from the person making the mistake be produced to a superior, as a means of keeping track of who makes the mistakes.

BERGER: A written memo?

NOLAN: A written memo. If there's a mistake, with facts wrong and requiring a correction, a memo should be filed saying why you made the mistake.

The third recommendation: the publishers of American newspapers should come to the realization that quality in American journalism requires the expenditure of money. To get the editorial talent to produce credible newspapers requires publishers to provide money for adequate staffing and, increasingly important, to provide competent counsel in First Amendment cases, which are multiplying, alas.

The fourth recommendation involved maintaining an outreach program involving readers, explaining the news business generally to readers, an effort that would require editors' involvement and also reporters' involvement. As part of this outreach program, we urge American newspaper editors to be just as open and responsive to the questions and criticism that our business gets as we expect other institutions to be open and responsive to the criticism those institutions get.

On the matter of journalism awards, we think that the proliferation of these awards has intensified our problems of credibility with the public. We urge that each newspaper itself provide a mechanism of awards that we could explain to the readers, for example: "We thought in the last year X story was good, X photograph was good." Nobody saw this as a form of shameless promotion so much as explaining what we do. And we don't want to rig news stories towards the anticipation of some prestigious award; we urge the abandonment of that practice, if it should ever go on anywhere. We also urge intense scrutiny of every outside award presented by a special industry or group, maintaining a skeptical attitude towards the meaning behind the donor's gift.

Our final recommendation concerns the all-important attitude American newspapers should have towards fairness. We need to maintain a skeptical attitude towards government and towards all institutions. But we also need to keep in mind our job, which is to maintain a daily sense of fairness to all concerned and to avoid cynicism at all cost.

BARBER: Thank you. Are there any corrections or additions from that group?

SEIGENTHALER: I'm just sitting here between my two friends from CBS, and the moment Marty mentioned a memo for the files on corrections, a bell rang in my head that said, "Benjamin, Benjamin, Benjamin," the Benjamin Report in the Westmoreland case.

NOLAN: We don't doubt that there will be all kinds of lawyers interested in these memos, not to mention the representatives of various newspaper guilds and unions who might wonder what these pieces of paper are destined for. So we realize there are people who are going to want to get their hands on them. But does that mean that you don't keep a record?

BLACK: Van, if you had the Benjamin investigation to do over, would you have a lawyer do it to make it privileged?

SAUTER: This is being recorded?

BARBER: Yes, it is.

NELSON: Go ahead. We won't tell.

SAUTER: Creed, I don't know what we'd do. When you have that kind of circumstance, the correct journalistic instinct is to assign somebody of credibility and authority within your organization to do an impartial examination of the issue. People who have pressing day-to-day responsibilities can't do it, particularly in a case like this involving volumes of material, as the trial attorneys have discovered. So you put somebody on the case, and the only way they can do the investigation is to commit stuff to paper, and that commitment to paper carries with it an incredible vulnerability. We have a circumstance here where it's going to be very difficult for journalistic institutions to investigate consequential issues brought to them from the outside. Our lawyers tell us that, even if we said we're bringing a lawyer in because there's a chance that we're going to be sued, the presence of that lawyer does not necessarily guarantee the protection of whatever document that lawyer produces.

NELSON: Even lawyer-client relation?

SAUTER: That's right.

NELSON: I thought work product was protected.

SAUTER: They say that you can find a lawyer for almost any purpose. They say that if this lawyer is brought in to investigate within your news organization, and that lawyer submits a report, and there is no lawsuit filed against you at the time, there's a high chance that report may then be obtained in later litigation.

CHANCELLOR: Van, what would happen if you said, "I don't have the report. I keep the ashes of it in this urn in my office?" I'm asking a dead serious question.

SAUTER: Well, we could have burned the document. But we produced the document under the assumption that we were going to convey that material to our employees and our public, and how we interpret it. I had some very distinct disagreements with the Benjamin Report. But it was a key factor in the ultimate statement that CBS News issued. So you could burn it, but that would be another violation of the basic intent.

CHANCELLOR: If you burn it before you know anybody wants it, is it a violation?

SAUTER: There are any number of possible shenanigans. The basic problem is that newsroom questions should be investigated by journalists. And we should be prepared to make the outcome of those investigations available to anybody in the public who cares. But there is a high degree of vulnerability if litigation flows from the incident. So I guess I would say we'd probably do it the same way again, though I wouldn't be surprised if people I work with shot me.

BARBER: Other points?

BOCCARDI: Maybe we should just say that newspapers should devote particular effort to accuracy, because it's the first step in this credibility issue. Without accuracy you can't achieve credibility no matter how energetically you reach out to the public. We should drop the notion of written notes and just stress accuracy as the beginning of credibility.

NOLAN: It used to be the *sine qua non.* Now it's a luxury option.

BOCCARDI: I don't think it's a luxury option. I think there are a lot of newspapers that are not as careful as they should be.

NOLAN: When I have to a correct a mistake, I certainly don't want to sit down and interrogate the reporter. I just say, "Give me a memo." If we have to, we print a correction. I make a lot of the mistakes myself, so I type my own corrections, and then I foul up the corrections too. So we say, "Due to an editing error...," or "Due to a reporting error...," etc. I don't know if that helps the reader, but we always do it. So the disposition of these crucial documents is not the issue; it's monitoring accuracy and making a daily attempt to get it right.

BARBER: Let's move on to management and Larry Jinks's report.

MANAGEMENT

1. Make a profit.
2. Stress credibility priority.
3. Cultivate active consciousness of readers and audience.
4. Exert community responsibility, distinguish from cheerleading.
5. Stress accuracy and fairness.
6. Endure in the above priorities.

JINKS: As one might expect with our group, there was less than total agreement on all points. But there was a keynote sounded early that nobody took issue with. Van Sauter said, "The greatest threat to editorial integrity is red ink," and there was appropriate concern for black ink in our discussion.

We decided that credibility as a journalistic issue is primarily a management concern. Publishers talk about it, and editors talk about it, but you do not hear a lot of talk about it at the water cooler or in the bar across the street. We feel that our franchises would be threatened by people not reading the paper or watching programs, that there is a fundamental business reason to worry about whether we have credibility with our audiences and our reading publics.

Central to the issue, however one defines it, is an active consciousness of readers and audience. Editors and publishers and broadcast managers are on the whole very conscious of reader and audience concerns. But in many cases, reporters and other staff members are not; who's going to read that story or who's going to listen to it are not high in their consciousness. We think that management is responsible for setting standards and seeing that they are carried out. There was some disagreement as to how this might be done, but most of us felt that it should be done in partnership with staffs. If reporters and copy editors and television producers, etc. are not as conscious as we think they should be, then that's a failure of leadership. We need to make sure that they are fully conscious.

We need to define community responsibility. When we are talking about local newspapers and local television stations, we need to spell out clearly the differences between cheerleading and intelligent concern. We need to emphasize in a variety of ways within our staffs the absolute essentiality of accuracy and fairness. We need to emphasize a constant concern for dealing with the people we write about, the people who take our newspapers or who listen to our television broadcasts, in ways that are decent and fair, and in the long-term best interest of our institutions.

BARBER: Thank you. Other additions or corrections for that report from your fellow managers? No? Anyone else have a parting comment before we adjourn for this afternoon?

CHANCELLOR: Mr. Chairman, if we're thinking about our credibility with the public, we ought to take note of the premise that we may have overused the First Amendment as a defense of our position in society. My own view is that we have used it too much, and we ought to put it in the bottom drawer for about 10 years. The reaction I get from the public is that every time somebody in journalism gets in trouble, he begins to holler about the First Amendment. Some people are offended by this. People are constantly reminded that the press has a special position in the American society, and we may be overusing that. Others are saying that we're using the Constitution to preserve our right to make money and to do other unspeakable things. We might want to talk about overusing the First Amendment and whether that is leading to an erosion of credibility.

BLACK: John, you'll notice in the ombudsman report I gave you, that when he speaks of arrogance, he says that readers do not understand and often resent the press's concern with the First Amendment. We've failed miserably in convincing the rest of this country that the First Amendment includes all of us. In our last libel suit, our defense attorney told all of us who were testifying for the paper not to mention the First Amendment.

HEWITT: The problem is we keep saying, "It's not our right to publish; it's your right to know." The public doesn't believe that. They say, "Come on, it's your right to publish." It's about time we stopped kidding them about their right to know; a lot of it is our right to publish.

BARBER: Well, friends, we could start tomorrow with a list of the points that have come out of your committees, and move from the specifics to larger issues of approach.

[The group adjourned until the next morning.]

Saturday Morning

BARBER: Good morning. We have our list of suggestions before us, an attempt not to be eloquent with your findings from your caucuses but rather just to say them simply. There were several other points for increasing credibility mentioned by individuals and by the whole group, such as the idea of short versus long articles, David Broder's idea of referrals for readers to places they could get other information, upbeatness of various forms, and Sandy Vanocur's interest in celebrity news. I'm sure there are many other ideas, but why don't we begin with the television group.

CHANCELLOR: We couldn't agree on one area, sourcing. I believe that you don't necessarily have to give the names of officials or policemen or prosecutors who give you information, but what we don't do well enough is to say that they are policemen or prosecutors or government officials, a problem more in television than in print. If we did more of that, we would be fairer with the viewers, which might make them feel that we were more credible.

BARBER: How about others in the television group? Would they say the same, identifying sources better, but not necessarily by name?

HEWITT: I wish that it were practical to have a requirement at every news organization that you could not use an unattributed quote, that you'd never say, "a high government official, etc." If the guy doesn't want to be quoted, don't use it. But it's just not practical on a daily basis.

SCHWARTZ: Don, do you use unattributed quotes?

HEWITT: I try not to, but I'm not in the same pressure cooker every day. But it would be a marvelous service to readers if it were practical never to say that we have learned something from somebody in some unnamed organization. I don't think you have to say, "a CIA agent named so and so." But I think saying, "a deputy director of the CIA" is better than "high intelligence source," or "an aide to the President" instead of "White House sources."

LAVENTHOL: That's the last time you'll say it.

HEWITT: That's right; I said it's not practical. But I have a feeling that part of our problem with the public is their wondering, "What the hell are they talking about? Who said that?"

SCHWARTZ: Part of the reason it's not practical is that we are manipulated by those people who give us information. Especially in the White House, they have learned that they can get their message across without taking responsibility for it. The most recent example is the way in which Reagan managed to communicate this whole tax proposal without for one second identifying himself with it. The media stood by and let him do it, and made believe that Ronald Reagan had not sat down with Donald Regan and worked out this whole scenario. I'm talking more ideally than practically, but if major news organizations were willing for a certain number of months to do what Don Hewitt is saying, you might smoke out a change in all this. Probably you would be sacrificing a lot in the process, but I do think it's a problem.

WOODRUFF: We discussed the exact same thing in our group, and decided that everybody would be better off if we used fewer or no unattributed sources, but it's just totally impractical.

CHANCELLOR: The problem exists not only in Washington, but also on the local television level and the local newspaper level. When, for example, Mr. Jones is arrested and charged with a crime, and then all of a sudden the local television station says he was arrested three times in California; where did it come from? Did the prosecutors leak it? Did his ex-wife tell you? If you just put in the paper that the guy was arrested three times in California, you're damaging his case, and you're operating on behalf of the prosecutors. I don't need the names. I need to know the direction of the compass. That's part of the story, of leveling with the readers and the viewers, and I think we're not doing enough of that. You don't always have to identify a source; we're not going to burn our sources that way. But you owe it to the people to tell them where it came from.

RENICK: How about a long-distance phone call to California to substantiate the information? I think this is basically a Washington problem. In Miami, it's been a long time since I can recall a story based on "a source said..." or "so and so has learned...."

SAUTER: This is a very interesting ethical issue for journalists to address, but an issue that really doesn't relate to the news consumers. They give the broadcaster or the publication the benefit of the doubt. They presume that if we attribute something to an inside source, it's accurate and fair, and they really don't care whether it comes from a deep background or whatever the source may be.

I don't have any research on newspapers, but for television, one of the reasons the consultants urge a diminishing of government coverage is that the viewers perceive the whole system as being so distant and so convoluted that they don't understand it. There's also a suspicion that the media and the politicians are involved in a dance, a dance that only they understand. There's a limited interest in news of government because there's an inherent suspicion, not a doubt about its truth, but an inherent suspicion about the whole process, and a lack of understanding of it. We really have to address the nature of the news coverage from Washington and the state capitals, and try to determine why it is incomprehensible to many viewers and readers, why they feel that the media and the politicians have this dance that they engage in, and how we can make that material more understandable and more desirable to the news consumers.

BOCCARDI: To some extent, we can take control of the problem of sources by putting a ban on using certain kinds of information anonymously. Take that story about the bank robber in California; you don't really want to say something like, "Sources said he's also a lousy father," where you get into the opinion area, character assassination, and political argument. You see a lot of that quoted anonymously. That's something that you can put a ban on. You can't ban anonymity, but there are things you can ban. You've got to stand up and push some of that back to the point where you get to the irreducible minimum, as in that lunch you were talking about yesterday, where over the shrimp cocktail they tell you about the MiGs. I don't know any way around that, and I don't think any of us does.

HEWITT: Returning to what Tony Schwartz said, I think it's just the opposite. Tony, we're talking about credibility. If you start pointing out that the Reagan administration has pulled the wool over your eyes, you erode your credibility with the government. That's something we haven't talked about. We are perceived as against the President; right or wrong, that's the perception out there. If you let somebody start saying on television, "Well, the President really isn't doing that. They're using somebody. Deaver is doing this, doing that." That should make you more credible, but the problem today is you're going to have big problems if you do it.

SCHWARTZ: It depends on how you cast it.

NELSON: We're already writing that in newspapers.

HEWITT: I know. And when we do it and you do it, that's one of our problems.

SCHWARTZ: That's a problem worth having. If the public doesn't believe you because you're telling them the truth, then the problem is educating the public better, not changing your style.

HEWITT: You've got a public out there who reads you and watches us, who adores this President, a beloved figure. But if you say that it's really not the President, that it's really Deaver, or tell them that Mrs. Reagan mouthed some words for him to say, then you're an enemy of the people.

BERGER: Lou Cannon wrote a story quite a while ago about the mistakes that Reagan has been making over and over again in press conferences. And the largest part of the mail he got was saying, "Why are you picking on the President?"

BRODER: What is the implication of what you're saying? Are you suggesting that that response ought to change the coverage?

HEWITT: No. What you're talking about is believability. You've got a lot of people out there who assume that you're making this stuff up because you're out to get the President.

BARBER: Could we concentrate on solutions, perhaps on Lou Boccardi's idea not to use anonymous sources for matters of opinion?

NELSON: One of the answers is to explain the motive of the anonymous source, wherever you can. In other words, if you're quoting an anonymous source on Capitol Hill about one of the Reagan administration programs, you say "a critic of the program."

VANOCUR: In the Duke seminar on news as fiction, Ward Just was asked the difference. He's a novelist, and earlier was a journalist. He said, "As a journalist I couldn't deal with motive. As a novelist I can deal with motive." Do we want to start getting into the motive game?

NELSON: Yes, you've got to be in the motive game.

VANOCUR: That's tricky.

NELSON: If you're quoting an anonymous White House source about somebody else in the White House, and you can find a way of saying that this is somebody who's been at odds ever since the administration started, you ought to do that. It says something about the credibility of the information you've got. On the other hand, the reader knows that it doesn't come from an unbiased source.

VANOCUR: Let me give you an example. I don't buy into the arguments about Jeane Kirkpatrick and the sexist motivations of charges against her. Do we really know what she has done to have alienated first Alexander Haig and then the White House staff? When we talk about it, do we really know whom she's at odds with and why?

NELSON: I think we do. We know they disagree on a number of things.

CHANCELLOR: We know how Shultz feels about her. There's a certain amount of evidence about that.

VANOCUR: Has he ever said so?

CHANCELLOR: No. Not in public.

BARBER: So the suggestion about motives is to identify the source as a critic, a champion, a supporter, something like that. Anything else on sources that would help?

SCHWARTZ: You could go one step further than Lou's idea, which is a very good one. At *The New York Times* now, you are not allowed to use an unattributed source if it is subjective and negative, but you can use a positive one. I'm not sure these distinctions have to be made this finely. It seems to me that any subjective characterization of any kind and particularly a negative one ought to come under much tougher scrutiny.

BLACK: I said that newspapers could improve their credibility by using fewer anonymous sources, but on television I think there is more of a tendency to use anonymous sources without ever talking to anybody. That's one of the points of the thing I presented here yesterday. [Negative reaction from group.] Well, all right. Let me read one of these things.

Hey, critics! Look here!

This was not the first time an American ship has drifted into Cuban waters, but it is the first time a U.S. aircraft carrier was sent in to assist. U.S. officials say it was the only prudent thing to do given the Cubans' unpredictability. But critics are likely to call this a major overreaction to a minor incident at sea.

—Rick Inderfurth, ABC News

BLACK: This is Rick Inderfurth of ABC News talking about that incident in which the "American ship drifted into Cuban waters," and "a U.S. aircraft carrier was sent in to assist. U.S. officials say it was the only prudent thing to do given the Cubans' unpredictability. But critics are likely to call this a major overreaction to a minor incident at sea." Now, he didn't talk to anybody. He's speculating on what anonymous sources are going to say.

BARBER: I thought for a moment you were going to remind me of those people who think that the whole space program is a fraud run from a studio in Houston or Burbank.

BERGER: We're talking about this in a vacuum. We're forgetting that people go on the air or write under a certain byline who haven't come from Mars; they have a track record. When David Broder tells me something, no matter how anonymous the source, I know he has weighed the evidence. He has thought about it. He has thought the report was worth making to the public because it had reality. It was important, and he knew what he was talking about. When

Hedrick Smith does it, or when Sandy does it, or when John does it, or Judy, we know that these people are not coming from high school, and that they know what they're doing.

BURGIN: They have credibility.

BOCCARDI: Everybody thinks they're David Broder. That's the problem.

SAUTER: That's what the management is there for; that's why there are editors. In terms of our audience, the broad audience, this is not an issue. Whether you have it or don't have it is going to have no impact whatsoever upon your credibility with your audience, because it's there, and therefore it has credibility. It's accepted.

NELSON: I don't agree with that as far as the audience of newspapers is concerned. There's concern that newspapers too often do not tell the sources of their news.

SEIGENTHALER: Beyond that, there are young people coming right out of journalism school who've been watching national television and reading local newspapers, who just can't wait to call somebody up and say, "All you have to do is tell me, and I won't quote you." That practice has to be reversed. It is a local problem for many local newspapers. It is a news management problem, and tighter control is badly needed.

NELSON: There's a tendency on the part of a lot of reporters now coming out of journalism school to use anonymous sources because they think it gives a story more standing. They've got the inside story. They're not just talking to somebody who's willing to be quoted on the record; they're talking to an insider who's talking only to them, whispering to them. And so they've got a very important story. That's one of the biggest problems. John Chancellor mentioned yesterday not having the educators' or the preachers' words in the paper anymore. How many quotes do you see in news stories now? Relatively few sometimes. Some of the best stories have a lot of quotes in them, but a lot of reporters think that if they've got quotes in the story, they're not doing their writing job.

BARBER: Let's ask Marty Nolan to wrap this section up, and we'll move on to the next caucus.

NOLAN: Don't forget, it's not just our problem. It's also the public official's problem, many of whom are ignorant. If you had a gun to their head and asked them what "background" and "off the record" mean, they don't know. My favorite rule (and I don't recommend it to others because it can get you in trouble) is: you peddle it, you get your name on it. A politician or political hack or assistant secretary or whoever walks up to you and starts to unload, tells you something, then says, "Oh, by the way, that's background, off the record." I say, "Too late, chump; your name's on it." I'm happy to say I've got some of the most benevolent people in the history of modern America mad at me because of it. I'm delighted. I wish I had brought a precious artifact which I'm going to donate to a media museum, a press release I received recently, quoting a source in City Councilor Kelly's office on what City Councilor Kelly was about, and right on top, it says "From City Councilor Kelly." A press release quoting a source in his own office! This is how far we have brought these clowns. We are responsible for feeding them the mystery, the inside. So it's our responsibility to call a halt to it. "Hey," as Jason Robards once said, "is anyone going to go on the record on this?"

BERGER: Marty, how big do you have to be to do that?

NOLAN: We have educated generations of politicians to believe it, not just the young reporters coming out of journalism schools. Any political hack thinks it's more powerful to be on background and off the record. I don't think the best reporters need to do that, and we ought to put a stop to it.

BRODER: It's probably easier for newspapers than television to do this, something we don't do very often: we need to take one step back. If you're involved in writing a story about the infighting over Jeane Kirkpatrick, and you're using a lot of unattributed information, you are trapped in that situation. There is nothing that prevents you, say, four days later, from stepping back and saying there is a battle going on within the administration over this. Nothing keeps us from describing the news process in the White House. Even at our paper, I don't think we have told people very clearly that a major part of what they read every day coming out of the White House is coming from Jim Baker, Dick Diamond, Mike Deaver, and so on. We can write about that, do that without breaking any rules. You cue your readers in. You tell them something that gives them a basis for making intelligent judgments about unattributed information in a lot of specific stories that they've read before and after that story.

BLACK: David, don't I remember that years ago Ben Bradlee propounded a policy against using unattributed sources?

BRODER: Yes, he did.

BLACK: How long did that last?

BRODER: Well, it lasted about as long as Bradlee's attention span did. (Laughter)

MATUSOW: Is that on the record, David?

BRODER: I've got some resumes I'd like to distribute.

VANOCUR: Both print and television ought to make a statement along the lines of what Ben tried to do. We can state that when public officials have background briefings, they should not be background; they should be briefings, and attributable. No more Kissinger lectures on the planes. No more little lines dropping about submarine pens in San Fuegos.

BARBER: But, Sandy, I gathered that people were saying that would be ideal but impractical.

VANOCUR: We ought to say there ought to be an end to background briefings with unidentified officials. It won't happen, but we ought to say that.

NOLAN: I think guerrilla activity is useful. My favorite paragraph in all the "high official on Henry Kissinger's plane" stories was the last. Bill Beecher just got sick of it, so in his final story he said, "And the high official on Henry Kissinger's plane got off the plane and entered a limousine with Nancy Kissinger." You've got to break the rules sometimes. We break our own rules, but we don't break theirs. Let's break their rules.

NELSON: Didn't the *Post* run a picture of Kissinger, calling him "the unidentified background official?"

CHANCELLOR: And David Brinkley went on the air saying, "A senior official aboard the plane, speaking with a German accent."

BARBER: Let's look at the second item on the print caucus's list: "Written memo by mistake-maker." Someone who makes a printed mistake should submit a memo explaining the circumstances.

NOLAN: Lou Boccardi can speak to that. It was his idea that such a memo should not go to the lowest relevant echelon of the news operation, that is, to the assistant city editor, or to the city editor. It should go to the assistant managing editor, or whatever the equivalent is for television. Is that right, Lou?

BOCCARDI: Exactly. If you move it up the chain a little bit, it gets a little bit more tense, though some tension would reduce the amount of it that gets through.

NOLAN: But Tony Schwartz tells us that at *The New York Times*, if you're involved in a correction, it goes in your file.

SCHWARTZ: The correction is attached in red to the original piece in your byline file. I had a very red file.

BERGER: But you have to have some kind of correction, or it'll get perpetuated in the paper in quotations.

BARBER: The file has the correction that was published, not a separate memo?

SCHWARTZ: No, not a separate memo. If in some way it was addressed in the paper and not published as a correction, it still will get in the file as a correction. In trivial cases, they don't tend to do that. If you said "age 17," and it was age 18, it was inconsequential and wouldn't get in.

SEIGENTHALER: I don't see anything wrong with our making a recommendation on such memos if it's couched in terms that say "maybe useful." I think all of us have talked with some regularity to counsel and got their advice on "should this be a matter of our file or should it be a part of your work paper?" I think the process of requiring the mistake-maker to go behind the error and address it in his own mind, so that he or she knows everybody else knows, is an important part of not making the error a second time.

BOCCARDI: That's the element of internal accountability.

PATTERSON: Mr. Chairman, I'd like to ask Van Sauter how badly he thinks he has damaged the Westmoreland case by the internal investigation he ordered.

SAUTER: The Benjamin Report was in effect removed from the trial. It has absolutely no impact whatsoever on the trial itself. It was, however, a guidebook for the plaintiff's attorney in terms of a discovery process.

SCHWARTZ: Wasn't it also a possible motivation for actually bringing the suit?

SAUTER: There are people who think that. But I think there's an overwhelming body of evidence that the suit was going to be brought under any circumstances.

SEIGENTHALER: Isn't it so that a less informed, less sensitive judge might have tilted the other way? It seemed to me that Judge Lavelle excised that from the jury's consideration because your lawyers very effectively made that case to him. But a less effective lawyer in another situation or a less sensitive judge might leave us all exposed.

BARBER: I imagine you all agree with the print group's item number three: "Spend more on salaries and counsel."

BURGIN: No, no. Wait a minute. Something got lost in the translation there. God knows that in the newspaper world we're all so well paid that we don't have to worry about salaries. What we're talking about there was travel, bureaus, research, ideas, newsgathering, all that.

NOLAN: We never mentioned salaries yesterday. The word never came up.

NELSON: We meant spend more on covering the news.

SEIGENTHALER: Yes, we meant an effort to tie the need for quality with the need for money to support the sort of things that Dave Burgin was talking about.

BARBER: What is the point about counsel?

NOLAN: "Competent counsel in First Amendment cases" is the way we phrased it.

BARBER: There's some disagreement on the next item: "Outreach to readers explaining the news business." Some of you think that when you open the lid of that can, people will look in, be disillusioned, find how rude and nasty you are, and thus decrease your credibility.

NOLAN: In the caucus, I used Bismarck's remark that "legislation, like sausage, is something that you really don't want to see being made." Our ombudsmen are these sausage *meisters*. They'll give you a tour of the sausage factory: "Now maybe you really like it, dear reader, and if you do, we'll give you every jot and tittle of this, how the reporter got misinterpreted by the editor," and so forth. Ombudsmen reports generally are pretty heavy going.

NELSON: All of us in the communications business do a very poor job of communicating to the public how we operate. I've seen instance after instance of people coming in and talking to me about it. When you talk to them about why you use anonymous sources and how you go about your business and how you really try to get at the truth, it's an eye-opener for them.

NOLAN: I think this is truly a psychological generation gap or something. Those of us who came into the business at a certain time were told nobody cares how the reporter gets the story.

NELSON: I think that's wrong too.

NOLAN: I know that. But didn't you hear that all the time?

NELSON: Sure. "Who cares about it, just give them the news. Don't say how much trouble you went to get it or what your problems were."

NOLAN: But explaining the news business is not necessarily sending some ombudsman as a sleuth.

WOODRUFF: Tell the public that you had a camera stationed three or four or five miles away from the ranch in Santa Barbara, and all that? The people really don't want to hear all that. If we did put a lot of that out there, the public would ignore it, except for some people who are as intensely interested in it as we are.

MATUSOW: The suggestion is not that we should explain more of the technical maneuvers. Every business has its technical minutiae, and I don't think the public really cares about it, other than some media freaks out there. Wasn't it David Broder who suggested taking a minute-fifteen before the press conference to explain what the reporters were doing at the press conference? Perhaps those broad and important issues that are misunderstood by the public need to be explained.

NELSON: Traditionally editors have said they don't care, that the reader doesn't care that you talked to eight officials and none of them would tell you a thing. They want to know what you found out. You explain that the White House has clamped a lid down on talking about certain subjects, and go to some length to tell that story. But it may turn some people off; maybe they're not interested.

BARBER: But you try to write it with the same criteria of newsworthiness as anything else.

BERGER: Would it help with anonymous sources to say, "Deaver wouldn't talk about it, Baker wouldn't talk about it, but we learned that, etc.; so we got by process of elimination the eighth person, who talked?"

BLACK: This technique can be used effectively if it's used selectively. Our editors have tried it from time to time when we've had some controversial story and a close call that we wrestle with. Then if you write a column explaining to the public why you do certain things, that can be useful. On the other hand, it has become faddish among some newspapers to bare the soul and tell everything that's going on in the shop. Our competitors in Louisville have a column by the executive editor every Sunday on the way the paper works. Boy, that is some boring reading! There is just not that much to say week after week that the readers are interested in.

NELSON: If it's week after week, I think you're right, and I'm not talking about just individual stories. In the news you're covering that day, you can sometimes explain the problems that developed in trying to get the stories.

BLACK: We've had good response in the right circumstances. If it's a controversial call, then you explain to the public why you do certain things.

BRODER: First of all, Marty, it's not just a generational change. The world has changed. When you and I were kids, DuPont went on the air saying, "Better things for better living through chemistry." Everybody said, "Fine. These are wonderful people handing us these great products." People don't believe that anymore. They want to know what process they are going through, and they've got good reason to want to know. They are no longer prepared to accept that what we are handing them somehow comes down from a divine source and is immutable. They want to know how it got there, how that stuff gets put together, because they have become very skeptical of the way in which large, powerful institutions deliver something that is an important part of their lives.

Second, Judy, we're not talking about what kind of lens you use to shoot the ranch, or whether I use a number five or a number three pencil. We're talking about essential ignorance of stuff that we regard as basic to our business. For example, the distinction among editorials, columns, and news stories, which all of us think is absolutely fundamental, is not understood by most of our readers. We have failed to communicate even the rudiments of what we think we're doing.

BURGIN: Agreed.

LAVENTHOL: I agree with what Dave Broder said. We can't do enough of this. It's probably boring to us, but I don't think it's boring to a good number of people who are both curious and skeptical about it. Most of us believe that we are wonderful people who are doing a great job, an important thing, and we're committed. But most of the people who view us, whether at a presidential press conference or anyplace else, don't see us that way. The more that we can show them what we actually do, the more it's going to put the media in less of an adversarial role, and fewer people will say, "It's your First Amendment, not ours."

BURGIN: I'd like to ask a question of the television people. What David Broder is suggesting is achievable and practical and simple in a newspaper context. For the television people, could I assume that the next time we have a televised press conference, somebody would say, "The President today blah, blah, blah." And then he's likely to be asked by Jack Nelson and Sam Donaldson and David Broder, all sitting up there in the front row, about this, that, and the other. Is that what we're talking about?

BERGER: They would explain why they're going to be nasty.

HEWITT: On Sundays at 7:00 we take the viewer along on the story, and they love that. You tell them what you did, how you got it, where you went. I think the game changed with Woodward and Bernstein. We found out that people were as interested in how they did it as what they found out, and that changed the whole game. At that point, we became news. Maybe that's good; maybe it's bad. But it's a fact of life that people are interested in Broder, interested in Nolan, interested in Nelson and Chancellor and Wallace and Brokaw and Rather. They want to know all that. In addition to news coverers, you guys have all become newsmakers. Maybe that's a terrible thing, but it's a fact of life. They like to know about your process.

SEIGENTHALER: It may be even more fundamental than Dave Broder puts it. I have a sense, particularly in local communities, that there is a resentment, bordering on hostility, for even the most basic performance of reporting. Reports of crime or reports that reflect adversely on local or state government inevitably draw this sort of response: "Why are you doing this? Why are you playing God?" It's very tough to say, "Well, that's what we do." But that's true. Stories hurt people, and sometimes hurt innocent people. I think that we can sell that, but I don't think we can sell the idea that we're playing games. Too often we do play games.

BARBER: Just a minute. Do you agree with the view that if they know you they'll like you?

SEIGENTHALER: No, I don't think it really makes any difference.

BURGIN: Let me have a follow-up question, as we say in the press here. I still don't see where television explains anything. I can see it very clearly in newspapers, and I think it's called for. But what is television going to do to explain things?

CHANCELLOR: Going back some years, in the Editor's Notebook pieces we would do sometimes two or three times a month, sometimes only once a month, we'd explain problems we'd had in coverage. When people would write in, asking why we were picking on whomever we were picking on that week, we might write a little something saying why it's important. We used to do it all the time and got a lot of letters from people saying, "We wish you did more of that." We could have done that Editor's Notebook every Friday night for a couple of minutes, and the audience would have loved it.

BURGIN: We still have a credibility problem. How can we explain why Sam Donaldson screeches over the helicopter?

CHANCELLOR: Easily. That's a good one to explain.

SEIGENTHALER: You asked if I agreed with the view that if they know us they'll like us. I don't, and I don't really think that's the way it was stated. It was stated, "If they know us, will they understand us?" I think understanding us is enough.

SCHWARTZ: First of all, there are different answers, depending on the particular institution involved. In a typical local news operation, if people ask why the first eight stories were either murders or fires, the answer can't possibly make the reader like you. If you force people in positions of power to ask that question, it may force them to answer beyond something about red ink. Don, I find it curious that today you're saying people are interested in knowing about how the news is gathered, but yesterday you were saying that ABC's attempt to explain the news was so boring that nobody watched it.

HEWITT: There wasn't any program about the news. They were talking about issues.

SCHWARTZ: The issue is uninteresting to people when it's abstract.

HEWITT: Reporters are glamorous people in America.

SCHWARTZ: I agree with you, but you take it one step further. The stories are interesting to people, and they want to know how the stories are gathered. But after the story is done, they raise questions. That's reflected on *60 Minutes* to some extent in the letters you run at the end. On their letters to the editor page, newspapers simply run the letter. They don't run a response; they don't create a dialogue. It remains just another one-way communication.

HEWITT: Answering letters in print is a very good idea, a great way to explain yourself.

BARBER: Sandy, would you wind this one up, and we'll go on to management?

VANOCUR: I'd like to add a note of caution. About 10 years ago, I heard Nick Williams say that the function of a great newspaper is to educate the elite and pacify the masses. I won't go that far, except I worry that in both print and television we might get hectored by what we're going through now into a kind of journalistic nannyism. I worry that we're so busy minding our manners and fretting about what we're doing wrong, that we forget our principal job: producing a news product. I think we're very dangerously near there. You have to do it on an *ad hoc* basis, one step at a time, but not forgetting what business we're in. The only cure is to hire people you think are professional and make sure they remain professional. We have got a lot of dogs in television who are not professional. We work for the esteem of our peers, and the emphasis should be on professionalism in both print and in television. That will go a long way toward resolving this problem, but I don't think that you can codify it.

BARBER: You mentioned the word "business," giving us our transition to Larry Jinks and the management team, whose 10 commandments begin with "Make a profit."

JINKS: Since I have the floor, I want to say something about what Sandy Vanocur just said. That premise is entirely wrong that there's a kind of an abstract sense of what journalism is about, defined by professionalism, that is somehow put in jeopardy by being conscious of your readers or your audience. I've heard elements of that around this table for the last day and a half now. The premise that we are somehow threatened by caring about how we come through to readers, is itself dangerous and self-defeating. Nothing in developing a consciousness of readers causes you to be weak or timid, or to fail in your fundamental mission. A part of your fundamental mission is communicating with people; it's absolutely essential to the fundamental mission.

Now I'll go to what you asked me to do, talk about the management report. Our premise was that none of this makes any sense unless you have a thriving enterprise.

NELSON: Could you link up your number one, "Make a Profit," with the revised number three of the print caucus, "Spend more on coverage and counsel?"

JINKS: Sure. Spending an adequate amount of money on a news report is entirely consistent with making a profit. When our company has bought newspapers, we have almost always first increased the amount of money spent on the news operation. Creed Black went to Lexington as publisher, and had two or three years in which his returns weren't looking very good. He was spending a good bit more money on his news operation, and he's now making a helluva profit. The points are entirely consistent if the job is being done by people who know what they're doing and who care about a news report as a fundamental product of the journalistic enterprise.

VANOCUR: Should we reword this item, "Make a profit?" C.P. Scott, the great editor of the *Manchester Guardian*, said the chief duty of a newspaper is to make a profit.

PATTERSON: May I suggest that we change it to Ed Lahey's wonderful equation: "All I ask of you as publishers is that you stay solvent."

JINKS: The point here is not to rewrite history, but to try to reflect what we agreed on within our group, that is, if we're talking as management, there's a fundamental business foundation to concern about credibility.

GARTNER: In other words, you can't be journalistically vigorous unless you're financially strong.

JINKS: Right.

NELSON: But can you be financially strong without being journalistically vigorous?

BURGIN: How about: "To be an artistic success, you must first be a financial success?"

BLACK: About number six, "Persist in the above priorities." In some respects, ours is a transient business. We have a lot of young reporters coming into a place like my paper, staying a few years, and moving on somewhere else. But the management has a particular long-term responsibility to keep the whole enterprise moving forward in a certain direction over the long haul.

BARBER: We thought we would have a little professor period, the "we" being Roy Peter Clark and Don Fry and I. I'm going to give you a very sketchy idea of what I think about this credibility business and how it might be fixed.

I agree with Don Hewitt that it is a miracle that you people do as well as you do, when, especially from a professor's point of view, one considers your time constraints. A professor's task is to take whatever he knows and stretch it out over 14 weeks of the semester. We're pretty good at that. I've had some experience rewriting television news scripts, but I could do it at leisure, not on deadline. I happen to be a fan of your line of work, especially of those of you who do it so well.

But there are some ways in which it can be improved. And the three things that I suggest are contradictory on the surface.

First, make the news more interesting. I don't mean to hype it, but as a civics teacher interested in the viability of democracy, I think there are far too many people out there who are not getting your message. The message is political realism. To be sure, the citizen needs to have the right values, but he also needs a realistic sense of what's going on. And citizens are not getting that.

One could go down a long list of indicators of vast public ignorance, largely obscured by the way public opinion polls are reported. Public opinion polls typically report that "62 percent of the American people last week said that they're for the deployment of the Per-

shing II missiles in Europe, provided that the NATO
forces otherwise arrayed will not be distorted in this,
and that House Foreign Relations Committee, et
cetera, et cetera, et cetera." What they really said was,
"Uh huh."

To put it positively, there's a great opportunity out
there for getting reality across to them better. That involves a concern of the sort that Larry Jinks was just
talking about, a real concern for understanding how
the message actually is getting across to people, not
just what they like and dislike, but how the message
is getting across.

For example, it's easy to show that network news
is presented with a vocabulary that's way beyond the
capacity of the average American, that the meaning
of the very words is unknown to most Americans. You
can show that empirically very easily. You just study
the words, and you see that people don't know what
they mean. It's sometimes said they catch something
from the context. I don't believe that. But even so, step
one is to put the news into English, and by English I
don't mean "Run Dick run," but Hemingway and Fitz-
gerald and that kind of punchy, simple English that
people can understand.

Another thing television could do would be to recap-
ture the enormous power of narrative. They gave narrative up by the historical accident that the news on
the radio used to be read from the wire service copy.
That wire service copy was composed for the purposes
of newspapers as a story with a lead, then dribbling
away down the side of the pyramid to the nothingness
that could be cut from the bottom. And so television
is presenting a drama consciously designed to become
less interesting as it proceeds, which is not the way to
win people. So you have this weird situation in which
the anchor gives away all the sex of the story up front.
If Dan Rather were telling the story of Little Red
Riding Hood, he would say, "Good evening. Last night
a wolf ate a grandmother. Now, here's Marilyn Berger
to give you the rest." What has Marilyn Berger got left?

BERGER: Thank you.

BARBER: In any case, too often all the correspondent in the field has left is a lot of emotion, a lot of feeling, stuff like that, and a sort of Aesopian epigram at the end that expresses the wisdom of youth in terms of ambiguity as a substitute for wisdom, that is, "On the one hand, on the other hand, the future lies ahead." It would be possible to make that story much more attractive by composing it in narrative terms, so that you take advantage of the most fundamental, human dramatic form. Those are just two little examples of television.

In print, the point about shortening things, having a realistic view of what people will actually read in the newspaper, is helpful. But think about the kind of narrative appeal that the *Reader's Digest* has to millions and millions of people, both at home and abroad over a long period of years. They're on to how to get information across in a dramatic way. So I'm saying there ought to be *more* drama.

The second point is perhaps contradictory to the first, that is, the danger I see in what I call the "drift of fiction," the boredom with fact that I perceive in a lot of modern journalism. The image of the reporter used to be the guy who went out and found out what happened and then came back and told you the facts. That was the excitement of it: reporters with Teddy Roosevelt at San Juan Hill, the war reporter coming back with the story. Then you got a generation of educated reporters like Broder and Wicker and Jules Witcover and all these guys, and the need for analysis became very important. Analysis and explanation and interpretation became all the excitement of it, producing the rise of the columnist. Now you've got something going in which "Insight" (as they call it in the *London Times*) is being valued. It's a poetic and metaphorical and emotional understanding of things. Television has contributed heavily to that; the typical television question is "How do you feel?" The news concentrates on the imaginative world, on subjunctivity, on news of the future, that is, the news becomes about what is going to happen down the road a little ways, a sort of anticipatory expectancy that you see so often in the presidential press conferences, about what is going to happen. That grows partly out of an interest in policy.

But what gets lost in fiction news and future news is reality testing. Journalists covering political candidates, for example, ought to ask questions about reality, ought to press candidates to reveal their assumptions and perceptions about how the real world works, in fact, not in speculation. No matter what questions journalists ask, the politician may lie or evade or distract. But there's virtually no chance of getting a factual answer unless you ask for it. So questions should be, not "How do you feel," not "What might you do sometime," not "What is your intention about the future," but "Tell us what happened," "Tell us what you did," "Tell us how that worked out," "Tell us what the cause of it was." Does the President really believe that the people being deported to El Salvador are not in danger of their lives? Does he really believe that his policies have not hurt anybody? News stories ought to test his realism, not in trivial detail, but as it fits his relevant facts. Now don't tell me that that has all been reported, because I know that. It has been reported. It has, however, been radically de-emphasized in modern news coverage.

Finally, research. I don't think we know nearly enough about how people use the news. There's a good deal of research going on, but I would like to see a lot more research which gets at what people actually do get out of the newspaper. Beyond pollings, we need exploratory research, where you sit down with people and say, "Now look, you read the paper this morning. Just look at it with me. What'd you get out of this? What did you do with this and that and the other thing?" For television, we need to know not just their sentiments, but also what they actually came away with in terms of understanding and information about the events that were reported. There is some resistance in your line of work, as in mine, to genuinely finding out how we're going over, because we're a little scared that we might find out that too much of what we give never gets taken.

Robert Hutchins of the University of Chicago said that in his darker moments, he felt the university was a babysitting operation, that we were just keeping the youth off the streets for four years, and that all of that effort of lecturing and testing and everything probably wasn't having much impact. That helps to explain why professors are not too interested in their impact on students, and I think there's probably some of that with you too. But the positive side would be lots more understanding, not just of the satisfaction of the reader-audience, but also their understanding and information.

Those are my points. Thank you.

You've heard from me, and now we're going to hear from Roy Peter Clark.

CLARK: Don Hewitt mentioned that one of the things that might be missing from this program was the voice of the people. So in order to rectify that, last night I called my mother, Shirley Clark, who lives on Long Island. (Laughter)

HEWITT: Terrific.

CLARK: I told her what was going on here, and I explained in detail and asked her reaction. Here are some of the things she has to say about the media and what she's been reading and looking at lately. By the way, David Laventhol, she reads *Newsday* and loves it, and she sends me clippings all the time. (Laughter)

Here are some excerpts from Shirley Clark. The first thing she says is: "They didn't have to pay, but *TIME* can't say that they won." Her maiden name is Marino, so the second thing she said is: "The press is unfair to Frank Sinatra." (Laughter) She said that she saw a program on media ethnics or media ethics, she wasn't sure which. (Laughter) So I figured it was about Geraldo Rivera. (Laughter) She asked, "Is John Chancellor really down there?" And I said, "Yes. What do you think?" She said, "He's got a nice way about him. Hey, he's part of the living room. I'll never forget the look on his face the day they tried to take him out of the convention." (Laughter) She said she was watching the inauguration, and she thought she saw tears in Dan Rather's eyes at one point, something moving had happened. She said, "That's nice to see. It shows they're human."

CHANCELLOR: Both eyes? (Laughter)

CLARK: My mother created an English teacher, but she never could get pronoun-antecedent agreement. And I said, "What about Creed Black?" And she said, "Who?" (Laughter)

In trying to sum this up a little bit and create some sense of closure, I want to leave with an anecdote, something as a media consumer rather than as any kind of an expert. I dedicate it to Marty Nolan, a graduate of Boston College. It concerns the last minute of the Miami-Boston College football game, which I think was one of the most exciting things on TV this year, and I'm hoping you had the chance to see it.

Bernie Kosar had just passed his team down the field to B.C.'s two-yard line, headed for the winning touchdown. There was a time-out with about 40 seconds left. The camera and the mike revealed Bernie all psyched up, screaming at his coach on the sideline as if he were objecting to the play called, and this is what the nation heard: "Let's play f---ing football. Let's run the f---ing thing in." In the booth, Ara Parseghian laughs: "I guess Bernie wants them to run it in." (Laughter) Run it in they did, followed by wild jubilation.

But the camera now shows Doug Flutie on the sideline with his coach. The lens seems to be inches from Flutie's face. He is as cool as can be, nodding and looking confident. Suddenly, his team is on the 50-yard line with only six seconds left, and the camera shows Bernie Kosar on the sidelines smiling and slapping hands with his teammates.

What follows is the pass of the century: 65 yards in the air, cradled in the end zone by Flutie's best friend, Gerard Phelan. Then a series of images: Flutie being held aloft by his brother; Phelan mobbed in the end zone; Kosar walking head down toward the locker room; and Flutie later walking around the field looking in vain for Kosar. We hear: "Where is Bernie? Where is Bernie?"

This was great television sports. Right there on the spot, the camera was in the quarterback's face; the mike was picking up every word, including the obscenities. That night I saw the thing about 10 times on TV. And yet I felt a little bit incomplete, and I tried to figure out what the heck was missing, when I realized I had a tremendous urge now to read about it, looking for narrative retelling of this terrific event. What I got from the reading of it was a little bit different from what I got from the seeing of it. I found out from reading that Flutie's scramble was intentional to give Phelan time to get into the end zone. And since Flutie says he can throw the ball 75 yards in the air, he had to "take a little off of it to deliver it to Phelan."

Narrative retelling, detailed reporting, and explanation. I mean this anecdote to reveal that there are things that television can do very well, and things that print can do very well. They are complementary in very important ways, as has been mentioned here. In looking for reform, we shouldn't fail to celebrate what each medium does best.

Thinking of another dramatic moment in sports history, I recall Bobby Thomson's famous home run in 1951, and I mention it since that home run is one of my earliest memories. I was about 3½ years old when it happened, and I remembered sitting in a tiny apartment (at least I think I remember) in the lower east side of New York, watching my parents, who were fierce Dodger haters, dancing in front of a 10-inch RCA Victor television screen. I've asked them, and to the best of their memory, the scene that they were celebrating was the so-called "Shot Heard 'Round the World." And I remember that tiny TV very well, and I even remember sitting in front of it and watching the test patterns.

I say that because I'm young enough to be part of a generation that does not remember life without television. And for a lot of us, TV viewing and reading are compatible and complementary activities, and that goes for news as well. In a previous seminar down here, David Halberstam said that print defines and television magnifies, and I think that's true. We agreed at another seminar here that William Greider's *Atlantic* piece on David Stockman began to have serious impact when a reporter started waving it at a televised press conference.

So I come up with my final observations about this conference from that point of view. I offer here a brief list of what I perceive as some shared values and strategies that might get us headed towards some of the goals that David Barber outlined at the beginning of the seminar. Marilyn Berger made a reference to the New Journalism and some of the problems related to it, and Don Hewitt talked about being in the reality business. Ms. Berger, I wasn't sure if you were talking about the New Journalism, the Old/New journalism, or the New/New journalism, since there are several different manifestations. Both television and print can follow John Hersey's advice that we redraw the line between fiction and non-fiction, between illusion and reality. Hersey says that the legend on the license must read, "None of this was made up." That goes for *The Washington Post* and *The New Yorker*. And we have problems with the nonfiction novel and docudrama. I'm not sure what we're going to learn about Robert Kennedy on television this week, or what we learned about Errol Flynn, but when history and reality are distorted by such events, it's one of our jobs as journalists to expose these distortions.

I remember criticism when one television network offered an artist's rendering of John Hinckley's trying to commit suicide in his cell, although no one had witnessed the event. It was decried as cartoon journalism, and rightly so. Even as we all seek to make news-telling more engaging, to delight and instruct the reader and the viewer, let's be careful not to blur the distinction between news and entertainment. Let's be careful about calling reporters "talent," for example, lest we turn Mike Wallace in his trenchcoat into Mike Hammer by mistake. Attention to this distinction will lead us to an even greater commitment, as has been said here, towards the process of verification and more careful attribution.

We didn't have a chance to have a critics' caucus here, but we should engage in more rigorous forms of media criticism (David Shaw and Hodding Carter) and media reporting as well. We are central institutions in American culture and should cover each other to enhance the good things we accomplish and to spur us to reform. Too much of current criticism is one-directional, print criticizing TV in snotty ways. We need more criticism of print on television, constructive criticism. I'm talking about solid reporting and explanation that helps us make links between what's happening in the media and what's happening in our lives. I have in mind a book such as Neil Postman's *The Disappearance of Childhood*, which talks about the effects of media and the current predicament of children. We need academics to be able to write and "put the hay down where the goats can get it," to write in clear English for a mass audience.

One of the things we haven't talked about much here is education, and that's an area where there is some hope. One of the things that might help us is to take a hard look as professionals at the tracking of students in journalism schools between broadcast and print. There are special needs for each medium, but the education of both print and broadcast journalists should perhaps be a little bit more monolithic; they all should be engaged in learning about government and economics, American culture, thinking, writing, and ethics. One journalism teacher I talked to was critical of the broadcast sequence, saying that there was too much emphasis on performance and not enough on journalistic values. Too much emphasis on hair, clothes, and voice, and students came there with that in mind.

I applaud the collaboration, for example, of newspaper and broadcast editorial writers, now underway through the National Conference of Editorial Writers. In the area of writing, for example, we have much to learn from each other. I can learn from John Chancellor how to write tightly, how to write for the ear, and how to create through my writing a human voice. As we try to improve our writing as journalists, finding new strategies, new definitions of news, new story forms, we do best to learn from each other.

I'm going to make this next point with some trepidation, remembering a comment that Malcolm

Muggeridge made in an essay called "The Fourth Temptation," where he says that if Christ were on earth today, praying in the desert, Satan would offer Him not three, but four temptations. Having failed in the first three, Satan would offer Jesus a chance to give His message on national television. (Laughter)

But having said that, I'm going to advocate that print and broadcast journalists should change roles, or better, use each other's medium to advantage. I've read Jack Nelson and David Broder to great benefit, but I really know them more intimately through television. We're better off as a nation because old Charlie McDowell can stick out his neck and squint his eyes, stick out his teeth, and in his own beautiful Virginian accent say things like, "Now, what we're talking about here is this thing called the deficit." (Laughter) When he says that, I'm ready to learn about it. And because of television, not just Richmond has learned about Charlie McDowell. This is less frequent, but I greatly admire broadcast journalists who write occasionally for print. I think that sends out an important message and gives the writer and the journalists a different kind of authority.

It's clear from our discussion that we have something of a public relations problem. We're often depicted on television shows and in the movies as behaving in packs. No less of an authority than Bernhard Goetz responded to reporters' questions on the occasion of his arrest with a single word: "Vultures." We need to start talking to each other and discuss what happens when we work in packs. How does our behavior change when Air Florida Flight 90 crashes into the Potomac and 50 reporters gather at Tampa Airport for a death watch?

The other thing we can do, stated over and over again here, is to explain ourselves better to readers and viewers. As a citizen, I should know much more than I do about how television programs are made, and I shouldn't have to wait until it's revealed to me in a libel trial. More and more newspapers have been revealing themselves to readers with good results.

Here's why this is important. Our mistakes are highly visible, especially our excesses. On the other

hand, many examples of our restraint are by definition invisible to readers and to viewers. You've all read
that a Marine family in Rhode Island had their privacy
violated by one television station. What you probably
don't know is that another television station established careful guidelines on how to prevent such abuse.
I know because I called up there and asked around. But
people in Rhode Island and in the nation don't know
that.

We need to engage in a continuing discussion of
shared ethical concerns. All the things we've talked
about this morning, privacy and disclosure, government secrecy, protection of sources, arrogance and accountability, fairness and accuracy, concern us both.

Raising awareness of the ethical issues may
restrain certain kinds of irresponsible activity. But
overall, ethics should not have and will not have a chilling effect on reportorial aggressiveness. In fact, it
should inspire it. When I look at most newspapers and
TV stations across the country, I do not see a hostile
or cantankerous press. I see a tame or lazy press. And
ethics discussions in this regard must include discussions of business ethics. Is the company spending its
profits to encourage editorial excellence? Is there a kind
of a "yin-yang" relationship that says, "We do our
business to make money, but we make money to do our
business?"

I wish newspaper reporters didn't have to write
eight stories a day, as some do. I wish some newspapers
wanted to hire my best college students at more than
$9,500 a year to start. And I wish some local TV sta-
tions would spend less on promoting their news teams
and more on building those teams.

So let me just list in brief summary these shared
values and opportunities for collaboration:

- Help redraw the lines between fiction and non-
fiction so that we can convey information with
authority, and give more emphasis to verification and attribution.
- Cultivate more enlightened criticism of the
media from many quarters.
- Collaborate in the training and continuing
education of journalists.

- Use each other's media to enhance our efforts to inform the public.
- Fight our images as arrogant and insensitive by revealing ourselves and our operations to readers and viewers.
- Finally, carry forth our discussion of ethics in ways that enhance rather than undercut our efforts to serve the public with our best work.

HEWITT: That's terrific! Great!

BARBER: Now, Don Fry.

DON FRY: Journalists really do differ from their fellow citizens. They tend to view the world in terms of stories, and they pay closer attention than any other group, except maybe nuclear physicists. Take Sam Donaldson, for instance. We regret Sam could not be here to demonstrate how to shout rude questions at helicopters, but I tend to think of him in his other public role, prying up the edges of answers on *This Week with David Brinkley*. Professor John Robinson studied viewer comprehension for eight television stories on BBC, and concluded that the average viewer could answer questions about fewer than three of them. Of 507 people asked, no one got more than six correct responses. He then asked 10 BBC newspeople the same questions: one got seven right, and the rest got all eight right. Robinson concluded that journalists and viewers are vastly different, requiring a rethinking of writers' assumptions about shared preconceptions. I would also conclude that newspeople pay closer attention to the world, and not just to the world of news.

We've been struggling here to find some concrete ways to deal with problems of credibility, but I want to step back from our close focus on details, and return to first principles. What functions do journalists serve? I would propose two: storytelling and sentinel duty. These duties did not begin last week or in the 16th century, but about 25,000 B.C., with the cavemen. So please fasten your seat belts while I rewrite the cultural history of the human race.

Cavemen (and cavewomen) had three kinds of storytellers, whom they called "Screamers," "Wordsmiths," and "Painters." The first group, the "Screamers," tended to shout extremely short stories in single incomplete sentences, such as: "Antelope Sighted!" or "Saber-toothed Tiger Right Behind Me!" or "Man Bites Mastodon." No, they did not develop into headline writers, but into radio newscasters. (And here I exclude National Public Radio, a late and very civilized development in our cultural history.) The second group, the "Wordsmiths," fashioned long narratives shaped like upside-down pyramids. This group educated the tribe in important subjects, such as whom to marry and whom not to, what to eat and which poison plants to avoid, what to wear to the inaugural ball and how not to distress mannerly persons, and the hypocritical nature of adults. They couched their lessons not in sermons or editorials, but in stories telling the history of the tribe and its members, past and present. "Hansel and Gretel" probably originated in this period, and still remains one of the best lessons for tots on the potential hazards of child abuse. The final group of storytellers painted their narratives on the cave walls, mostly in the form of stylized food animals, surrounded by gesticulating tribal hunters. The flickering firelight probably conspired with the bumpiness of the cave wall to make the figures appear to move. This form of storytelling proved extremely effective, but it promoted a perhaps fatal hazard, a danger Judy Woodruff and Gene Patterson warned us about in yesterday's session. Ubiquitously on European cave walls, we find another picture, the outline of a hand. But artists did not *paint* these hands on the walls; rather, they spread their palms and fingers against the stone and sprayed red ochre around them, leaving a perfect handprint. Once you see the potential of your personalized hand on the cave wall in front of all your friends, who can resist becoming a television news star? Pictures beckon inevitably to the ego.

So now you understand the origin of the storytelling side of journalists. Sentinel duty follows logically. People who tell stories well usually do so for two reasons, because they understand human beings, and because they pay attention to telling details. So the storytellers, whether they screamed things or spoke tales or painted hunting scenes, also became the lookouts for the tribe. The tribe depended on them to stay awake and notice things, particularly to spot dangers. The dangers included natural disasters (such as landslides or citrus-killing frosts) or violent animals (such as muggers) or hostile tribes (such as Nazis or Neo-Nazis or the next Nazis). Gradually the sentinels had to keep an eye on the tribal leaders themselves, because the leaders tended to share the food unfairly and to lie about territorial imperatives. This latter aspect of lookout duty required special skills for ambiguity, and the storytellers probably invented the device of unnamed sources about this time. (Laughter) Very late in the human race's development, the sentinels discovered they had to keep an eye on each other; their success as storytellers had made them very rich and powerful, and therefore almost as dangerous as the tribal leaders.

Why am I telling you all this gibberish about the cavepersons? Because little has changed; we still make our fortunes as sentinels and storytellers. But something has changed. We suddenly fear that the tribe might trust the leaders more than they trust us. Yesterday Don Hewitt asked repeatedly, "What is this credibility you guys keep talking about?" Good question, Don, keep asking it. Allow me to risk an operational definition: credibility is the trust we earn every day by alerting the people and telling something like the truth. And how do we do that? Journalism 101: accuracy, fairness, balance, completeness, and all the other traditional values of our profession.

The skeptics here in this room say that we have no credibility problem, at least not yet. But remember what we do so well: we stay tuned up for the coming dangers so we can tell stories of warning to the public. I can just barely make out one of those dangers shambling towards us out of the murk. He looks a little like Joe McCarthy; no, he looks more like Jesse Helms. He's not alone, and he has a target in mind larger than Dan Rather, larger than Van Gordon Sauter, larger than three networks. Maybe we should stop scrutinizing each other so hard and sharpen our tools.

Thank you.

BARBER: Thank you. Now we have a last hour together for you to say all that needs to be said about credibility. Barbara?

MATUSOW: I was very glad Roy brought up the business about more vigorous media criticism and the one-directional criticism. The original point of departure of this seminar was the increasing or long-standing hostility between print and television. Newspapers are adding immeasurably to public disgust with both media by encouraging their television critics to write about television in the most vituperative, intemperate terms. TV has a lot to answer for, as does print. There seems to be an area in television in which civility is entirely lacking, and that is the TV critic. And the more surly, nasty, snide, cynical, and vicious they are, generally speaking, the more highly they are paid. They are fun to read; we'll all admit that. But the general feeling of this group is that the public does not really distinguish that much between television and print. For example, TV critics have written about ratings, making them seem near monstrous in the public eye, which, of course, is a lot different from circulation, which, as we all know, is holy. The public begins to think that newspapers and television are only out there to make a buck, to increase ratings or to increase circulation. They have no understanding at all that the average reporter just gets turned on by the story, and so does the average editor, but they don't see every story in terms of profitability. The public regards appeals to the First Amendment as cynical and hypocritical, because they think the press is only in it for the dollar. The TV critics have a lot to answer for in stirring up this kind of contempt.

RENICK: How would you suggest television should respond?

MATUSOW: Not by attacking in print. I like what Roy Clark says about more vigorous media criticism from all quarters. As near as I can count, only nine newspapers in the country have media critics. Every newspaper over 75,000 has a TV critic, but only major publications like *Newsday* and *The New York Times* and a few others have anybody looking at the broader questions of the media. I like the suggestion of having more criticism from other quarters, not just the media looking at themselves, but also inviting government officials and others, victims who have had an experience with the press, to submit their voices too.

RENICK: What about the word "critic?"

SCHWARTZ: Don Hewitt used to say to me when I was writing about television for *The New York Times*, that the problem is that television is a variety of things: news, entertainment, sports. The critics on nearly every newspaper in America are assigned to be critics of every aspect of television. They are considered to be equally qualified to do a critical piece about a documentary on arms control, and then to turn around the next day and do a review of *Three's Company,* and the following day to analyze the adequacy of sports coverage on *Wide World of Sports.* Obviously they are not genuinely qualified to do all of those things, short of the most extraordinarily eclectic talent. *The New York Times* has made one step in the right direction, separating fact from fiction in criticism, so that there is now a critic assigned to factual things on television, essentially news, and another critic assigned solely to the show business of television. Second, the vituperative nature of criticism is in part a management problem. With no disservice to Creed Black, it is a reflection of people who are intrinsically hostile to television, who have not spent that much time in a television station, and have no sense of the distinctions between the two media. If you are going to do criticism, if you deem criticism to be worthwhile, then you have to make a basic assumption that there is value in what you are criticizing. And so it is critical that newspapers who assign critics to do either kind of criticism should do it in a constructive rather than destructive context.

HEWITT: I once asked Sidney Gruson, "Would you hire a baseball writer who hated baseball? Would you hire a dance critic who hated ballet? Would you hire a theater critic who couldn't stand the theater? You keep hiring television critics who hate television. And I think I know why you do it. (And I know this is going to go on the record.) You do it because Abe Rosenthal doesn't like television." Almost everything pro-television in the pages of *The New York Times* is pro-PBS, which takes no advertising dollars from *The New York Times*.

SCHWARTZ: That view has now actually changed. *The Times* employs three people writing about television instead of one, and at least two by any definition are knowledgeable and sympathetic to television.

MATUSOW: In Washington we have a critic who never says anything good about PBS.

HEWITT: Tom Shales is probably the best of all of them.

NELSON: Yes, he loves CBS and can't stand ABC.

HEWITT: I withdraw that.

NELSON: But he is the prime example of a vituperative TV critic. He writes some of the strongest, most anti-television copy I have ever seen.

HEWITT: The *New York Daily News* has no bureau in London, has no bureau in Moscow, has never had anybody in Beirut. But they've got four people writing about us. That is ridiculous.

MATUSOW: That is not ridiculous. Tony Schwartz mentioned that nobody would expect one person to be expert in criticism of sports, news, drama, etc. I run into a lot of TV writers around the country. They are just overwhelmed because they're supposed to keep up with all the new technologies, to keep up with all the programming trends in cable, plus all the programming trends in over-the-air TV. It's a highly volatile field, and most papers now have one person doing it. You could easily use at least three people, somebody to review, somebody to write about new technology, etc.

LAVENTHOL: Don Hewitt's and some other comments that I've heard here over the last couple of days reflect where some of us are coming from, but probably don't reflect the views of most people in the newspaper side of the business these days. The idea that newspapers in their criticism, or in the way they cover it, or whatever, are still fighting the battle of not wanting TV to succeed, that ended 20 to 25 years ago.

HEWITT: Sure. You guys have come into the business now. Your parent companies are all in it.

LAVENTHOL: No, I'm not talking about parent companies. I'm talking about working newspapers. Newspapers wouldn't run TV logs, they wouldn't cover it, and so forth. But that was over 20 years ago, and it's probably only people like us who can even remember the issue. If you talk to most people in the newspapers, they'd say, "That's silly. We cover TV. It's maybe the most important media influence in this country, and we cover it." So I don't think that's the reason why newspapers may not do a good job in covering TV.

On the question of the critics, most newspapers' television critics are critics like theater critics, like movie critics, like music critics, in that they're working out of the genre of the critic. And most critics are vituperative. Read John Simon. (Laughter) He isn't writing about TV, and the traditional style of the critic is to be clever, to turn a phrase, to praise occasionally, and most of the time to dissect. Certainly part of the tradition, not necessarily a good one but part of the tradition, is that the more vituperative you are, the cleverer you are, the better critic you are. And if you have absolute standards, you know you're only going to like three plays every decade because you're writing for the history books, and the same with TV.

What Tony Schwartz said certainly makes a lot of sense. The television entertainment critic, who is judging the stage in the living room, is one thing. But an information critic or a media critic, who is both explaining and evaluating news and information on television, is really a pretty good idea.

SAUTER: A few months ago, after what I consider outrageous judgment by a television critic/writer, who relied upon an inside source who requested anonymity, I went to our station people and offered to give them a budget to hire newspaper critics. It was an absolutely intemperate, irrational act on my part. (Laughter) They said, "We don't want one." And I said, "What do you mean?" And they said, "Well, they're not news. It's not important." That is an absolutely erroneous response on their part, but then we got into a more sophisticated discussion about how do you criticize the newspaper without doing some of the things that so offend us. Now we're hiring Peter Boyer, who, like Ron Powers, will be doing a fair amount of observation about newspaper and television ethics and performance. There's a lot of value in it. It's very unfortunate that local stations do not cover newspapers, because newspapers are a significant force in the community.

GARTNER: Why don't they?

SAUTER: The assumption has been that it doesn't matter, that people don't care. That's not the case. A second reason is (and I'm not speaking for my stations) an assumption about stations, that there's a very distinct fear that if you start being critical of the newspaper as the newspaper is critical of you, then the newspaper is going to increase the intensity of its criticism of your station. The newspapers are not involved in truly competitive environments; we are, and we have a vulnerability there.

I used to say the greatest threat to our credibility is not a Westmoreland trial or the Cooke incident or the Insider column. The greatest threat to our credibility is telling stories our viewers and readers don't understand. That is a significant problem for the news media, and particularly in our coverage of government, we have a serious problem in telling stories in a fashion that the people will understand, believe relevant to their individual concerns, and respond to by seeking more information. Newspapers, radio, and television have turned off a great deal of interest in government. If there is citizen apathy about government and about the election process, we bear a certain accountability in that area, and at some point we're going to have to address it.

But beyond the government, there's a larger concern. Don Fry referred to the BBC study. I've never done that kind of study here; but I'd like to. But I certainly see a tremendous number of indications that many stories that are told (and I presume many stories that are read) are not understood, that there's no skill displayed in making those stories relevant to the interests of the people reading or watching. That has to be a serious factor in our ultimate credibility. It doesn't speak to our telling the truth; it doesn't speak to these people liking us or disliking us; it really speaks to their willingness to read and listen.

We have a citizenry that believes in what we say. It's a citizenry that wants to like us, and that's particularly the case in television. The problem that citizenry has with us is that we're a one-way communicator. We throw this paper on their door, we push this stuff down the television tube, and they have no way to communicate back. A lot of what they communicate back is not anger, it's not indignation; they want to be heard on any number of issues. They want to ask questions about why we do as we do. We have been unable in publishing and broadcasting to establish forms for a dialogue with our consumers. The op-ed pages aren't it, and the letters to the editor aren't either. I don't know how one goes about it.

On one level, reporters have a general disdain for the consumers of news, or a lack of interest in them. The managers, who are normally very skilled at marketing, have not addressed this communications gap. We really have to know a lot more about how our consumers feel about our product, and at some point, we're going to have to show the courage and have enough managerial credibility to go to the people who actually write and produce these stories and say, "This is what your consumers think of your work. This is what they say they need. This is where they find us performing with a shortfall." We need to share in that. The managers know a lot about the marketing process and a lot about the consumers, but we have kept that information from the reporters. On one level, you want to do that, because you do not want them to skew their journalism to meet other kinds of needs. But I think this area is where our credibility problem truly exists.

NELSON: I'd like to agree with what Van Sauter said, particularly about government reporting, and the most recent examples of it really jump out at you, our coverage of the deficit and of arms control. Every day we have several stories about the deficit; we just move it a little bit ahead. We do the same thing on arms control, and we've done it on other issues. But you have to do it because it's going to be on page one of the *Los Angeles Times*, on page one of *The Washington Post*, on page one of *The New York Times*, and it's going lead on all three national networks. We'll have one development one day saying that Reagan's plan is now going to call for 40 billion dollars of cutting the deficit, and the next day we'll come back and say that they changed to 45 billion, and the next day we'll come back and say that Dole says it has to be 50 billion. We've been regurgitating the story, but in Los Angeles, the editors expect us to follow that development day in and day out, and AP and UPI do the same thing. We look at the wires, and they've got the daily development moving ahead just a half-inch or something. I'm not saying that it shouldn't be chronicled, but you've got to do something other than a page-one story and a lead on the networks every day with a small development on a story that people are sick and tired of.

BRODER: In newspapers, we have to find a format or free ourselves up to say, "If you've just started coming to this story, here's what you need to know. Here are the basics of it. If you've been reading it every day, skip this. But if you really want to know what the hell people are talking about with the deficit, here is something you can latch on to." We don't do that in any way.

There is a service that you could perform for the press and for the community which would not necessarily risk any enmity or exacerbation of bad feelings. I'll give you two examples. My paper recently hired a new movie critic. Because of our inhibition about self-promotion, I don't know a thing about this guy, where he's coming from, what his taste is, what his values are. If any of the local Washington television stations had sat this guy down for five minutes and said, "Tell us a little bit about what kind of movies you like and what makes you like them," that would have been a service to the Washington community.

We have a new managing editor, Len Downey, who runs the news conference where the front page stories are picked every day. It would seem perfectly legitimate and helpful if the Washington television stations sat down with Downey and said, "What's important to you, and how do you decide what's going to be on the front page of *The Washington Post?*" That's a legitimate story that would have been of help to the community.

SAUTER: You're absolutely right that Downey should be known to the consumers of that newspaper and that community. But we would end up doing what the *Washington Journalism Review* did, and we would be less concerned about Downey and more about the internal machinations of the company, which is exactly what the newspapers do to us.* I don't know whether that's good or bad; but we obviously need to get into the business of reporting about newspapers. But we're not, and I gave you a couple of reasons why we're not.

RENICK: Once we asked for just still photos of the critics at the newspapers, and they were shocked. They wanted to know what we were about. (Laughter) What was this insidious request based upon? (Laughter)

---

* Robert Kuttner, "The Royal Succession," *Washington Journalism Review* 7.1 (January 1985) 22-34.

SCHWARTZ: For a dart board, for a moral threat.

SAUTER: Let me tell you one quick story. Ron Powers reviewed the coverage of the Democratic National Convention by *The Washington Post, The New York Times,* and the *Los Angeles Times,* and he reached the conclusion that the *L.A. Times* did the best job of covering the convention....

NELSON: By far. (Laughter)

SAUTER: By far. Within 48 hours the *L.A. Times* had a full-page ad saying, "Ron Powers says the *L.A. Times* did a better job of covering the convention."

NELSON: Also, our publisher Tom Johnson, had the transcript out immediately afterwards, showing it to everybody at the convention.

MATUSOW: If you think the TV people are sensitive about criticism, you ain't seen nothing until you see the TV turning their focus on the newspapers. Another day, Powers ranked political reporters, who was out and who was in. It was the talk of the entire convention. I went to lunch, and there were some Washington-based columnists who were "out," and all the newspaper reporters were sitting around talking about it, buzzing about it. And Theodore White said, "That isn't fair. They make their living that way!" (Laughter)

BLACK: I want to respond to one of Van's points. You underestimate the safety valve for newspapers provided by the letter to the editor columns and op-ed page. When I was in Philadelphia, we obviously weren't able to run all the letters, but we ran maybe 10 percent of them. In Lexington, we can run almost all of the letters we get. We make a deliberate effort on the op-ed page to get points of view that differ from ours. If somebody calls me, or calls the editor, and says, "Boy, you're just all wet," we say, "Well, write an op-ed piece." We actively recruit community columnists. We have about a dozen ordinary citizens out there who write columns for our op-ed page. This does give readers a sense of access and a chance to talk back that television doesn't provide, and that is a major difference in the two and in the public's perception of them.

SAUTER: It's a source of great concern within our company that we don't have that process.

SCHWARTZ: Van, you've talked about this problem that people understand too little of what they're being told. The area of greatest failing is local television news as a whole. Precisely the opposite is the problem, that people understand too well what they're being told. In general, they are being told that we are going to do this news almost purely as a form of entertainment. We are going to deliver you the biggest crimes, the biggest fire, the most attractive celebrities who are in town. We will not hire someone to cover the mayor in New York City, who is a show biz mayor. Not one station in New York City covers the mayor of New York. We will not cover the city council; we will not cover the state legislature; we will not talk about government; we won't talk about neighborhoods; we won't talk about business or economics. On any given 11:00 broadcast, the likelihood is that you will have three fires, four crimes, and two "Mr. T testifies in an incest case." The expectation level is that you're not going to get news, and I don't know whether this is even a credibility issue so much as it is a failing of journalism. But across the country in local news, you have a destructive diminishing of the whole journalistic process.

PATTERSON: I've been struck over the last two days at the amount of frustration felt around this table about the Teflon President, a guy who can spend more red ink than any president in history, and yet the public doesn't blame him. In Beirut, he falls on his face, comes home, and nobody blames him. I have not heard anybody here really analyze just what he's doing. We could learn from Mr. Reagan; we in the press could take a lesson from him. He can get away with anything he wants to. Talk about power! Look at the power he's got, and the people trust him with it, even when he misuses it. We can make a couple of mistakes, and the public comes down on us with both feet. So, what's going on here? What's the secret? And what can we learn from Ronald Reagan?

Number one, he's a friendly fellow, while we're perceived as being very unfriendly people. He seems to wrap himself in the flag at all times, and we're regarded as unpatriotic when we question him. We bare our fangs and curl our lips and bark and lay our ears back, and the public sees that, because we're on television just like Ronald Reagan. They never see him do that. When he cups his ear and listens for Sam Donaldson to yell at him, he smiles. He never gets angry at anybody. As a result, the people trust him; as a result of our incivility, the people don't trust us.

This is a little more than cosmetic, and it deserves a place in the list alongside these other substantive concerns that we've expressed. Instead of simply criticizing Mr. Reagan for having gained the trust of the American public, we ought to analyze ourselves in contrast with him and see why we've lost it. If we lowered our voices a little bit instead of running in a pack the way our peer pressure directs us, we could change the direction of our peer pack. We should listen to Solzhenitsyn, who spotted our weakness in his Harvard talk, that we are pursuing fashionability. He was astounded when he came to America and looked at the media, which he had heard was a free press full of independent people.

This problem also goes back to Woodward and Bernstein, to Mike Wallace, to what we have accepted now as the norm for what it takes to succeed. You have some powerful examples in print and television media. In the print media, I look at David Broder, by far the preeminent political reporter and columnist in Washington, and if the power of example can teach a new direction for peers, Broder is setting a standard I hope we follow. He's fair. He's firm. He doesn't lay his ears back and curl his lip. I hope we would slowly learn that that's the kind of people that not only the public trusts, but we trust.

We ought to pick up on what David Barber said yesterday, that the televised press conference has become a place where reporters are seen impolitely asking cream puff questions. I wonder if we might change that around to politely asking hardball questions.

HEWITT: Gene, I don't mean to be defensive, but you mentioned Mike Wallace. (Laughter) How do you explain the fact that Mike Wallace wins a landslide victory if there is a news election, as Ronald Reagan won in a national election? If the people are so turned off by that kind of thing, why do they tune in by droves every Sunday night to watch Mike Wallace take somebody on?

PATTERSON: Don, you're going to have to ask somebody who's done the psychological study, like Barbara Matusow, because there is no doubt there's a love/hate relationship out there in the American public with the Dan Rathers, with the Mike Wallaces. They've got the hard edge, and the people are fascinated with them, as some women are fascinated with bad men. (Laughter)

MATUSOW: Maybe that's the answer.

PATTERSON: They will say, "Yes, I watch him every time he comes on because he fascinates me."
"Okay, what do you think of him?"
"I just detest him."

HEWITT: Like my father reading Westbrook Pegler.

BERGER: All of us are fighting with each other, the television people with the written press, and the written press with television people. But every time we are cited by the opposition, if I can use that term, we are thrilled. The *L.A. Times* takes out an ad when Ron Powers on television says they are terrific. When we would have a story in *The Washington Post*, we would ask, "Did the networks pick it up?" When the networks have a story, they say "Did *The Times* or *The*

Post pick it up?" It becomes a ratification of the story if the other people pick it up. So there's not that much opposition. It's that old jealousy.

SEIGENTHALER: I want to ask Lou Boccardi what he thinks of the Associated Press's media coverage, and I ask it to make a point that there are many newspapers outside the East Coast axis that rely on AP for an awful lot. I'm not specifically asking whether you think Fred Rothenberg does a good job. But it's interesting that his name has not come up here, and I suggest that most people around this table might not even know that he's assigned to that beat.

BOCCARDI: Since AP is a member organization, you all own a piece of us. It's been our judgment so far that we are not in the best position to undertake the kind of deep and perceptive journalistic criticism that a media writer ought to get involved in. We cover media stories, but that's different from media criticism. AP is so much a part of all of you that media criticism is something we're going to leave to somebody else. It may be a mistake in judgment; it may be one we change, but that's why you don't see a great deal of media criticism in the AP.

SEIGENTHALER: If you moved an occasional piece by somebody like Barbara Matusow without relying on her as a constant media reporter or critic, that would substantially enhance that part of the report. She's not looking for a job, and I said, "like Barbara." (Laughter).

BOCCARDI: I think we do television coverage or criticism more than adequately. We do not do media criticism of print, where there is a conflict for us. Television stations and networks are members of AP as well, but there's been the tradition there of the TV column in a framework different from print.

HEWITT: If the networks also own a piece of you, why is it okay for you to review Dan Rather versus

Tom Brokaw at a convention, and not David Broder versus Marty Nolan or Jack Nelson?

BOCCARDI: There's a tradition there of TV criticism.

HEWITT: What do you mean "tradition?" We're not that old.

BOCCARDI: I'm going back to the beginnings of television. There have been television columns and television criticism in virtually every newspaper in America.

NELSON: Is TV represented on the AP board of directors?

BOCCARDI: Yes. There is one person right now, Dick Wald of ABC. His predecessors were Reuven Frank, Bill Leonard, and Julian Goodman. On the board there are three people from the broadcasting industry, narrowly defined. But 11 of the 18 newspaper publishers or editors have very substantial broadcast interests, so there's a very loud and substantial broadcast input into the AP board.

SAUTER: I think Fred Rothenberg does a very good job. While I was enraged with him last week, he is a very effective and responsible television critic. Would the AP do a story such as the one in the *Washington Journalism Review* about what they described as a "struggle for succession" in *The New York Times*? (Laughter)

BOCCARDI: We wouldn't do it in the highly-speculative way that *WJR* did it.

SCHWARTZ: Would you do it if it was Mobil Oil?

BOCCARDI: Probably not.

GARTNER: That's not the kind of story the AP does about anybody.

HEWITT: Would you do it if it were Van Sauter?

SAUTER: No, well, wait a minute, they do it about me.

HEWITT: I mean, give me a break, guys.

MATUSOW: Lou, I talked to one of your top reporters about that story, and it wasn't all that speculative. There were some quotes in it and so forth, and this top reporter told me there was no way AP would touch that story.

BERGER: She's quoting an unnamed source. (Laughter)

MATUSOW: Even quoting Sulzberger or Bradlee, there was no way that the AP would touch that story because of their being such powerful members of the social circle.

BOCCARDI: No, that's not the reason at all. We reported on the struggles of *The Times* when the assistant managing editorships were shaken up a year or so ago. We went into all that. The fact that we have not done a speculative story about *The Globe, The Post,* and *The Times* in the fashion of the *Washington Journalism Review* is a reflection of the fact that we have not felt that that kind of media criticism is something we should do.

HEWITT: But if it were television news having a struggle, would you do that?

BOCCARDI: It would fall under the province of the TV critic, in all likelihood.

HEWITT: This is central to what we've been talking about. We have been taken out and put in with show biz.

BOCCARDI: You're ignoring the explanation I gave, which is that because of the peculiar nature of the AP and its relationship with the newspapers of the country, there is a reason for us not to be indulging in that.

GARTNER: Are you covering, for instance, the dispute between *The Times* reporter over his notes and The Newspaper Guild and everything else? Are you getting into some of the pretty dicey issues on all of that, or are you just covering it as a routine, five-paragraph piece? That's a great story.

BOCCARDI: I don't have total recall of what we've said about it, but we're covering that issue as a power struggle within the newspaper. Of course.

VANOCUR: With time running out, I'd like to address myself in purely television terms on two issues: civility and content. First, in television I do not see that comparable David Broders will follow John's and my generation. Although I can't quite identify them yet, what I can see coming along are gunslingers.

On content, Tony is right about the legislature of New York not being covered. No Los Angeles station covers the Sacramento legislature, where you've got really colorful characters, including Willie Brown, who may be the most interesting politician in the country. The reason may be that they don't know how to go about covering a legislature. The most famous legislative story is Bill Greider of Kentucky looking down, being appalled, and an old veteran looks at Greider's face and says, "Greider, you think they're bad? You ought to see the people who sent them here." (Laughter) You can do good stories on legislatures because they directly affect citizens of that state much more than the Congress does.

On the content of other things, no network news show did a story on James Beard's death. Look at the amount of space it got in *The New York Times* and *The Washington Post* and on the wires. This is a familiar person. There is videotape of him cooking. You could get Julia Child on. That is a good story, and I'm telling you we're running away from such good stories.

The reason why we have so many Washington stories on television news is that it's cheap. You don't have to send a camera crew out on the road, first class. You don't have to pay hotel rooms for them. It's cheap, it's available, and it's boring. We really have to sit down and get away from that daybook, and start to think about what is news and what is interesting to us, and hope that it will be interesting to our viewers.

NELSON: *The New York Times* and *The Washington Post* always used to set the agenda for what was being covered. To some extent, that's still true, but the networks help set the agenda for it too. For example, in Los Angeles, if a story runs on the networks, and we don't have it on our schedule, we get a call immediately about it. It's been going on for some time, for the 10 years I've been bureau chief.

CHANCELLOR: I remember something that Walter Lippmann said once, and it goes a little bit to what Sandy is talking about and what we're all doing, and maybe why we have a credibility problem. Lippmann said, "Journalism must give mankind a picture of the world on which it can act." I guess James Beard is part of that, but I'm not exactly sure why. Especially in television, especially in local television, and in a lot of newspapers, I wonder if we haven't missed that goal. We've gotten tied up in other perceptions of the world, and the readers and the viewers don't think that we're trying to give them that picture of the world on which they can act. There isn't any sense of cohesion in a lot of the editing of the papers and the production of the programs. We have failed in some way to get across to the public the essence of the craft, which is to enable people in a democracy to make decisions based on information.

There is room for a very broad spectrum of information and news in what we report. The whole function of the business is to inform and to make people better citizens if they chose to be. I sometimes think we miss that.

WOODRUFF: I'd like to pick up on being too removed from what's going on out there in the country. I don't know if there's any way to do anything about it, but it's true that most of us live either in New York or in Washington. Perhaps those of us around this table are exceptions, but too many of us just talk to each other. We just read what each other writes and what each other broadcasts. There really is a need for more of us to get out to read more that isn't conventional, that isn't being read just in our own cities, and to get a sense of what's going on. Don Fry said earlier that we need to be informed not just on the news, but also on what's going on in the world that's outside the news. That really goes back to the whole point of what we're all about as journalists.

HEWITT: We've left out one very important thing about television. John Chancellor said we've got to help people make decisions. We in TV are unique; we do something that the newspapers don't do. We provide a big conduit from events to living rooms. You guys go there, and you report a state of the union. We put it on the air. It comes right from the Congress to a guy's living room.

CHANCELLOR: That's not journalism.

HEWITT: No, now wait a minute. That's one of our problems. There's a guy at home saying, "Hey, I watched it. I saw it. Shut up. I'll make up my own mind. I don't need John Chancellor to tell me anything about that. I was there. I was at the same event he was at." That is one of our big credibility problems: your readers don't go to the same events you write about, but our viewers go to the same events we report about. And in many ways they say, "Just let us watch. Shut up, and we'll make our own decisions." All of America has been at every big event, and sometimes they say, "I was there. I saw it better than you did. What do you think I am, dumb? You gonna tell me what the guy said?"

BLACK: Let me put that in the words of one of our readers. This was a letter that I got that I didn't read yesterday, but the basic complaint was about television's invasion of privacy in the case of the families of the dead Marines. At the end for good measure, this person wrote, "In most walks of life we can find some obnoxious, insensitive, and arrogant people that the public has to contend with. It seems that television collects more than its share. I do not claim to be an Einstein. I do speak, read, and understand English when spoken, and I feel very capable of forming my own opinions. So I do not need Dan, Tom, Walter, or John to tell me what I just saw and heard, and what it means to me." (Laughter) And I think that's exactly right.

BARBER: So with the creed, we reach the end of the Mass. I want to say a double thank you, first for the instruction that you have given me over the last day-and-a-half, which I value very much indeed. It's remarkable how good you are in a didactic and pedogogical way, and that has been marvelously interesting to me. But also, not being a journalist, I can dare to thank you on behalf of your civilization. (Laughter)

SEVERAL: You're welcome. (Laughter)

BARBER: We have to be thankful to you for maintaining the great conversation which is democracy, in its civility, in its factuality, in its realism. It couldn't work without you, and it does work insofar as it does because of what you do. So I express that thanks.

Now it's appropriate that we end with our poet laureate, Martin Nolan.

NOLAN: This is the *Ite Missa Est* of the program. (Laughter) I have just a handful of historical witnesses, and I begin with Thomas Jefferson, not because he was a great man and a great writer, but because he has the most credibility of any witness, because he was the most gossiped-about political figure in our history. As he said, "Every shaft of calumny which malice and falsehood could form has come from the press toward me." He concluded, however, in my favorite Jeffersonian quote: "It is, however, an evil for which there is no remedy. Our liberty depends on the press, and that cannot be limited without being lost."

As Professor Barber would instruct his students, there's no sense in just quoting the great. How about the not-so-great? Take James Buchanan...please. As other politicians, he was frightened by new technology, and he wrote in a letter to James Gordon Bennett, the great entrepreneur of the penny press: "I do not know whether the great commercial and social advantages of the telegraph are not counterbalanced by its political evils. No one can judge of this as well as myself. The public mind throughout the interior is kept in a constant state of excitement by what are called 'telegrams.' They are short and spicy, and can easily be inserted in the country newspapers." Now, doesn't that sound like our favorite media critic of all times, Spiro T. Agnew? In 1969, one year after that great seminal event of television's incredibility that Sandy Vanocur talked about, the Chicago Conventions that happened in front of everybody, and everybody said, "Oh, no, it didn't happen," Spiro T. Agnew became the ultimate media critic who blamed the messenger for the bad news.

And when he fell and Nixon fell, in the hydraulics of human nature, we rose. And everybody loved us, briefly. The great movie that influenced so many people, of course, was a terrific movie. Naturally the young people are going to be influenced by a movie that shows derring-do and heroes who go after corruption, and they expose a massive governmental coverup and bring down corrupt officials. Of course I refer to *The Front Page* starring Pat O'Brien and Adolph Menjou. (Laughter)

The one time I was ever quoted in the Society Section of *The Washington Post* was at the premiere of *All The President's Men*, and I didn't know what to say. David Israel was covering it, and he said, "Give me a quote." And I said, "Okay. This is a typical Washington party: no one can breathe; no one can hear; no one can think. I thought Jason Robards was terrific as Walter Burns despite the League of Nations." (Laughter)

As Van Sauter said, "A million hired girls and motormen's wives need to know what's going on." As David Broder and John Chancellor will tell us, Chicago is the first place in modern American journalism. Where do you think television learned all the tricks of the ambush interview and of the staged event? It's our dear friend of my youth, the "rusty knife in the riverbed" theory. You're covering a so-so murder, and you're afraid it's going to peter out, so you say "Hey, Chief, that looks like a rusty knife in the riverbed to me!" (Laughter) Headline: 'NEW CLUE FOUND IN COED SLAYING!'

I don't like much television criticism, and I wouldn't allow it in papers, though it gets by sometimes. We occasionally have editorials that criticize television, and I don't let them go by. "Look, when we're perfect, let's criticize John Chancellor." There's not nearly enough reporting; there's not nearly enough telling me about the profit structure of CBS; there's not nearly enough reporting about what Ted Turner is doing. There's not nearly enough reporting about local television, about why Channel Five has been bought by Metromedia and what that means.

I like innovation in papers. We need it. My favorite of the week was in *The Orlando Sentinel*. On the editorial page they had an obituary appreciation of James Beard, which saluted him in the best way possible, by printing his recipe for banana nutcake. (Laughter) The only time I've ever seen a recipe in an obit or an editorial. (Laughter)

The ultimate practitioner of the Chicago-style journalism has a message for us all, Finley Peter Dunne's Mr. Dooley. He wrote essays at the turn of the century, and he got away with saying such outrageous things because he did it in dialect, because "what would a humble ole Irish bartender on Archie Road know about a few things?"

About 1900, he talked about the practice of journalism. He said:

> A man knocks at your door early one
> morning, and you answer in your nightie. "In
> the name of the law, I arrest you," says the

man seizing you by the throat. "Who are you?" you cry. "I'm a reporter for the *Daily Sleuth*. Photographer, do your duty." (Laughter) You're hauled off in the circulation wagon to the newspaper office, where a confession is ready for you to sign; you're tried by a jury of the staff, sentenced by the editor-in-chief, and at 10 o'clock Friday the fatal trap is sprung by the fatal trapper of the family journal.

The newspaper does everything for us. It runs the police force and the banks, commands the militia, controls the legislature, baptizes the young, marries the foolish, comforts the afflicted, afflicts the comfortable, buries the dead and roasts them afterwards.... (Laughter)

They used to say a man's life was a closed book. So it is, but it's an open newspaper.

That phrase I love, "comforts the afflicted and afflicts the comfortable." Well, whatever our ethics problems are, whatever our credibility problems are, we're going to have no trouble if we remember that it is our duty to "comfort the afflicted and afflict the comfortable." Thank you. (Applause)

BARBER: Thanks to you all.

1. Opinion Surveys Conflict On Public View of Press

By MAXWELL McCOMBS and LAURA WASHINGTON

Newspapers sense an anti-press mood in the country, but how deep-seated is it? How much do they *really* hate us out there?

The only practical way to attempt to answer this question is to ask the "they"—readers and nonreaders of newspapers and magazines, viewers and nonviewers of television news, listeners and nonlisteners of radio news.

But a comprehensive look at the many polls that have attempted to gauge the public's perception of the press leads to but one firm conclusion: The answers are inconclusive. Depending on the question asked, the time of the sampling, the manner of interpreting and other variables, the press can come out near the bottom in public esteem, in the middle or, surprisingly, even near the top.

For example:

• The Harris Survey—the most quoted measurement on this subject—recorded a drop from 29% in 1966 to a low of 14% last year in the number of people with "a great deal of confidence" in the "people in charge of running" the press. The press ranked third from the bottom among the 11 national institutions included in the survey.

• That same Harris Survey, however, also measures—but doesn't report—those who have "some confidence" in various institutions. In 1982, for example, 61% of those polled said they had "only some confidence" in the press. When the 14% with "a great deal of confidence" is added, the press scores 75% on the confidence scale—down only four points from its combined 79% in 1966.

Maxwell McCombs is chairman of the Department of Journalism at the University of Texas at Austin. Laura Washington was a senior at Syracuse University majoring in journalism and political science when this article was published. This article, originally titled "Opinion Surveys Offer Conflicting Clues as to How Public Views Press," appeared in Presstime (February 1983) 4-9. Reprinted by permission.

• A variety of polls have given newspapers poor grades for believability, accuracy and bias, but a high grade for fairness.

• A separate Harris poll in 1978, assessing public confidence in 20 industries, gave newspapers above-average marks.

• In two Gallup polls since 1975, journalists were accorded relatively high ratings for honesty and ethical standards.

• In a 1981 *Los Angeles Times* poll, the media ranked first—ahead of business, government and labor—in public esteem for honesty and integrity, and for doing the most "to promote the public good."

Taken together, the seemingly conflicting data support the notion that public attitudes toward the press are complex, and that quick and easy interpretations of that data are often misleading. An added complication is the shifting focus of attention among the various polls. For example, some ask the public's view of the press, others of the media, others of newspapers, journalism or TV news. Still others intersperse the terms.

A classic example of the complexity was the 1981 report of Canada's Royal Commission on Newspapers. It simultaneously found 78% of Canadians agreeing that "Newspapers tend to sensationalize the news" and 72% agreeing that "The daily newspaper helps make your community a better place to live."

Newspapers present many faces to the public—and there are many publics. The examination here of the scattered and fragmentary evidence on public opinion about the press takes into account the widely varying perspectives used to interpret these outcroppings of public feelings. This examination also notes the widely varying facets of press performance held up to public scrutiny.

While that effort at bringing some order into a complex portrayal does not dispel entirely a pessimistic view of the public mood, it does encourage a more sanguine view of where the press stands with the public. The public's perception of the press clearly is more positive than is widely believed.

Three perspectives. Three different perspectives commonly are invoked to "explain" the public's negative attitudes toward the press.

Some critics and researchers assert that the public's negative image of the press is part of a broader *lack of confidence in all major institutions* in our society, including government, business and labor. Any anti-press mood simply reflects the public's disenchantment with the press as one of the nation's major institutions.

Others, however, claim that a *"badnews syndrome"* has created an anti-press mood. One example of this view is the assertion that the recent outbreak of libel suits with large awards against the press indicates that the public "blames the messenger" for bringing bad news.

Third, some analysts, in particular journalists themselves, contend that an anti-press mood is the *reaction against editorial excesses* and other unethical journalistic practices.

This examination of the scientific evidence on public opinion toward the press explores both the extent of an anti-press mood and how well each of the proffered explanations accounts for public feeling.

Declining confidence. The first perspective cited as an explanation for anti-press attitudes points to the overall decline of public confidence in key societal institutions. This also is the position most often and consistently measured by polls.

The Harris Survey measuring public confidence in national institutions since 1966 has documented this decline in public regard for all our major institutions.

Thirteen times across two decades Harris has asked a cross-section of adults nationwide to rate their level of confidence in 11 institutions, including Congress, major companies, and the press: "As far as people in charge of running (each institution) are concerned, would you say you have a great deal of confidence, only some confidence, or hardly any confidence at all in them?" (See chart, page 186.)

Since 1966 the press has received one of the lowest confidence ratings of all the institutions measured. Last year its confidence rating sank to an all-time low of 14% expressing "a great deal of confidence."

The press was near the bottom of the list, just above Congress (13%) and organized labor (8%). Medicine, the military, and colleges ranked at the top with ratings of 32%, 31% and 30%, respectively. All these ratings signify the public's apparent lack of confidence in the leadership of the nation's major institutions.

While this interpretation of the low confidence rating of the press is indeed accurate, it is not complete. It fails to offer a comparative framework. Public confidence in the press also must be compared across the 16-year span with the ratings of other institutions.

A comparison of the confidence rating for the press in 1966 (29%) with its rating in 1982 (14%) yields a change score of minus 15 percentage points. In contrast, the change scores for nearly all the other institutions are considerably greater. For example, medicine dropped 41 points, major companies 37 points, colleges 31 points and Congress 29 points.

Confidence ratings are not available for the White House and television news for the entire 16-year span.

But for the other eight institutions, excluding the press, the median change from 1966 to 1982 was 30 points. (See graph, page 187.) In fact, in terms of percentage points, the press has experienced the least decline in confidence among the institutions measured.

Also clouding the interpretation of the Harris Survey is the inherent subjectivity involved in the terms themselves. What, for example, is "a great deal" of confidence, 75%? 100%? What is "only some" confidence, 40%? 60%? What is "hardly any" confidence, 1%? 25%?

When the "great deal" and the "only some" confidence ratings for the press are added together for 1982, the resulting 75% is only nine points below the combined figure for the leading entry, major educational institutions. The press's combined figure ranges from a low of 69% in 1972 to a high of 81% in 1979. For the past three years it has been a steady 77% (1980), 75% (1981) and 75%. Nevertheless, the press's combined figure last year still placed it ninth out of 11 institutions rated.

But these combined scores again show that the public's confidence in the press is far more stable than its regard for most of the other institutions assessed in the Harris polls. When the "great deal" and the "only some" confidence ratings are summed, the decline for the press is only 4 percentage points from 1966 to 1982. Only the U.S. Supreme Court shows less change across the 16 years.

Regardless of the interpretation of the Harris numbers, any anti-press mood readily can be characterized as part of a broader lack of confidence in all institutions rather than an isolated instance of public criticism of only the press.

It is also interesting to note that the great-deal-of-confidence change score available for television news, minus 17 points (comparing the 1973 and 1982 confidence ratings), is almost identical to that of the press. TV news' 1982 confidence rating, 24%, suggests that it also encounters credibility problems.

Other comparisons. The findings of other surveys which seek to compare the press to other institutions on honesty and ethical standards also offer support to the view that while people do question the credibility of the press, their declining lack of confidence in other institutions is greater.

A 1976 Gallup Poll of 1,524 adults, in which respondents rated the honesty and ethical standards of people in a variety of fields, found journalists ranked fourth among 11 professional categories. Thirty-three percent rated journalists as "very high" or "high," below medical doctors' 55%, engineers' 48% and college teachers' 44%.

A 1981 Gallup Poll of 760 telephone respondents yielded similar findings: 38% of those surveyed rated journalists high on honesty and ethical standards, while 44% gave them an average rating.

Likewise, a 1981 *Los Angeles Times* poll of 1,170 adults nationwide indicated that the public gives high marks to journalists for their commitment to honesty. Although only 25% of the respondents said "journalism" in America is "essentially ethical," the "media" were most frequently selected as the institution with the highest standards of honesty and integrity—36%, compared with 17% for business, 16% for government, and 12% for labor.

The media also came in first when respondents were asked to rank institutions in terms of which "has done the most to promote the public good." Thirty-six percent said the media, 17% business, 17% government, and 16% labor.

The same survey asked respondents whether the media, business, government, or labor "should have its power cut back for the good of the country." Only 12% favored a reduction in the media's power, compared to 14% who said business's power should be reduced, 35% who said government's power should be cut back, and 21% who said labor's power should be cut.

The results of a 1978 Harris Survey which polled a national cross-section of 1,347 adults sums up the public's perception of newspapers compared to 19 other industries, including oil, drugs, health care, insurance, telephone, steel, liquor, banking, and airlines. Newspapers scored 2 to 14 percentage points above average in such categories as quality of products and services, labor relations, and attending to customer complaints.

These empirical results from various studies and surveys documenting the public's perception of the press point to the inescapable conclusion that the public's opinion of the press is indeed complex. On the one hand, the results indicate that a strong majority of the public views the press in a critical light. At the same time, the findings show that compared to other major institutions in our society, the press stands well in the public's eyes.

Part of this seeming inconsistency is due to the nature of the polls themselves.

Variations in the wording of questions designed to measure public attitudes often can produce different results. The complexity of the term "press credibility" and its numerous synonyms also accounts for inconsistencies in the findings. As Professor Eugene F. Shaw of Temple University noted in a 1976 *ANPA News Research Bulletin*, "While media credibility has received much attention in the past few years, what people really mean by media credibility has remained obscure and uncertain."

In order to understand the public's attitude toward the press, then, one must examine some of the specific attributes that people refer to in rating the credibility of the press. Among these attributes explored in recent empirical research are:

- Believability
- Accuracy
- Fairness
- Bias.

Believability. A 1981 Gallup Poll found that only three out of 10 Americans said they believe most of what they hear and read in the news media, whereas a greater number—five out of 10—said they believe only *some* of the news.

Similar findings are reported by Yankelovich, Skelly and White. Only four out of 10 Americans said they "always or usually" believe newspapers. The study again shows, however, that newspapers have relatively strong believability compared to other institutions.

Comparisons of historical data to recent findings demonstrate the public's growing tendency to regard television news as more believable than newspaper news.

The Roper Organization has consistently asked respondents which medium—radio, television, magazines or newspapers—they would be most inclined to believe if they received conflicting reports of the same news story. Before 1961, newspapers were cited as the most believable, but since then, television has been regarded as increasingly more believable. Today, five out of 10 people say they are most inclined to believe television as compared with two out of 10 who put their trust in newspapers.

This is consistent with the 1981 *Los Angeles Times* poll in which 61% of those surveyed said television was the most reliable, with only 26% regarding newspapers as the most reliable.

Accuracy. Another component of credibility, accuracy, has a significant impact on newspaper readership. In a 1976-77 study for Ottaway Newspapers, reported in *ANPA News Research Report* No. 29, Robin

Cobbey found that the perceived accuracy of newspapers influences how often people read them. And findings from a number of polls conducted over the years suggest that Americans' views toward newspaper accuracy are becoming more negative.

In 1939, 68.4% of those surveyed in a Roper poll said they felt that newspaper stories are almost always or usually accurate as to their facts.

In 1958, the Gallup Organization asked Americans what their own experience has been with newspaper reports of things they know about personally. Again, a large majority, 70%, said newspapers were accurate in their treatment of the news.

However, when the same question was asked of Americans in late 1979, perceived accuracy of newspapers dropped sharply: Only half (47%) said their newspaper had the facts straight, and one in three (34%) said the facts were inaccurate.

The *Los Angeles Times* poll offers more evidence that the perceived accuracy of newspapers is declining. When asked to select words that best describe newspapers—the choices were "fair," "powerful," "accurate," "arrogant," "superficial," "informative" and "sensational"—only 14% picked "accurate." Most people chose "informative" (38%) or "fair" (35%). Similar to Gallup's 1979 results, the *Los Angeles Times* found that almost one-third of Americans said the media are usually inaccurate in reporting news they know about personally.

Fairness. Although Americans have a poor opinion about the accuracy of newspapers, their attitudes toward the fairness of newspapers are far more favorable.

In the *Los Angeles Times* poll, about seven out of 10 people said the media are usually fair in reporting news they know about personally.

The public's opinion of the press as fair is not new. Over the years, it has consistently scored high marks on this attribute. For example, a Roper poll for *Fortune* magazine in 1937 found that almost seven out of 10 interviewees said they regarded the press as fair.

The public also views that fairness as an essential component of freedom of expression. Public Agenda Foundation Researchers John Immerwahr, John Doble and Jean Johnson concluded in the 1980 report that the public's definition of freedom of expression is based on a strong commitment to a principle of fairness. That is, people believe that the presentation of diverse viewpoints, including minority points of view, maximize free speech. They therefore want and expect the media to provide balanced treatment of controversial issues and political opponents. As a result, the public supports "fairness-enhancing" laws that would require the media to present alternative viewpoints, thus enhancing freedom of expression as defined by the public, the foundation report stated.

But Leo Bogart, executive vice president of the Newspaper Advertising Bureau, questions the foundation's ability to measure precisely public attitudes on freedom of expression. He argues that the issue is complex and that "asking a question and recording the answers does not in itself give us an understanding of public opinion." In short, fragmentary empirical results may simply reflect "instant public opinion" rather than well-thought-out views or deep-seated beliefs.

The results of a 1980 Gallup Poll give credence to Bogart's criticism. Gallup found that about three-quarters of the American public were unable to respond when asked if they knew what the First Amendment to the Constitution is or with what it deals. In addition, six in 10 Americans with a college background expressed a "lack of awareness" of the meaning of the First Amendment.

Bias. The press long has received poor ratings on bias, another attribute of credibility.

Polls conducted by Gallup and Roper in the late 1930s found that many Americans believed newspapers slanted the news in favor of big advertisers, friends of the publisher, and friendly politicians.

When asked by Gallup pollsters if they thought newspapers left out stories unfavorable to companies advertising in the paper, five out of 10 respondents agreed. Roper found that a similar ratio believed newspapers "soft-pedaled" news unfavorable to friendly politicians and friends of the publisher.

In the 1970s, Yankelovich, Skelly and White found that a strong majority of the public still feels that newspapers report biased news. Seventy-two percent of the public said that it is definitely true or probably true that television and newspapers slant the news and distort events.

But the definition of bias seemingly has changed since the 1930s. Seven out of 10 people indicate that they define bias as "putting too much emphasis on bad news and not the good" rather than showing favoritism to certain groups. This finding adds some support to the "bad news syndrome" as an explanation for an anti-press mood.

"Bad news." Indeed, the second perspective cited as an explanation for the public's anti-press attitudes is this "bad news syndrome." Numerous public opinion polls indicate that Americans' most common complaint about the press is its continual reporting of bad news.

Such findings imply that the public seeks to avoid troublesome news and believes that if the press played down the bad news and reported more good news, life would be better. In short, according to this view, the public holds the press responsible for the pervasiveness of bad news, and its recourse is to "blame the messenger" who brings it.

However, the public's reaction is the result of a more complex criticism than the mere complaint that the press reports too many unpleasant facts and events, according to a 1980 report by the Public Agenda Foundation. Its findings suggest that Americans use "bad news" as a catch-all term. When the public criticizes press coverage of bad news, it not only refers to the constant reporting of disturbing news, but also often refers to the presence of sensationalism, hype and questionable news judgment, and the lack of feature stories, local news and "soft news."

One example cited of the public's readiness to "blame the messenger" responsible for bringing bad news is the recent rash of libel suits that have resulted in large verdicts against the press. The Libel Defense

Resource Center found in a study of 47 libel cases that reached juries in 1980-82 that the press lost 42 of them. In more than half those cases, awards exceeded $100,000; several were in the million-dollar-plus category.

These large awards against the press suggest that the public regards journalists as doing an unacceptable job in reporting the news.

Washington press lawyer Bruce Sanford, general counsel of the Society of Professional Journalists, Sigma Delta Chi, sees additional significance in these jury actions. "Punishing awards may be the public's way of saying that there are not satisfactory vehicles in the country for registering displeasure with the news media," he said in a recent interview.

However, any linkage between public perceptions of too much bad news, ascribing the blame to the press itself, and such punitive responses as large libel awards remains more a matter of conjecture and interpretation than of firm evidence.

Journalistic practice. A third major perspective advocated as an explanation for an anti-press mood centers on journalistic practices, particularly in investigative reporting. For example, the spring 1981 Janet Cooke case and subsequent highly publicized examples of the press's shortcomings certainly did not enhance credibility.

Although a *Newsweek* magazine poll found that 58% of the interviewees said they believed Cooke's fabricated Washington Post story about an 8-year-old heroin addict to be an isolated incident, 33% said they think reporters often make things up.

A 1981 *Washington Post* poll also concluded that four people in five credit the news media for exposing corruption of public officials "a great deal" or "a fair amount."

Still, many people express negative attitudes toward some of the tactics used in gathering information. A 1981 Gallup poll reported that eight of every 10 Americans approve of investigative reporting, but more than half of those surveyed disapproved of such techniques as having reporters not identify themselves as reporters, or paying informers for their information.

In contrast, respondents to the *Los Angeles Times* survey said they do not think the media should be less aggressive in their reporting. Most said the media should be more aggressive in their reporting on government and business leaders and at least as aggressive as now on labor and church leaders. The poll also concluded that 53% of the public thinks the media use their right to freedom of expression responsibly.

These findings seem to contradict other data which suggest that the public holds the press in low esteem, thus signifying the complexity of public attitudes toward the press.

The public. What do research organizations mean when they refer to "the public" in making generalizations from their data? It is obvious from the evidence already presented that the public's attitudes toward the media are certainly multidimensional.

In a study of public knowledge about and public attitudes toward the media, reported at the International Association for Mass Communications Research in Paris last September, University of Illinois researchers D. Charles Whitney and Steven B. Goldman also assert that the existence of several "attitude publics" accounts for the wide variation in the survey findings. These publics are defined by their demographic characteristics, with education playing the most significant role in determining an individual's attitude toward the press.

The *Los Angeles Times* reported in its 1981 survey that both education and age have major impact on an individual's perception of the media. The higher the education level of the respondent, the more likely he or she is to describe newspapers as "powerful" rather than "fair" or "accurate." Conversely, the younger the respondent, the more likely he or she is to describe the press as "fair" and "accurate."

Education, as well as income, also affects an individual's reliance upon newspapers for information. Most people claim that television rather than newspapers is their primary source of information for political, economic and sports news. The more educated the respondent, however, the more likely he or she is to cite newspapers as the primary source of such news.

The same relationship exists for individuals with higher incomes. These demographic differences reinforce the point that there are many different publics viewing the press's performance, making the accurate measurement of the "public's" perception a difficult endeavor indeed.

Press responses. Newspapers, at least some of them, have responded in a variety of ways to improve their performance in reaction to their public image. But steps such as appointing ombudsmen to handle reader complaints and critique in-house news standards; printing daily correction boxes, guest editorials, editor/publisher columns and "action lines"; and other innovations may not be enough.

One who has measured the public's perception of the press, Pollster George Gallup, suggests two general approaches. He urges journalists to renew their sense of professionalism, which is essential to a responsible press, and he stresses the importance of educating the public to increase its awareness of its basic freedoms.

Such efforts also should be coupled with more systematic monitoring of the public mood. The assessment here had to construct a picture of public attitudes toward the press from fragments never planned as part of a larger mosaic. Our ability to collect public opinion data often outstrips our ability to integrate this information.

Isolated and fragmentary efforts at gauging public opinion often commit the fallacy of assuming uniform views toward a monolithic object. But there is great variation among newspapers, and segments of the public focus their criticism on many different attributes.

While it is technically feasible to measure many different attributes of daily newspaper performance, how many of these evaluations are more than "instant public opinion"?

Systematic monitoring of public opinion will indicate which facets actually influence behavior, ranging from cancelled subscriptions to letters to the editor.

Systematic monitoring also will identify where a strong professional response by newspapers is needed to ameliorate any anti-press mood.

The confidence question

"As far as people in charge of running (each institution) are concerned, would you say you have a great deal of confidence, only some confidence, or hardly any confidence at all in them?"

	1966	1971¹	1972	1973	1974	1975	1976	1977	1978	1979	1980	1981	1982
Medicine													
"great deal"	73	61	48	57	49	43	42	43	42	30	34	37	32
"only some"	22	--	36	31	38	41	45	44	43	45	50	49	49
"hardly any"	2	--	9	10	11	12	1	11	14	19	14	11	16
Education													
"great deal"	61	37	33	44	40	36	31	37	41	33	36	34	30
"only some"	32	--	47	37	44	43	48	46	40	48	49	52	54
"hardly any"	4	--	14	15	14	17	17	12	13	14	13	11	14
Television news													
"great deal"	--	--	--	41	32	35	28	28	35	37	29	24	24
"only some"	--	--	--	43	51	48	53	54	48	48	54	60	53
"hardly any"	--	--	--	14	16	16	15	16	16	13	16	15	22
Organized religion													
"great deal"	41	27	30	36	32	32	24	29	34	20	22	22	20
"only some"	32	--	39	35	40	39	42	41	38	44	43	46	48
"hardly any"	9	--	15	22	22	20	25	22	22	28	31	27	27
U.S. Supreme Court													
"great deal"	50	23	28	33	34	28	22	29	29	28	27	29	25
"only some"	30	--	43	40	45	44	48	47	41	52	52	54	54
"hardly any"	8	--	16	21	17	22	22	18	21	15	18	14	17
The military													
"great deal"	61	27	35	40	29	24	23	27	29	29	28	28	31
"only some"	28	--	42	35	44	45	50	48	44	46	52	53	51
"hardly any"	4	--	12	19	22	25	21	17	21	19	17	16	17
The press													
"great deal"	29	18	18	30	25	26	20	18	23	28	19	16	14
"only some"	50	--	51	45	49	53	51	55	53	53	58	59	61
"hardly any"	14	--	21	21	25	19	25	23	22	17	21	22	23
Major companies													
"great deal"	55	27	27	29	15	19	16	20	22	18	16	16	18
"only some"	35	--	44	44	49	50	55	52	56	50	53	60	59
"hardly any"	4	--	16	20	33	26	25	23	17	27	27	21	20
Organized labor													
"great deal"	22	14	15	20	18	14	10	14	15	10	14	12	8
"only some"	42	--	44	41	47	41	47	43	40	47	51	48	50
"hardly any"	17	--	24	32	30	37	35	36	38	39	32	36	40
White House													
"great deal"	--	--	--	18	18	--	--	31	14	15	18	28	20
"only some"	--	--	--	36	52	--	--	52	50	61	55	48	56
"hardly any"	--	--	--	41	27	--	--	12	31	19	25	22	23
Congress													
"great deal"	42	19	21	29	16	13	9	17	10	18	18	16	13
"only some"	45	--	51	49	61	52	52	54	47	57	59	61	65
"hardly any"	6	--	14	16	21	30	33	25	38	20	21	20	21

Source: The Harris Survey
¹Data not available for "only some" or "hardly any" responses.

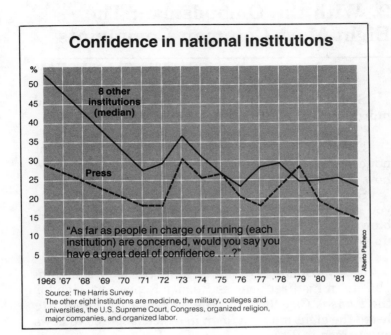

Confidence in national institutions

%

8 other institutions (median)

Press

"As far as people in charge of running (each institution) are concerned, would you say you have a great deal of confidence . . . ?"

1966 '67 '68 '69 '70 '71 '72 '73 '74 '75 '76 '77 '78 '79 '80 '81 '82

Source: The Harris Survey
The other eight institutions are medicine, the military, colleges and universities, the U.S. Supreme Court, Congress, organized religion, major companies, and organized labor.

2. With the Ombudsman: The Eight Most Common Complaints

By RICHARD P. CUNNINGHAM

She gazes over the rim of a cocktail glass and murmurs:

"I never knew anybody like you existed."

Every ombudsman has had the experience, but none of them get excited about it anymore; they know how the scene is going to play out.

She's going to ask, "What kind of complaints do you get most often?" And the ombudsman's going to blow it, because no one of them has ever really come up with a specific answer.

Until Casey Jones.

Casey (Donald D.) Jones kept track of the complaints in his first year as Reader Representative for the *Kansas City Star* and the *Kansas City Times*. He listed the eight most common in a recent speech to news executives in Phoenix, Ariz. The list:

- Inaccuracies
- Newspaper arrogance
- Lack of fairness and balance
- Disregard of privacy
- Insensitivity
- Contempt for the community
- Glorification of the criminal and the bizarre
- Bad writing and editing

By "inaccuracies" Jones said he meant "plain old errors of fact....These kinds of errors of fact do more to undermine the trust and confidence of readers than any other sin we commit. Some reader is an expert on every story we write. That reader knows the facts. If the story is negative, that reader can point to the smallest error of fact to cast doubt on the whole story."

Arrogance: "Readers see many papers unwilling to admit errors. They see reporters and editors trying

Richard Cunningham was an associate director of the National News Council. This article originally appeared in Editor & Publisher (March 19, 1983) 40. Reprinted by permission.

to set themselves up as a privileged class....They do not understand and often resent the press's concern with the First Amendment. We have failed miserably in convincing the rest of this country that the First Amendment includes all of us."

Unfairness: "I've been amazed, too, by many readers who have a more highly developed sense of fairness than some reporters. Readers are quick to pick up on hatchet jobs. They don't like them. Often these readers get on libel juries. They want both sides of a story. They don't want in a news story the opinions or biases of editors and reporters."

Privacy: "The privacy problem that bothers the reader is more emotional than legal. He seems to intuit that public figures are fair game. What the reader resents is the disregard by papers of the privacy—or probably a better word is the old-fashioned word 'feelings'—of individuals like himself who, for no fault of their own, are thrust into the news.

"They resent photos that show grief-stricken families. They resent photos of the victims of fires and accidents. They resent photos that hold someone up to ridicule. The reader empathizes with the helpless, the hurt, the grief-stricken, the victim of tragedy."

Insensitivity: "For the most part, papers today are much more sensitive to race, religion, sex and color than in the past. But we are a long way from being perfect. A recent AP story and cutlines talked about Indian squaws. I don't recommend going on one of the nearby reservations and using that term....Most staffs have persons who represent various minorities. It might take a little humbling, but why not ask that person—would this offend anyone of your race or religion or sex?"

Contempt for the community: "Many readers feel that the ownership by chains of once locally-owned newspapers and television stations leaves the business, political and cultural leaders more or less disenfranchised....There is the perception that chain-owned newspapers and television stations are the fast-food restaurants of the news business. Everything is fried in the same batter—a batter packaged in New York or Los Angeles and shipped in for local consumption."

Bizarre: "We put the funeral of the head of a biker gang on page one and relegate the funeral of a civic leader to the death page. The reader doesn't like to see the actions of a few protesters being given front-page play. Too often, they feel, the opinions of the majority are given scant attention....Editors need to stand back 15 yards and ask if the way we handle a story doesn't give it more importance than it actually deserves."

Writing: "Readers—older readers particularly—are quick to complain about bad grammar, poor spelling, looseness in language, obscenities and profanities. Many readers complain about recent fads in news writing—fads like the Jello-lead—that long drawn out introductory to a major story with the real news buried somewhere in the sixth or seventh paragraph.

"Surprisingly," Jones said, "many readers—despite our protestations that they do not—seem to understand the problems and pressures of getting news. They can understand error. What they can't understand is the extremes to which many reporters and editors will go to keep from saying, 'We were wrong.' "

3. Journalism Under Fire

By WILLIAM A. HENRY III

*It may well be that the public reacted cumulatively with
a judgment that the press had it coming.*
> —Robert McCloskey,
> former *Washington Post* ombudsman

They are rude and accusatory, cynical and almost
unpatriotic. They twist facts to suit their not-so-hidden
liberal agenda. They meddle in politics, harass
business, invade people's privacy, and then walk off
without regard to the pain and chaos they leave behind.
They are arrogant and self-righteous, brushing aside
most criticism as the uninformed carping of cranks and
ideologues. To top it off, they claim that their behavior
is sanctioned, indeed sanctified, by the U.S.
Constitution.

"J'accuse!" The rallying cry of crusading reporters
has been taken up in reply by a citizenry that seems
more mistrustful than ever before. Public respect for
journalism has fallen dramatically in recent years,
threatening one of the foundations of the country's
democratic system. The National Opinion Research
Center, which found in 1976 that 29% of the popula-
tion had "a great deal of confidence in the press,"
reports that this year that figure fell to a new low of
13.7%. The most vivid indication of the souring attitude
toward the press came when the Reagan administration invaded Grenada and excluded reporters from the
scene. Journalists argued impassionedly that the
press's freedom and the public's "right to know" were
at stake. But to many of their countrymen, the lack
of coverage seemed inconsequential—even gratify-
ing—as if laryngitis had silenced a chronic complainer.

*William A. Henry III is an associate editor at TIME magazine.
This article originally appeared in TIME (December 12, 1983)
76-93.*
Reprinted by permission of TIME.

NBC commentator John Chancellor, in a *Nightly News* broadcast, voiced the press vision of what was happening: "The American Government is doing whatever it wants to, without any representative of the American public watching what it is doing." But many in Chancellor's audience rejected his premise that journalists stand in for the people: in 500 letters and phone calls to NBC, viewers supported the press ban in Grenada 5 to 1. ABC anchor Peter Jennings said that "99%" of his mail from viewers on the issue supported Reagan. Newspapers also protested the exclusion, and evoked the same sort of response: the trade publication *Editor & Publisher* found, in an informal survey of about a dozen dailies, that letters to the editor were running 3 to 1 in favor of the Reagan Administration's exclusion of the press. *TIME*'s 225 letters on the issue ran almost 8 to 1 against the press.

The support for excluding the media was far from universal, but much of it was expressed in gleeful, even vengeful terms. Further, many of the more thoughtful respondents seemed to reach beyond the battlefield issue to reflect deep, far-ranging resentment of the press. Linda Warren of West Hollywood, Calif., wrote to the *Los Angeles Herald Examiner*: "Journalists are so out of touch with majority values, such as honor, duty and service to country that they are alienated from the very society that they purport to serve." Duane Bloom of Golden, Colo., argued in a letter to *The Denver Post*: "The media have frequently misused sensitive and explosive events as opportunities for personal glory and financial gain." Conceded *New York Times* editorial page editor Max Frankel: "The most astounding thing about the Grenada situation was the quick, facile assumption by some of the public that the press wanted to get in, not to witness the invasion on behalf of the people, but to sabotage it."

The dispute over Grenada seemed to uncork a pent-up public hostility. It reinforced a perception that journalists regard themselves as utterly detached from, and perhaps even hostile to, the government of their country. Another factor in provoking distrust is the suspicion that journalists care little about accuracy. When *The Washington Post, The New York Times* and *New*

York Daily News all discovered, during 1981 and 1982, that they had printed stories that reporters had embellished or invented, much of the public took these extreme cases as typical of journalism and expressed delight that major news organizations had been humiliated.

The mistrust has been heightened by several celebrated libel suits, particularly by General William Westmoreland and Los Angeles physician Carl Galloway against CBS and by Mobil Corp. president William Tavoulareas against *The Washington Post.* Each raised worrisome doubts about the objectivity of prominent journalists, and called into question the techniques used to shape a story.

Indeed, libel verdicts have become a telling measure of public eagerness to punish the press. According to Stanford University law professor Marc Franklin, since 1976 nearly 85% of 106 major libel verdicts by juries have been defeats for journalist defendants, and almost two dozen involved damage awards of more than $1 million. "Juries are the American people," says Eugene Patterson, editor of the *St. Petersburg Times.* "They want to punish us." The Supreme Court may share some of the mistrust. Since 1972, it has ruled against journalist defendants in all four libel appeals it has heard.

The failings of journalists have been compounded in the public's mind by the perception that as their power has increased, so has their presumption of self-importance. Says William Woo, editorial page editor of the *St. Louis Post-Dispatch:* "Arrogance, insensitivity, sensationalism, the sounding of First Amendment alarms at every provocation—these have all lost the press sympathy." Such attitudes are particularly grating to a large segment of the public that has come to see the press as primarily interested in its own profits and renown. "There is no longer a prevailing feeling that the press is fighting to right a wrong," says Chicago attorney Don Reuben. "The sense is that the press is venal, out to make a buck."

This decline of respect has been evident in popular culture: the image of journalism has shifted in movies from the diligent crusading in *All the President's Men* to the reckless destruction of people's lives in *Absence of Malice,* the corrupting collaboration with Nicaraguan revolutionaries in *Under Fire* and the intrusive buffoonery in *The Right Stuff.*

The press's unpopularity has political implications that the White House has been quick to grasp. "I think resentment toward the press has been stepped up by the public relations genius of the Reagan administration," says *Boston Globe* editor Thomas Winship. For all its affability, and its candor on issues it hopes to publicize, the administration has been as vigorous as any other in recent years in its attempts to control the flow of information and thereby define the nature of public debate. At various times, the President has proposed strict rules on contact between officials and reporters, used the FBI to track down embarrassing leaks, and moved to reduce the scope of the Freedom of Information Act and to impose lifetime government censorship on tens of thousands of officials who have had access to classified information.

When the U.S. military decided to exclude the press from Grenada, the White House was receptive. According to some sources, the inspiration was the British government's restriction, but not outright ban, of the British press during the Falklands war. There was little fear that the President and military would lose the battle for public opinion if the operation went smoothly. Says White House communications director David Gergen, who has tried to temper the Administration's anti-media sentiment: "Unfortunately, kicking the press is a sure-fire applause line with almost any audience."

Nonetheless, the Joint Chiefs of Staff have asked Winant Sidle, a former public affairs officer at the Pentagon, to help develop guidelines for press access to future military actions. Contrary to some public suspicions, secrecy is not the problem: the press has always been willing to respect agreed-upon security strictures. Nor are logistics necessarily an obstacle: a small group of reporters can act as a "pool" for the rest of the press. Although Sidle has not completed his proposals, his main worry seems to be that the press is too negative. Says he: "They are always looking for somebody to hit over the head."

The press, by its nature, is rarely beloved—nor should that be its aim. Too often it must be the bearer of bad tidings. Since World War II, journalists have covered the turmoil of the civil rights movement, conveyed vivid scenes of domestic protest and battlefield gore during the Vietnam War, and participated in the collapse of a presidency. Within the past two years, the press chronicled the pain of 10% unemployment. Increasingly, this bad news has been brought by the emotional medium of TV, which can seem rudely intrusive at both ends of its electronic linkage: at the scene of suffering and in the privacy of the viewer's living room.

Moreover, the time-honored image of the reporter—sketched in *The Front Page* as a low-paid but high-spirited regular fellow drinking beer with the police as the city edition is put to bed—has given way to a persona shaped by television: the anchorman or anchorwoman, cool, comely, and paid far more than the President.

Print journalists contend that when television became an accepted part of the news business, its you-are-there intrusiveness and emphasis on conflict tarnished the reputation of the entire profession. Says *Washington Post* executive editor Ben Bradlee: "Television has changed the public's vision of the reporter into someone who is petty and disagreeable, who has taken cynicism an unnecessary extra step." Robert Maynard, editor of the Oakland (Ca.) *Tribune,* agrees: "When people see a TV person shoving a mike in front of a grieving relative, all of us in the press appear to be boorish and ghoulish." TV executives reply that print can get away with more aggressive behavior because it is gray and abstract rather than immediate. "The printed press does not show the reporter asking the question," says NBC News president Reuven Frank. "What is peculiar to television is that the intrusiveness is part of the story."

As the power of the press has shifted from local newspapers to national networks, the public seemingly has added the news business to the list of remote institutions that it mistrusts simply because of their size. Says *Chicago Tribune* editor James Squires: "The press used to be something accessible, owned by the fellow down the street. There is no access now. It is too big and far away." The growth of the press as a business has led to consolidation, so that most cities now have one pre-eminent newspaper, often owned by a large chain. In many cases this has given papers the resources necessary to do their job better, but has also reduced the chance for readers to find editorial voices suited to their tastes. In addition, today's young journalists, often moving from city to city to climb the career ladder, tend to lack loyalty and sensitivity to the communities they cover, further aggravating the public's alienation.

The roster of complaints against the press is diverse, even contradictory, but there is an instructive consistency to the questions that the public asks most often: Are reporters scrupulously accurate, or will they reshape a quote, ignore a fact, even concoct an anonymous "source" in order to make a point? Are they fair and objective? Why are there so many leaks, and do reporters care about threats to national security? What value should reporters place on a person's right to privacy? What purpose is served by the preoccupation with "investigative" reporting?

The most fundamental of these questions is: can you believe what you read or see? The credibility of all journalists was damaged in 1981 when *Washington Post* reporter Janet Cooke was forced to return a Pulitzer Prize after admitting that she had invented the title character of "Jimmy's World," a portrait of an eight-year-old heroin addict. A month later, *New York Daily News* columnist Michael Daly admitted that he had made up the name of a British soldier who, he reported, had shot a juvenile in Belfast, Northern Ireland; the story was proved to contain other factual errors. Daly acknowledged that he had changed details in a number of other columns, but contended, in classic "New Journalism" fashion, that altering the facts had not impaired his rendition of the truth. The rash of fraud infected *The New York Times* seven months later, when its Sunday magazine published a report from Cambodia by freelancer Christopher Jones. In fact, Jones had written the story while at his home in Spain and for part of it had plagiarized a 1930 novel, André Malraux's *La Voie Royale*.

Journalists rightly pointed out that these deceptions were oddities—most stories of consequence are covered by a variety of news organizations, and the pressure of competition makes it all but impossible to fake a story from, say, the White House. Indeed, the fabrications of Cooke, Daly and Jones were quickly exposed, partly as a result of probing questions from other news organizations. Cooke and Daly were fired, and Jones was dropped from the *Times*'s freelance roster. But the spate of trickery underscored a fundamental vulnerability of the press: editors rely almost absolutely on the honesty of their reporters.

Much more common than willful inventions are errors that result from overaggressive reporting and inadequate checking. Says Robert MacNeil of PBS's *MacNeil/Lehrer NewsHour*: "More and more people have had the experience of being interviewed or being at an event that has been covered, and they know what they see on the screen is not the way it was." The *Kansas City Times* alleged, during a series on athletic recruitment practices, that the mother of a Wichita State University basketball player had received a new automobile and a house as a payoff for her son's success with the team. After another paper, *The Wichita Eagle-Beacon,* looked into the story, the record was corrected: the money for the purchases came from the settlement of a medical malpractice suit.

The *Atlanta Journal-Constitution* published a long front-page retraction in August of a 1982 series of front-page stories alleging that people who worked at, or lived near, a plutonium plant in Aiken, S.C., were suffering in disproportionate numbers from a rare blood disease. "We discovered that our reporters obviously had confused statistics and scientific data," wrote editor Jim Minter. "We did not ask enough questions as the series was being prepared." One key cause of this kind of error: a tendency among young reporters to believe the worst, to see a potential Watergate, hence their fame and fortune, in almost every story. Says editor Rosann Doran of the Broomfield (Colo.) *Enterprise* (circ. 18,200): "Every kid I get out of journalism school wants to have some major exposé under his byline. Sometimes they cannot accept the fact that something is not crooked."

The "investigative" impulse worries many news executives. Says editor Maynard of the Oakland *Tribune*: "We are too hungry for blood—it sometimes seems to readers that we will not do the story unless we can do someone in." The suspicious attitude among reporters leads to negativism in news coverage. The outlook of today's generation of journalists was formed during Watergate and Vietnam, when figures of authority seemed so often to be the proper adversary. Many citizens regard this hypercritical approach as a form of bias. Says Mobil's top public relations executive, Herbert Schmertz: "There has developed a premise in journalism that it seems to succeed when it systematically undermines public confidence in institutions and leaders. I don't think the public likes that."

On television, the posture of perennial mistrust has been promoted by the success of CBS's often excellent *60 Minutes,* which has been among the nation's most popular programs for the past six years. In its edited form, the show has elements of high melodrama: most of its investigative pieces are playlets in which a Lone Ranger journalist corners a villain, not with a gun but with an interview. Real life, however, is not so neat, and the confrontations are rarely so conclusive. This was seen during a libel suit in May brought by Los Angeles physician Carl Galloway, who was accused by *60 Minutes* of complicity in insurance fraud. Galloway lost his case, but won the consolation of making *60 Minutes* look silly: film edited out of the report showed the CBS team rehearsing interviews, or repeating them until they got the answers they wanted. In an attempt to force an impromptu interview just outside the clinic featured in the exposé, CBS anchor Dan Rather chased a man, whose identity he did not know, around a parking lot.

The distorting effect of the confrontational style was also evident in a 1982 CBS documentary, *The Uncounted Enemy: A Vietnam Deception,* which alleged that General William Westmoreland, when commander of U.S. forces in South Vietnam, was part of a "conspiracy" to mislead the public and perhaps President Johnson about the strength of enemy forces. Correspondent Mike Wallace, the most feared questioner on *60 Minutes,* challenged Westmoreland on events more than 15 years old and reduced the general to flustered confusion. But after an internal investigation, CBS concluded that the charge of conspiracy was "inappropriate," material supportive of Westmoreland's position had been minimized, and network rules had been violated to give unfair advantage to Westmoreland's accusers. CBS News will defend the program in a $120 million libel suit by Westmoreland scheduled for trial next year.

Tone, even more than the facts, was at issue in the suit against *The Washington Post* by Mobil executive Tavoulareas. U.S. District Judge Oliver Gasch, who tried the case, ruled that Tavoulareas had not met the legal standards for proof of libel, and overturned the jury verdict. But he added, "The article falls far short of being a model of fair, unbiased journalism."

Journalists contend that very few factual errors arise from the kind of ideological or political bias that critics, especially conservatives, often allege. Says Mark Ethridge Jr., a professor of journalism at the University of South Carolina and the former editor of the *Detroit Free Press*: "I find it particularly objectionable that none of our critics will give us credit for stupidity. To them it is always a deliberate distortion." Indeed, even with the best of ability and intentions, reporters find it difficult to ensure that a story is totally sound. Nonetheless, conservative critics argue that almost beyond debate there is a discernible liberal bent among reporters and editors at the major national news organizations. ABC interviewer Barbara Walters concedes, "The news media in general are liberal. If you want to be a reporter, you are going to see poverty and misery, and you have to be involved in the human condition."

In a 1979-80 survey of 240 editors and reporters at the commercial networks, PBS, *The New York Times, The Washington Post, The Wall Street Journal, Newsweek, U.S. News & World Report* and *TIME*, political scientists Stanley Rothman of Smith College and S. Robert Lichter of George Washington University found that 48% believed that the government should guarantee jobs, 68% argued that the government should narrow the income gap between rich and poor, and 88% held that the U.S. legal system favors the wealthy. On social issues, 90% believed that women should have a right to an abortion, and only 25% considered homosexuality morally wrong.

Journalists who admit that they are liberals—or conservatives—deny that their personal values show up in their reporting. Conservative critics reply that a newspaper's political leanings are evident in the choice and treatment of stories. Certainly there is often an edge to news reporting in *The Washington Post*, as in this skeptical lead from a Page One piece on Nov. 8: "President Reagan yesterday celebrated the 'heroic rescue' of American medical students from Grenada in a ceremony climaxing a White House effort to put the best political face on the invasion of the Caribbean island and the terrorist bombing in Lebanon that killed at least 230 U.S. servicemen."

Perhaps the most sensitive allegations of bias are those that cropped up during the Grenada controversy: that journalists are not patriotic enough. "You feel sometimes like they are not on your side in a war," says John Lane, a former commissioner of Chaffee County, Colo., who served in Vietnam. Fred Barnes, national political reporter for the Baltimore *Sun*, asserts in the December issue of the conservative monthly *American Spectator*, "The coverage of Central America in recent months points up one of the ugly truths about the American press: the better the news, the less of it you get. As the war began to turn against the Communist guerrillas in El Salvador, there was a palpable dip in the attention paid to it." Shirley Christian, who won a 1981 Pulitzer Prize for her reporting from Latin America for *The Miami Herald*, argued in the March 1982 issue of the *Washington Journalism Review* that much of the American press corps during Nicaragua's Sandinista revolution was "on a guilt trip" about past U.S. support of the repressive Somoza regime, and thus overlooked warning signals of doctrinaire Marxism among the Sandinistas.

Most journalists insist that they stay detached from news sources. But many admit to a hazardous exception. They readily cooperate with prosecutors, obtaining inside details about impending arrests and indictments in exchange for providing publicity at an opportune moment. Initial publicity can virtually convict an accused person in the public's mind. When Feminist Ginny Foat, then president of the California chapter of the National Organization for Women, was about to be arrested for a murder that happened 18 years ago, news organizations were tipped off. Pictures of the arrest appeared on all three networks and in dozens, perhaps hundreds, of newspapers. Foat, who was acquitted after less than two hours of jury deliberation, claims with some justice that from the moment of her arrest, the press wrote about her as though she were guilty. Says she: "They believed what a lot of people believe, that if you are arrested, you must be guilty."

Often, the mere disclosure that someone is "under investigation" is enough to derail the target's career or wreck his personal life. Last year, every major Boston news organization reported that the Massachusetts attorney general was pursuing charges of corruption within the state department of revenue. The allegations came from an ex-convict, employed by the department, who was caught extorting a bribe and who offered to testify against his superiors. One of the three men whom he accused—but only after a prosecutor put the name forward—was a long-time close friend of then Governor Edward King. The scandal ended whatever chance King had of winning a second term. For King's friend John Coady, the consequences were far more grave: while the inquiry was under way, Coady was found hanged in the attic of his home, and his death was widely reported as a virtual admission of guilt. Then the two other accused employees were tried and acquitted. That turnabout last month prompted the weekly *Boston Phoenix* (circ. 83,650) to attack the city's news organs, including itself; it placed special blame on the dominant daily *Globe* (circ. 515,000). Said *Phoenix* publisher Stephen Mindich: "It is a clear example of irresponsibility, and it creates distrust among the public." *Globe* editor Winship replies, "It was an important, live story. We were evenhanded then, and we are re-examining it now."

Many complaints about the press have less to do with the accuracy or fairness of stories than with the techniques used to get them, which have gone so far as breaking and entering, electronic bugging, impersonation, entrapment. Says Walter Jacobson, anchor of CBS's WBBM-TV in Chicago: "I do not believe there should be any restrictions. I have had to use all sorts of ruses to get information, but I do not feel I have to be honest with public officials who are never honest with us." New Orleans television reporter Pierre DeGruy posed as the owner of a film production company in order to obtain interviews with young male prostitutes, then aired footage in which the youths' faces and voices were recognizable. He has some regrets: "We scammed them to get them to tell us the most intimate details of their lives. Now that I have done it, I have serious problems with it." Undercover reporting was once widely accepted in print journalism, and is still praised by many editors as the only way to get certain kinds of stories, many of which serve the public well.*

But standards are changing: The Pulitzer Prize board denied awards to the Chicago *Sun-Times* in 1979 and to the *Los Angeles Herald Examiner* in 1982, at least partly because their reporters used false identities. The *Sun-Times* set up a saloon business and paid bribes to city officials; a *Herald Examiner* reporter claimed to be an illegal alien and took a job in a garment-industry sweatshop.

Another controversial technique is the use of unnamed sources. At best, reporters may subject themselves to manipulation by a person who passes on information for his own motives; at worst, readers suspect that the anonymous source may not exist. In some cases, reporters seem to feel that using a "deep throat" lends a touch of glamour—a signal that they are in the know. Relying on unnamed sources is often necessary. Most major publications, including *TIME*, get background information at official briefings or

---

*Nellie Bly, perhaps the most celebrated turn-of-the-century journalist, got herself imprisoned in order to expose jail conditions for the New York World; Feminist Gloria Steinem became a Playboy bunny to research a 1963 report for Show magazine.

through interviews of behind-the-scenes participants. In such cases, the source justifiably insists on anonymity. "The alternative is not to do a lot of stories the public ought to see," says *Wall Street Journal* executive editor Fred Taylor. But editors have become more aware that anonymous information must be used carefully. Michael Carlin, producer in charge of investigative stories at Atlanta's WAGA-TV, says, "The more I use anonymous sources, the less I like it. The more critical you are of someone, the greater the demand for a public accuser."

Some of the most controversial actions of journalists come when their desire for a good story causes them to collide with an individual's right to privacy. When 239 U.S. servicemen were killed in a terrorist attack in Beirut, the homes of the victims were surrounded by reporters and camera crews seeking to record the families' grief. When word came over the wires that Private First Class Michael Devlin of Westwood, Mass., was the first confirmed casualty from that state, reporters besieged his mother. Recalls Christine Devlin: "They are on top of you before you have a chance to get the family together. Why should people have to know how you look or feel under those circumstances?" At Camp Lejeune, N.C., a TV crew reportedly paid children to go door to door in areas closed to the press to find out which families were awaiting word of a potential death in the Beirut explosion. Said an outraged Marine officer: "You people will stop at nothing. Everywhere you go, you leave a smell."

In perhaps the most tasteless single snippet of this deathwatch footage, a CBS News crew taped the actual moment when Marine officials arrived to report to his family that Corporal Timothy Giblin of North Providence, R.I., had been killed. First shown on the CBS *Morning News,* the sequence was replayed that evening on, among others, the CBS-owned station in Chicago. As the tape finished, anchor Jacobson apologized: "I am sorry, that film should not have been shown. It was inappropriate." NBC chose not to air similar footage its crew shot at a Marine's home in California. Said anchor Tom Brokaw: "We looked at it and said, 'That is a blatant intrusion,' and we did not put it on." Nevertheless, the footage had been shot. Indeed, nearly every local TV station in America airs comparably intrusive interviews with the survivors of fires, auto accidents and other calamities that may have claimed family members. Newspaper and news-magazine reporters and photographers can be equally intrusive when covering personal tragedy.

Restraint does not come naturally to most journalists. Indeed, some of them argue that the best way to avoid accusations of bias is to go anywhere they can and publish absolutely anything they believe is newsworthy. CBS was accused of following this damn-the-consequences policy in October when it aired videotapes of the arrest of automaker John De Lorean on cocaine trafficking charges, even at the risk of imperiling the chance of finding an impartial jury. The tapes were of dubiously lawful origin—CBS acquired them from *Hustler* publisher Larry Flynt, who bought them from a clerk at a law firm that had briefly represented De Lorean—and they did not break news that would otherwise have gone unreported: the actual footage was scheduled to be introduced into evidence at the trial. The network's rationale, according to CBS News president Edward Joyce: "It was newsworthy because this was the first time we actually saw the government making an arrest in this type of case."

This lack of restraint sometimes even extends to cases involving children. When it turned out that a previously identified kidnap victim in Chicago, an 11-year-old girl, had also been raped, the *Sun-Times* published the girl's photograph with the word "rape" next to it. The *St. Paul* (Minn.) *Pioneer Press* published the names of parents who had been charged with child sex abuse, identifying their children as among the victims. Says managing editor Deborah Howell: "We felt readers had a legitimate interest in knowing if their children had associated with the accused parents, but it was hard. I know what this does to little kids."

Often, news executives who might otherwise be restrained rush the news into print to avoid being scooped. The Oakland *Tribune,* however, chose to run that risk when it learned that mass murderer Juan

Corona had wanted to enter a guilty plea at his long
and costly ($5 million) re-trial, but was dissuaded by
his attorneys. Editor Maynard kept the story secret until the trial was complete. He explained: "There was
no doubt in my mind that if we had printed the story,
it would have caused a mistrial, which could have
forced yet another trial and the expenditure of still
more millions."

A special set of ethical questions concerns the elite
of American reporters, the Washington press corps. Indeed, much of journalistic behavior that the public says
it finds objectionable is seen chiefly in telecasts from
Washington: rudeness to high officials, prosecutorial
shouting of questions at press conferences, overt attempts to trap an interview subject with trick questions, "instant analysis" of speeches that viewers have
just seen for themselves. Another blow to the image
of all journalists was struck in Washington last Friday when White House spokesman Larry Speakes announced that he had trapped two reporters purloining
internal White House memos. To prove that some
writers on the White House beat were snooping,
Speakes said, he prepared a "scam": fake messages,
one about the timing of President Reagan's re-election
announcement, were left out to see who would pick
them up and pursue the stories. Said Speakes: "They
both bit like snakes."

Apart from manner and attitude, there are other
grounds for criticism: reporting from Washington
tends, inevitably, to be highly speculative and to rely
heavily on anonymous sources and undocumented
assertions. Critics also fault the capital's press corps
for preoccupation with politics and frequent failure to
delve into the performance of government agencies,
which spend the bulk of the nation's budget.

Perhaps the most troubling issue for Washington
reporters is the growing use of leaks by government
sources. The term leak implies a breach of security and
calls to mind the image of a disgruntled lower-level
employee seeking to embarrass his boss. In fact, in
almost every modern administration, the majority of
leaks have come from top-rank presidential aides,
Cabinet members and other senior officials who want

to get information or a point of view across to the public. Last week, for example, Reagan's top aides indicated their displeasure with Martin Feldstein, chairman of the Council of Economic Advisers, through a leak by "a senior White House official" to Knight-Ridder newspaper reporters. The purpose of leaks is often manipulative: to pretest public reaction to a plan, outflank a colleague or sabotage a rival policy proposal. There is an added appeal: Journalists are so accustomed to treating the closed-door side of Washington as the "real" one that they tend to report unattributed information with less skepticism than they bring to public pronouncements.

For all its faults, and all the public outcry over them, the press has many claims to make in its defense. To former Vice President Spiro Agnew's much repeated charge that journalists are "elected by no one," editors have two valid responses. The first is that some institutions in a democratic society must be able to stand apart from the electoral process so that they can risk making unpopular decisions. Federal Appeals Court Judge Irving Kaufman of New York has likened the press to the judiciary in that respect. Said he: "Both sustain democracy, not because they are responsible to any branch of government, but precisely because, except in the most extreme cases, they are not accountable at all. Thus they are able to check the irresponsibility of those in power." The second argument is that journalists are elected by their readers and viewers every day. During the past decade, in response to public demand, the number of broadcast hours devoted to network and local news increased sharply, and Ted Turner's Cable News Network provided the first 24-hour news service. The average American now spends about four hours a week watching newscasts. The newspaper industry has been shaken by failures and mergers that have stilled dozens of "second" voices in cities, but the 1,700 U.S. dailies still command an estimated readership of at least 110 million people a day. Moreover, consumers have some choice: there may be only local-monopoly newspapers covering their communities, and local TV stations may simply follow the papers' lead, but there are numerous ways to get national and international news.

The competitive urge among these multiple sources of information leads to excesses, but it also contributes to a self-correcting process. When one news outlet reports a story badly, rival organizations can score a coup as well as honor their craft by setting the record straight. Indeed, most irate critics of bias in the press cite stories from other parts of the press to prove their case. For readers of almost any ideological stripe, the perceived or actual bias of some publication can be offset by the availability of others. In soliciting subscriptions from new readers, the conservative weekly *Human Events,* for example, cites the "distortions of the major networks and your daily newspaper" and offers as an antidote its own pages.

Sophisticated readers know that by comparison with the highly ideological press in Western Europe—or, for that matter, the noisy, brawling, relentlessly partisan and even corrupt papers that were the norm when the First Amendment was written—the modern U.S. press is distinctively balanced. By the standards of the late 19th and early 20th century era of "yellow journalism," the American reporter today is a model of responsibility and restraint.

Most important, U.S. journalism is generally good. Reporters and editors are better educated than their predecessors and are readier to take on difficult topics. Partly as a result of the influence of television, which has made the world seem smaller, many local newspapers now publish considerably more international news, and not all of it is revolutions and earthquakes. Social trends, which newspapers long overlooked because they were not events that happened the day before, are now covered thoughtfully. In recent years, the press has learned to report about economics, education, medicine, science and the computer revolution as fully and discerningly as it follows crime and politics. Says *Washington Post* editor Bradlee: "It is strange that so much criticism is coming now, because I honestly believe that the quality of the American press is better than ever. When we set out to do something ambitious and relevant to a problem, we do a helluva job."

Despite the criticisms and controversies the press provokes, it successfully produces hundreds of substantive stories, large-scale and small, that hold government to account and bring the public important information. Perhaps the best overall performance during the past year was the persistent probing, by several news organizations, into improprieties at the federal Environmental Protection Agency, including alleged favoritism to business interests and, at best, lax enforcement of regulations. Despite the Reagan administration's seeming determination to dismiss the evidence of pervasive EPA wrongdoing as a press vendetta, the reporting eventually led to top-level resignations, the appointment of a capable new administrator and, last week, the perjury conviction of former EPA official Rita Lavelle.

The public interest has been served by a steady spotlight throughout the year on waste and mismanagement at the Pentagon, another branch of government that fiercely resists scrutiny. Stories, ranging from cost overruns on weapons systems to price gouging by contractors, forced the military to step up its own investigations. As always, journalists provided community services that are too easily taken for granted: when river flooding knocked out telephone service in Louisiana in April, most radio and TV stations managed to stay on the air to broadcast safety information. There have been innumerable enterprising individual efforts. Samples:

• Associated Press reporter Bill Vogerin's series, investigating claims that water theft by farmers was drying up the Arkansas River, prompted state and federal officials to review irrigation and conservation practices.

• The *Los Angeles Times*, in a 21-part series, explored the economic, social and political diversity of its region's three million Hispanics.

• Pam Zekman of WBBM-TV in Chicago discovered that the city's police had for years underreported crime statistics for political reasons.

• The *Los Angeles Herald Examiner* last week ran a vivid but not alarmist six-part series on Los Angeles County's youth gangs (estimated membership: 40,000), which are believed responsible for 1,000 murders over the past four years.

- ABC News devoted 52 hours in February and March to crime topics. Notable among the segments was a hardheaded yet optimistic *Nightline* report on the relative success that Patuxent Institution, a state prison in Jessup, Md., has achieved in rehabilitating inmates through education and psychotherapy.
- *Washington Post* reporter Neil Henry demonstrated the kind of useful purpose that undercover reporting can serve. Posing as a destitute drifter, he was hired as a migrant laborer in North Carolina. He chronicled work under wrenching conditions, yet his carefully modulated stories managed to be fair to both the labor recruiters and the down-and-outs they signed up to harvest tomatoes.

Many of these stories were controversial. Yet unpopularity is not always a cause for alarm; it can be instead a healthy sign that the press is performing its role. Says author David Halberstam, who won a Pulitzer Prize for reporting in Vietnam: "The more we do our job of questioning accepted norms, the more we can expect to be questioned."

Still, growing numbers of news executives recognize a real problem in the public discontent with the press, especially the perception that journalists are arrogant. At the most basic level, dealing with this problem requires coming to terms with motivations, the forces that drive individuals to become journalists and the attitudes they take when pursuing a story. Reporters have sometimes lost sight of the fundamental truth that their job is to provide a service to the community rather than to seek the glamour and glory that now often seem to draw people into the craft. News organizations are trying in a variety of ways to make themselves more self-critical and more accessible to the public and to attune their reporters to asking themselves, "Is this fair?" rather than, "Will this make Page One or top of the evening newscast?"

Perhaps the most basic obligation is for editors and reporters to be tougher on themselves when mistakes get into print or on the air. One helpful source of pressure: A commitment to correct errors publicly. "In the old days," says Cameron Blodgett, executive director of the watchdog Minnesota News Council, "the way to deal with a complaint about a mistake was to yell, 'There's a nut on the line,' and hang up." In the past few years, many newspapers have created a standing format for corrections. The Louisville *Courier-Journal* runs its admissions of error on the front page of the local news section under the headline "Beg Your Pardon"; its sister paper, the *Louisville Times*, uses the blunt designation "We Were Wrong." Some newspapers, including *The Seattle Times, Charlotte* (N.C.) *News* and *Observer* and *The Miami Herald*, mail out questionnaires to the subjects of certain news stories to ask whether they feel they were treated accurately and fairly. When the *Los Angeles Times* in April found that a business story had grossly misrepresented the cost overruns on Lockheed Corporation's C-5B military transport plane, the newspaper ran a corrective follow-up that was twice as long as the erring story, CBS's *60 Minutes* has, on the air, looked critically at its stories and techniques, and CBS and ABC have explored journalistic ethics in a series of roundtable documentaries.

To provide a further court of review, more than two dozen newspapers have appointed ombudsmen or "reader representatives." Some news executives argue that having an ombudsman shunts complaints aside. Says editor James Gannon of *The Des Moines Register:* "The person who should handle the complaints is the editor, not someone in a corner with no real power." Others contend that editors are too busy and too closely tied to their staffs to be able to handle complaints thoroughly. Most critics of the press agree with James Atwater, a former *TIME* senior editor who is dean of the University of Missouri School of Journalism. Says Atwater: "We need much more self-examination and a whole flock of ombudsmen. This is a very heady business, and we need a moral compass."

Some newspaper and TV news organizations have assigned beat reporters to cover the field of journalism. Among the most respected is the *Los Angeles Times*'s David Shaw, who occasionally reports on his own employer with cool objectivity. Says he: "Too often, newspapers view what they do as too arcane for the public to understand or as a state secret that is none of their business." Other newspapers and stations send

editors to community meetings to field questions. In
a few states or regions, journalists have cooperated in
forming American counterparts to Britain's Press
Council. These boards attempt to judge the rights and
wrongs of complaints, but have no enforcement powers.
The National News Council, founded in 1973, has never
won the wholehearted support of major news organizations, and has been boycotted by some. News executives
question whether any organization can oversee the
complicated, diverse American press, and note that
such councils rarely have adequate research help.

The crucial role of journalism in a democracy is to
provide a common ground of knowledge and analysis,
a meeting place for national debate: It is the link between people and institutions. Without the information provided by newspapers and TV, citizens would
have little basis for deciding what to believe and whom
to support. Just as a pervasive mistrust of police could
cause a breakdown of order, a growing hostility to the
press could sever the ligaments of a workable society.

Moreover, without a strong and trusted press, people would have almost no way to keep their government and other big institutions honest. Government,
particularly the Federal Establishment, has vast
powers to mislead the people and manage the news.
Officials can conceal impending actions until their effects are irreversible. Other big institutions—
corporations, unions, hospitals, police forces—prefer to
cloak their decision-making process and their performance from the scrutiny of the public, whose lives may
be deeply affected. And despite the passage of shield
laws to protect journalists from having to reveal
sources, they are regularly subpoenaed to testify about
what they have reported.

Journalists became so aggressive partly because
they knew, contrary to the widely held public view, that
they were Davids fighting Goliaths. As the press itself
grows into a more powerful institution, it must be
careful how it uses its strength, whether it faces an ordinary individual or a president: the attempt to uncover
can too easily turn into the impulse to tear apart.

Freedom of the press, like any other freedom, can
be dangerous. But Thomas Jefferson, who suffered at

the hands of journalists as much as any contemporary politician, insisted that protecting the press at its worst was an essential part of having the press be free. Said Jefferson: "It is so difficult to draw a clear line of the separation between the abuse and the wholesome use of the press....I shall protect them in the right of lying and calumniating." Moreover, the press, however forceful, has no power to indict or impeach, no power beyond what is granted by its audience. A journalist can expose a situation, but cannot compel an indifferent public to change it.

In an earlier era, and one perhaps more optimistic about human nature, Union General Irvin McDowell reported before the First Battle of Bull Run: "I have made arrangements for the correspondents of our papers to take the field, and I have suggested to them that they should wear a white uniform to indicate the purity of their character." Probably no one talks of journalists that way today, and perhaps no one should. But for the sake of American society, as well as for its own sake, the press must try harder to wear white. It must be more responsive to public concerns. Barry Bingham Sr., chief executive officer of the Louisville newspapers and a former chairman of the International Press Institute, puts the case with forceful simplicity: "You cannot hold on to a free press if it behaves irresponsibly. The idea that our mission is so high that no one should question our performance is illogical. The higher the mission, the more responsibly we should carry it out."

4. Confidential Sources: Testing the Readers' Confidence

By GENE FOREMAN

A lot of us in the newspaper business are worried about credibility these days. Truth, after all, is our basic commodity. If the public does not believe what we publish in our newspapers, it is logical to expect that its next step might be to stop buying what we print. We worry about credibility even though Lou Harris, the pollster, tells us to take heart: more Americans expressed "high confidence" in the press in 1983 than in 1982. But that vote of high confidence came from only 19% of the people answering Harris' poll questions—and we had a lower confidence rating than those running organized religion, the White House and Congress.

With all the fretting about believability, I think we ought to take a close look at the number of times our news stories attribute information not to people with names and titles, but to "sources"—and to their redundant cousins, "informed sources." I do not suggest that this is the only basis of our credibility problems, but many of us in the profession feel that heavy reliance on unnamed sources engenders suspicion and distrust. *By the very act of taking someone else into our confidence, we strain the confidence our readers have in us.* David Shaw, the media critic of the *Los Angeles Times,* has observed of this pervasive practice: "Reporters who write stories based on statements they do not identify for their readers are, in effect, asking their readers to trust them, to assume that the reporters and their editors have evaluated the source's credentials and credibility." A few readers may readily grant us that prerogative; most, I fear, resent being asked. Just as our profession has matured and become

Gene Foreman is managing editor of the Philadelphia Inquirer. This essay originally appeared in Louis Hodges, ed., Social Responsibility: Business, Journalism, Law, Medicine 10 (1984) 24-31. Reprinted by permission.

more sophisticated in the last generation, so, too, has our readership. There is skepticism, even cynicism, among our readers. We invite their wrath when we keep secrets from them, when we tell them: "Trust us."

Even the very best newspapers in the country, I think, deal excessively in blind sources. Recently *The Washington Post,* in the course of 3,000 words on Central America, avoided mentioning a single source by name. *The New York Times* published a 600-word analysis on the flights of American fighters over Lebanon, supporting its finding not by names and titles but by descriptions like these: "foreign and American intelligence analysts," "retired intelligence officials and others," "analysts," "critics of Reagan administration policies," "foreign intelligence analysts," "a NATO officer with experience in the area," "Middle East intelligence sources," "the majority of those consulted," "an American source," "an Arab source" and "other sources." In fairness I point out that these two newspapers have expressed concern about the practice. *The Washington Post,* for example, tried unsuccessfully in 1971 to force the government to put its official briefings on the record. They gave up, according to executive editor Benjamin Bradlee, because the rest of the media would not go along. *The New York Times* probably more than any other newspaper restricts the use of unidentified sources, insisting on qualifiers (such as the adjective "Western" in the phrase "Western officials") to give readers some hint of the sources' probable allegiances and possible biases.

Last fall our staff at the *Philadelphia Inquirer* had a series of discussions on fairness and accuracy. One of the subjects we spent considerable time on was the need to limit unnamed sources to those giving information truly essential to our readers and not obtainable in any other way. In the ensuing months I noted with satisfaction that we did seem to be cutting down on "sources" stories. It took a routine piece two weeks ago to make me realize I was being complacent. The story was about the actor Harrison Ford's spending some time with Philadelphia police detectives to prepare himself for a role in a new movie. In the five-inch story one of our police reporters, who happens to be an exceptional digger of facts, got carried away in quoting a "source" and a "police source." To these anonymous observers he attributed such hardly crucial bits of information as the plot of the forthcoming film and the fact that Ford had the police commissioner's approval for this field work, as if he could have done it otherwise. Once again, we're trying to get the word out on our concern about the "sources" problem.

The Washington Post's Bob Woodward and Carl Bernstein, in their Watergate investigation, influenced our profession in countless ways. Their story relied heavily on the use of confidential sources. But does that mean that using anonymous quotes is, in the abstract, a good thing? Here is what Woodward himself has to say about anonymous sources: "I think it's a bad habit that has developed—and a lazy one. Getting it on the record is the ultimate solution." Speaking for the National News Council's 1983 report on the use of unidentified sources, Woodward went on to say that with a little more digging, a reporter "generally can go back and get it on the record." I wonder how many emulators of Woodward and Bernstein, plying their trade on papers across the country, are aware of how Woodward really feels about anonymous sources. By their own success Woodward and Bernstein may have inadvertently contributed to the bad habit.

Woodward's assessment is supported by a 1982 study for the American Society of Newspaper Editors by the journalism school at the University of Iowa. Analyzing stories from a half-dozen large papers scattered around the country, the researchers found upon interviewing the reporters that in about one-third of the stories the anonymous quotes could easily have been avoided. In some cases the reporters did not know why their sources needed protection. In others, the reporters concede that they could have persuaded the sources to go on the record. In still others, the information attributed to blind sources was not crucial and indeed was duplicated elsewhere in the stories.

In addition to inviting distrust by our readers, blind sources expose us to other dangers.

One is the threat of defamation suits. Robert Sack, a well-known libel defense lawyer, was quoted this way by the National News Council: "It becomes very difficult when somebody has sued you, and you say, 'I had no actual malice or I wasn't negligent. But I can't tell you who I talked to in order to be as certain as I am.' " Sack warns us that a plaintiff's lawyer can spot the phrase, "according to confidential sources," and knows that he has "a hell of a fish on the hook and that he can at least have a lot of fun playing with it through the courts."

In criminal cases there is another danger: a journalist may be threatened with a contempt-of-court citation and jail for failing to identify sources on the witness stand. Shield laws afford much protection, but the courts have shown a willingness to brush them aside when they are seen as conflicting with a defendant's Sixth Amendment rights to a fair trial.

The problem of blind sources is compounded when the source is allowed to attack someone from the safety of anonymity. The accused never knows where the assault is coming from. Blind pejoratives are inherently unfair.

Finally, the overuse of anonymous sources makes the newspaper vulnerable to the possibility that it will be manipulated by those sources. They have their own axes to grind and trial balloons to float. By printing their ideas without their names, we allow them to use us.

So why not ban the practice of quoting confidential sources and be done with it? The solution is not so simple. I have already cited the classic example of Watergate as a story aided significantly by unidentified sources. Our mission, remember, is to serve as a conduit of information to our readers. That flow of information would be greatly diminished if we flatly ordered our reporters to write nothing that they could not attribute by name and title. One of the strengths of the press is that our reporters can talk with people that government investigators often cannot or will not consult; they give us information only if we keep their identities confidential. Their status in the community, their careers, perhaps even their lives might otherwise be in jeopardy. When we accept the conditions of confidentiality, it is a sacred trust. We decide that the information is more important than the identity of the provider. In Vietnam, for instance, there were ranking officers who disagreed with the way the war was being fought. Of course they could not be quoted by name, rank and serial number, but reporters were able to portray the vital policy debate by granting them anonymity.

Our thrust should be to devise subjective guidelines that would permit the publication of crucial information even without a named source when the circumstances warrant it. Just as important, these guidelines should discourage the use of unnamed sources when the case for their use is less than compelling.

I have a set of guidelines to offer for consideration. For valued advice and counsel in constructing these guidelines, I want to thank Bill Marimow, who with Jonathan Neumann did the painstaking reporting work that helped the *Inquirer* win a Pulitzer gold medal for public service in 1978.

At the outset, I would like to make clear that I am directing my remarks at confidential sources who are actually quoted in news stories. There are, of course, confidential sources who provide us tips that can be checked out elsewhere and reported in the paper without even mentioning the tipster. I do not think anyone has any problem with that, as long as the source's possible self-interest is kept in mind and the story is evaluated on its merits.

I also propose to short shrift a couple of other confidentiality issues because I detect little disagreement about them. So I will just say here that good reporters avoid creating *composites,* which are combinations of different characters. As far as I can tell, the verdict is just about unanimous that this is fiction writing, not reporting. It is also my impressions that *pseudonyms* for characters in stories should be used only rarely and with reason for protecting innocent people. Top editors should be involved in such decisions, and the technique should be prominently disclosed to the readers.

The first guideline I offer in evaluating confidential sources is: *the use of unnamed sources in a news story should be a last resort, not just an easy alternative to documenting the information from the public record or quoting someone willing to be named.* In short, there is no substitute for digging. In the brief story about the actor who rode along with detectives as they went about their homicide investigations, there was no indication that the reporter had even tried to interview the actor himself or his agent or the movie company. Any of these would have been more knowledgeable about details of the movie than the secret police source. As I noted earlier, the University of Iowa researchers found repeatedly that the reporters could have gotten people to talk for the record if they had tried. David Shaw has written that the competitive rush for Watergate disclosures induced many reporters to let traditional standards for attribution slide badly. Shaw said, "Getting into print first, with a story from an unnamed source, was often thought to be better than being second, with a story from a named source." Shaw also noted that Watergate spawned a whole generation of young "investigative reporters" who felt that their editors and readers would be impressed by their savvy in referring to "informed sources" even though they were perfectly willing to be quoted by name.

The second guideline: *it should be clear that the source's physical or economic well-being might be jeopardized if his or her name is revealed.* Thus we apply another test, one that must take place before the information is accepted with the stipulation of confidentiality. The writer should not simply assume that a source would be "more comfortable" not to be quoted by name; there should be evidence of real jeopardy.

The third guideline: *the information provided by the unnamed source must be very important. The story should be one that helps a newspaper's readers make informed decisions about their government or community. The information from the source should be crucial to the story, not tangential to the theme.* Again, this is a sort of "needs" test that we should apply along with the first two before allowing a veiled source to be quoted in the paper. It is intended to separate the truly significant, essential story or passage within a story from the nice-to-have-but-not-really-necessary. At the *Inquirer,* we learned the hard way to apply this rule. In a piece about why major motion pictures were slow in reaching Philadelphia theaters, we spent the first two-thirds of the story's length expounding on what all the named sources agreed was the crux of the matter: the distributors control when and where a movie will be shown, and they allow films to spread out into the country only after making their splash in the media centers of New York and Los Angeles. Near the bottom of the story we mentioned that when it came to asking a favor to get a particular movie earlier than usual, Philadelphia exhibitors were not likely to be successful because they were such an irascible bunch. The story quoted an anonymous source several times in alleging that a certain exhibitor paid bills late so as to earn interest on the money withheld, and used its market clout to violate its contract by cutting short the run of a film that turned out to be a poor draw. To our chagrin, we learned after publication that we could not substantiate the accusations made by the anonymous source. And we found out that the source was in fact a competing exhibitor, something the editors of the story had not known or asked about at the time. It was an object lesson for us. We realized that the information, even if it had been scrupulously true, was simply not essential to the story. For that matter, the story itself was not one that, to quote the guideline, "helps readers make informed decisions about their government or community."

The fourth guideline: *to help readers evaluate the information, the unnamed source should be described as fully as possible without giving away the identity.* So often we attribute statements simply to "sources" or "informed sources" or "reliable sources." I would argue that semantically they are the same thing; we should not be quoting anyone who is not informed or reliable, and our readers should be astonished if we did. Using those terms amounts to nothing more than a plea to the reader that we are not making the whole thing up. Certainly, they impart no information. Of course, we should not risk giving away the identity of a person to whom we have promised confidentiality, but usually there is a way of characterizing that person that does not isolate him or her. Instead of a "source," why can we not say "one of the participants in the negotiations" or "a police officer familiar with the department's procedures in administering promotions tests?" Assuming that more than a handful of people fit those descriptions, the additional information helps the reader weigh the source's credentials. The less we ask the readers to depend solely on our word that the source is qualified, the better off we are.

The fifth guideline: *if an unnamed source is quoted making derogatory statements about someone, such a statement must be one that enhances the public's understanding of a crucial issue. Here, reporters and editors must apply additional safeguards: the statement should be corroborated by public record or by named sources, or the source should have an impeccable record of reliability as well as direct knowledge of the facts.* On this point I probably would encounter disagreement from many journalists, who would argue that under no circumstances should a blind derogatory quote be permitted. I accept the principle but feel that there has to be flexibility to deal with the rare exceptional situation. The additional safeguards I mentioned were intended to reduce the possibility of unfairness. Of course, in any situation in which a person is mentioned in derogatory fashion, he or she should have an opportunity to respond.

Now the sixth and final guideline: *reporters have to be free to use their judgment in granting confidentiality to sources while gathering the facts. However, it should be understood that the agreement of confidence is between the source and the newspaper, and that the reporter can be expected to identify the source to his or her editor.* This is yet another area where honest men and women disagree. There are editors who insist that no one on the paper but the top editor can authorize confidentiality. Although recognizing that there are horrible abuses—which are, of course, the point of this article—I do not see how such a policy could help but inhibit a newspaper's ability to gather the news. Not to allow discretion would be to put our reporters in a straitjacket. The reporters, in my opinion, have to be relied upon to make judgments on the spot. The reporter's editor would naturally be bound by the agreement of confidentiality granted by the reporter—that is, he or she could not attach the name to the quote—but nevertheless has the option of deciding whether to use the quote at all. On the other extreme, some journalists would argue that the agreement of confidentiality is between the source and the reporter *as an individual* and no one, not even the reporter's editor, can be given the identity. Although I would not insist that an editor has to know the identity of each and every source quoted, I do feel that the editor has the prerogative of asking—and getting an answer. Reporters do not put stories into the paper, editors do.

What we have in the guidelines I have laid out is a series of tests to apply in the reporting and editing process. We methodically ask questions: Is there any way to get the statement on the record? Does the source seeking anonymity really stand in jeopardy if identified? Is the information really important? Can we give the readers some idea of how qualified the source is? Is the information derogatory to any individual and, if so, have we gone extra lengths to make sure we are being fair? I am convinced that if every reporter and editor went through this checklist before publishing an anonymous quote, our papers would contain a lot fewer anonymous quotes. And the flow of truly essential information to the public would not be diminished in any significant way.

In closing I want to suggest one more test, this one offered in the National News Council study by Richard Smyser, editor of the *Oak Ridger* at Oak Ridge, Tennessee. Smyser divides people who give us information anonymously into two distinct groups: "sources" and "sourcerers." He has a high regard for "sources," whom he describes as "good guys" who have information of importance to the public on things that are amiss but whose careers or jobs would be jeopardized if they were identified as the communicators of that information. He has revulsion for "sourcerers," people whose goal is to use the press, and ultimately the public, as a means to an end. One way he has to tell them apart is to go back periodically and look over all the information his paper has printed without attribution.

"Give it the test of time," he says. "Read last year's non-attributed news this year and see how it stands up."

The on-the-spot tests I have suggested—and Dick Smyser's test of time—have a common goal: to help us achieve a higher degree of reader confidence. I am convinced that by needlessly resorting to unnamed sources we undermine our cherished credibility and dilute our effectiveness as an institution. For us as journalists, there can be no higher mission than to guard, and reinforce, our reputation for truth.

5. TV Newsman Dumps on TV News

By WILLIAM F. WRIGHT

Charles Kuralt was at his affable, rumpled best. But behind the wit and folksy charm of CBS's roaming correspondent was a biting attack on his own medium for the way it handles the news.

Kuralt, delivering the annual Scripps Lecture in Journalism at the University of Nevada-Reno (March 29), said by-and-large television news is more show business than news business. He urged journalism students to think twice before getting into it.

Kuralt said television station managers who "don't know anything about news and don't care" were the main problem, followed closely by the outside "news consultant," who is a "breed of scoundrel" who is "everywhere in the land giving bad advice.

"First, he tells the station manager, you must have ringing bells and flashing graphics to seize the attention of the sap at home who might otherwise be inclined to read a book or play with his children. Then, you must keep the show moving to dazzle the sucker. Put those reporters out there live at the scene—it doesn't matter what scene—and make them talk loud and fast. The successful station is going to be the one that masters the staccato pace and the one-sentence interview and the car wreck on the highway," Kuralt said.

He said many stations have a rule that "no story is worth more than 90 seconds.

"These wretched consultants would cut the *Iliad* or *King Lear* to 90 seconds. And the station managers who employ them eagerly follow their contemptible advice, and in city after city the news is cheapened, and the viewer is cheated," he said.

William F. Wright is a graduate teaching fellow in the School of Communication at Pennsylvania State University. He wrote this article while a Visiting Reynolds Professor of Journalism at the University of Nevada-Reno. This article originally appeared in Editor & Publisher (April 14, 1984) 13, 32. Reprinted by permission.

All this, Kuralt said, has led to a "very depressing state of affairs around six o'clock in the evening all over America. Urgent electronic music plays, the lights come up, and an earnest young man or woman says to a camera, 'Good evening, here is the news.' This is said very urgently and with the appearance of sincerity—most often by an attractive young person who would not know a news story if it jumped up and mussed his coiffure."

Kuralt, whose new prime-time CBS series *The American Parade* premiered recently, incorporating his popular *On the Road* reports, said he mourned the passing from television of such journalists as Edward R. Murrow, Robert Trout, Charles Collingwood and Eric Sevareid.

"They were giants to me as a kid, and they are no less giants to me now," he said. "They were reporters and thinkers and splendid users of the language. Words counted with them, and they made words count."

Murrow, he said, "warned that a television set is just a box with wires until good people make it come alive with good programs. But evidently nobody was listening. The shining promise of the box with wires has too rarely been kept. And now, somehow, even the promise has lost its brilliance. Imagination and creativity have been dimmed by daily reality."

Kuralt said there are good writers still working in journalism, "but the giants are all gone—the ones who established the standards for television journalism. I don't know where the great reporters will come from to hold up the standards for another generation."

He said that perhaps he was being too cynical—that "maybe the best television news directors will all be elevated to station managers. Maybe good judgment will replace greed in the front offices. Maybe a comet will come from heaven and burn all the news consultants to ashes."

Kuralt, 49, who began his journalism career as a reporter with the *Charlotte* (N.C.) *News* before joining CBS in 1957, urged journalism students to "think about it awhile" before going into television news.

"I am afraid I must say that television news, as it is practiced in most places, is not the field in which a serious journalist would wish to live," he said.

Kuralt said there are "few satisfactions in television journalism, either in giving it or receiving it. It is easy and fast and it pays well, and it goes by without anybody noticing very much.

"The real rewards—both in the giving and the receiving—are in the patient, hard work of the careful writer who seizes a fact or an event out of the air as it flashes past and hammers it like a blacksmith on his anvil, and tempers it, and, dissatisfied, discards it and rekindles the fire in the forge, and comes back to it until at length it becomes a useful and pretty thing—a bit of truth," he said. "Television news is papier mache. Real writing is wrought iron."

6. Our Image Problem: A Paradox

By CREED BLACK

Custom dictates that each outgoing ASNE [American Society of Newspaper Editors] president make a few observations on the state of our craft. As we open this 1984 convention, then, I want to examine with you a paradox that has received an extraordinary amount of attention since we met in Denver last year.

It is this:

On one hand, most thoughtful students of the American press agree that our newspapers are doing a better job today than ever before in this nation's history. On the other, we are buffeted almost daily with new pronouncements of a crisis of public confidence which—in the words of that familiar *TIME* magazine cover story—threatens "one of the foundations of the country's democratic system."

How do we explain this?

We start, I think, by trying to keep a sense of perspective. Disenchantment with the free press, after all, is not a phenomenon of the late 20th century.

As editors, we like to quote Thomas Jefferson's statement that "were it left to me to decide whether we should have a government without newspapers or newspapers without a government, I should not hesitate a moment to prefer the latter." We need to remember, however, that this same Thomas Jefferson also said that "even the least informed of the people have learnt that nothing in a newspaper is to be believed."

That, of course, was before the days of opinion polls telling editors how poorly they rank in public esteem.

For further perspective, we need to remember that the press is not alone among American institutions which—the pollsters tell us—have suffered public

Creed Black is chairman and publisher of the Lexington Herald-Leader. These remarks were delivered to the ASNE convention, Washington, D.C., May 9, 1984. Reprinted by permission.

distrust in an era of profound political and social upheaval.

But the press has been especially vulnerable during this period because it has been the bearer of the bad tidings which have shaken the faith of many Americans in all our institutions.

As Ruth Clark points out in the new readership survey she will discuss with us later this morning, in the six years since her last survey, "the United States has undergone inflation, recession, unemployment, international crises, and developing concern about its prestige abroad and its ability to compete in world markets. Underlying all, as many national polls have shown, is a deep-seated anxiety about the danger of nuclear war—not in the distant future, but in our lifetime."

That kind of news does not make pleasant reading. The theory that we get blamed for it has been advanced so often that it's almost a cliché. Yet all of you, I'm sure, can cite personal experiences to illustrate its enduring validity and pertinence today. Let me mention just one of mine:

I was executive editor of the *Chicago Daily News* when the police and the hippies clashed at the 1968 convention there. That clash, you will recall, was later described by a special investigating commission as a "police riot." In its immediate aftermath, however, we got such an outpouring of angry mail directed at our coverage and commentary that I asked one of our reporters to read all those letters and see what lessons might be drawn from them. His memo to me concluded with these words:

"The essential impression one gets from wading through scores of these letters is that emotion has replaced reason and fact. People are very stirred up, and there are many who justify the beating of anyone with whom they disagree. These people do not believe in free speech, free press, or free assembly, and there are a hell of a lot of them. They want a scapegoat; if the hippies won't fill the bill, the press will."

Note that word "scapegoat." We'll return to it later.

The sentiment described in that 1968 memo, believe me, lives today. My public statements as your president in protesting the exclusion of the press from Grenada inspired a number of letters from around the country. One of the harshest said this:

"Yes, our lying, Communist-loving, un-American (news?) media lost the war in Vietnam....If they ever decide to drop the liberal media ahead of the troops so they can be treated like the rest of our enemies I would volunteer again just to try once more to help clean up some of the worst enemies this country has ever had."

This notion that the American press was somehow responsible for what happened in Vietnam is a classic example of blaming the messenger for the bad news. The problem with it, of course, is that it just isn't so.

No less a critic than Alexander Haig said recently he has been tempted to blame the press for the loss of Vietnam. But that, he said, is a bum rap. "Policy lost Vietnam. Bad policy."

"So why has the role of the media been so inflated?" That question was asked—and answered—by George Herring, a professor of history at the University of Kentucky, in his highly regarded book *America's Longest War: The United States and Vietnam, 1950-1975*. His answer:

"In part, no doubt, because it offers a handy, in some cases self-serving, explanation for an apparent anomaly: how the world's greatest power could be defeated by a small, backward nation. A British scholar once identified as a central trait of our national character what he called the illusion of American omnipotence, the belief that the difficult we do tomorrow, the impossible may take a while. When we encounter failure, we naturally look inward for explanations—and scapegoats."

Scapegoats. There's that word again.

The possibility that we will be made scapegoats for unpleasant news is, then, an occupational hazard. Surely, however, it is not one we can shirk out of concern for our standing in the latest image poll.

Nor can we shrink from the solid investigative reporting which seems to upset some of our readers. The irony here is that because newspapers *are* better than ever, we may be gaining unpopularity in some circles as we improve in the performance of our historic watchdog role. But that, too, is a risk that goes with the territory. "The more we do our job of questioning accepted norms," as David Halberstam has said, "the more we can expect to be questioned."

In most cases, of course, those who question and criticize us are quick to assure us that all they want is a fair press. My observation after four decades in this business, however, is that what most of them really want is a favorable press—and that they confuse the two.

One further explanation for our standing with the public is, of course, our own fallibility. Lester Bernstein, the former editor of *Newsweek,* reminded us of that in a recent *New York Times* review of Jody Powell's new book, *The Other Side of the Story.*

"News people are indeed fallible," Mr. Bernstein wrote. "At their worst, some can be careless, stupid, insensitive, lazy, arrogant, biased and vindictive. Most galling of all, they can be obdurately unrepentant."

Sure. But at their best many can be careful, intelligent, sensitive, hard-working, fair-minded men and women who regard newspaper work as a noble calling, who take their responsibilities to their readers and the democratic process seriously, and who are today more willing to investigate, admit and publicly correct their errors than at any time in the past.

Finally, I come to what I have become increasingly convinced is one of the major reasons our public standing seems to have declined while our performance as an institution has improved.

It is that the public lumps the printed press and television together in something called "the media" and makes little if any distinction between the two. The result is that we are blamed for the sins and shortcomings of what television—which remains basically an entertainment medium—calls news.

This, of course, is not an overnight development.

Exactly 20 years ago, as chairman of your Freedom of Information Committee, I submitted to this convention a report calling attention to what I described then as a relatively new element in the perennial "free press vs. fair trial" controversy.

That new element, our report said, "is the extent to which television is complicating matters for all news media." As evidence, we cited a report from the Civil Rights Committee of the New York Trial Lawyers Association which opened with this statement:

"As television has reached its maturity it has become more and more clear that its special visual impact requires that traditional rules governing the publicizing of the arrest of persons accused of crime must be re-examined. The growing number of instances where televised reporting of arrests has clearly jeopardized a fair trial for the accused has aroused the bench and bar as well as many responsible segments of the public at large."

The report then came to the following melancholy conclusion:

"Inquiries by the Committee on Civil Rights in connection with this study have persuaded us that any reliance on voluntary restraints by the television industry is largely doomed to failure."

That, I think, helps explain why 20 years ago we suddenly found ourselves fighting a rash of new restrictions at a time when most American newspaper editors—sensitive to earlier excesses in some sensational cases—were exercising an unprecedented degree of self-restraint.

And just as the printed press was tarred then with the television brush, so we still are two decades later.

I said earlier that I had received some angry mail this year from around the country. I've also fielded some hostile comments and questions from audiences at public appearances I've made on ASNE's behalf.

A striking thing about all this is that when these critics get down to specifics, more often than not they unleash a litany of complaints about television. I could spend the rest of the morning citing chapter and verse, but I hardly think that is necessary. My guess is that every editor in this room has had the same experience.

But if all those folks out there who are unhappy with "the media" sometimes fail to make distinctions between our newspapers and television, that doesn't mean there aren't any. There are distinctions—and they are profound.

First, television is in no small part show biz.

"There is a tension between substance and theater" on TV, Walter Mondale—who's certainly had his share of experience with the medium—said recently. As of 1984, theater seems to be winning.

Speaking recently of the current crop of newcomers to TV news, Walter Cronkite said, "I suspect that if television didn't exist they'd be in acting."

Perhaps you saw *Editor & Publisher*'s account last month of a university lecture in which Charles Kuralt—surely one of the wisest and most literate figures in TV news today—deplored what he called a "very depressing state of affairs around 6 o'clock in the evening all over America." He described it this way:

"Urgent electronic music plays, the lights come up and an earnest young man or woman says to a camera, 'Good evening, here is the news.' This is said very urgently and with the appearance of sincerity—most often by an attractive young person who would not know a news story if it jumped up and mussed his coiffure."

Second, what is breathlessly introduced on TV this way often is not news at all—or at least not significant news presented in enough depth to give it meaning.

Television, said Mr. Kuralt, is afflicted with station managers who "don't know anything about news and don't care" and consultants who give them this kind of advice:

"You must have ringing bells and flashing graphics to seize the attention of the sap at home who might otherwise be inclined to read a book or play with his children. Then, you must keep the show moving to dazzle the sucker. Put those reporters out there live at the scene—it doesn't matter what scene—and make them talk loud and fast. The successful station is going to be the one that masters the staccato pace and the one-sentence interview and the car wreck on the highway."

Charles Kuralt was talking about local TV news. The networks, however, are not exempt from the electronic gimmickry that puts a premium on high visual impact.

TV news, NBC correspondent John Dancy told *The Wall Street Journal* recently, "always favors the simple story, not the complex issue." ABC correspondent Brit Hume, talking of coverage of the presidential campaign in Iowa, put it more colorfully: "You can always get on the air with pigs."

Furthermore, what the networks call news is in fact a mixture of news, analysis, opinion and speculation.

"I think the White House would rather have a straightforward record of the president's activities," CBS *Evening News* producer Howard Stringer told *TV Guide*. "We don't do a presidential diary. We're closer to analysis."

Well, newspapers do analyses, too. And we give our opinions. But we strive daily—and, in my judgment, usually successfully—to separate the news from the commentary and label the latter clearly for what it is.

As *Newsday*'s media writer Tom Collins said recently, however, "TV journalism has evolved into a highly personalized style. TV reporters are free to interpret, analyze and speculate in ways newspaper reporters don't do and shouldn't be able to do."

Third, television provides little opportunity for dissent or criticism by its viewers or the subjects of its coverage.

The networks have no such mechanism at all. Some local television stations do permit limited viewer reaction, but the time they give to it doesn't begin to compare with the space devoted by any newspaper to letters to the editor.

Fourth, and similarly, television has developed no standard mechanism for correcting its errors. I said earlier that American newspapers today are more willing than ever to investigate, acknowledge and correct their mistakes. But when, I ask you, was the last time you heard a TV newscaster do the same?

So, what can we do about the problem that television is creating for newspapers?

For one thing, we can follow the advice offered in *The ASNE Bulletin* earlier this year by Stanley Cloud, executive editor of the *Los Angeles Herald Examiner*, that we curb the use of that troublesome word "media."

"The gradual replacement of 'the press' by 'the media,'" he wrote, "has had the effect of blurring and, lately, all but eliminating the distinctions between various purveyors of information....By acquiescing in the use of 'the media,' we play directly into the hands of those who benefit from riding the coattails of serious, responsible journalists."

Another thing we can do is make sure our readers understand the distinctions between newspapers and TV. There's no reason we have to suffer in silence under the heavy load of television's baggage.

And we can always hope that television news will improve as it grows up. While that 20-year-old report from the New York Bar I mentioned earlier referred to TV's maturity, it is in fact still in adolescence at most—having been around no longer than American newspapers had been back in the early 1800s.

The printed press itself has come a long way since then—but we still have a long way to go. If newspapers are better today than ever, they can and should be better yet. Our challenge is to make them so.

Meanwhile, let's not become totally obsessed with our image. It's easy—but dangerous—to inflate the problem out of proportion.

Some highly vocal support of the Reagan administration's decision to keep the press out of Grenada, for example, is frequently cited as clinching evidence that nearly everybody out there hates us. Yet a Louis Harris survey last December showed that a majority of Americans—by a 2-1 margin—were convinced that the government was wrong in that policy.

And another Harris poll last year suggested that, as in so many other areas, public opinion has its cyclical ups and downs. For the first time since 1979, Lou Harris told the APME [Associated Press Managing Editors] convention last November, the number of adult Americans who have a "great deal of confidence" in the media had risen in the past year.

Ruth Clark found in her survey, furthermore, that while more than half the persons interviewed believe that newspapers *in general* are biased and inaccurate, they have a quite different perception of the papers they actually read most often: 62% consider their papers fair, and 84% regard them as accurate.

It is one thing to address legitimate concerns about our shortcomings, which I readily acknowledge despite all I've said today. But it is quite another to be paralyzed by our critics.

I keep near my desk an inscribed quotation from an editor of an earlier era, Herbert Bayard Swope, which says it all: "I cannot give you the formula for success, but I can give you the formula for failure, which is: try to please everybody."

As every editor knows, a newspaper can generally avoid controversy and criticism if it will publish everything that people want published, suppress any news that may be unpleasant to anyone, close its eyes when it sees some wrongdoing, and remain silent when vigorous leadership that might offend someone is needed.

That, however, would produce a daily bulletin board, not a newspaper. And newspapers, ladies and gentlemen, are our business.

For all its flaws, the free American press has served this nation well for 200 years and continues to do so today. I'm proud and grateful to have had the honor and opportunity this year to serve as one of its spokesmen, and I look forward to its future with confidence.

Thank you.

7. Journalism and the Larger Truth

By ROGER ROSENBLATT

When journalists hear journalists claim a "larger truth," they really ought to go for their pistols. *The New Yorker*'s Alastair Reid said the holy words last week: "A reporter might take liberties with the factual circumstances to make the larger truth clear." O, large, large truth. Apparently Mr. Reid believes that imposing a truth is the same as arriving at one. Illogically, he also seems to think that truths may be disclosed through lies. But his error is more fundamental still in assuming that large truth is the province of journalism in the first place. The business of journalism is to present facts accurately—Mr. Reid notwithstanding. Those seeking something larger are advised to look elsewhere.

For one thing, journalism rarely sees the larger truth of a story because reporters are usually chasing quite small elements of information. A story, like a fern, only reveals its final shocking shape in stages. Journalism also reduces most of the stories it deals with to political considerations. Matters are defined in terms of where power lies, who opposes whom or what, where the special interests are. As a result, the larger truth of a story is often missed or ignored. By its nature, political thought limits speculative thought. Political realities themselves cannot be grasped by an exclusively political way of looking at things.

Then, too, journalism necessarily deals with discontinuities. One has never heard of the Falkland Islands. Suddenly the Falklands are the center of the universe: one knows all there is to know about "kelpers" and Port Stanley; sheep jokes abound. In the end, as at the beginning, no one really knows anything about the Falkland Islands other than the war that gave it momentary

---

Roger Rosenblatt is a senior writer at TIME magazine. This article originally appeared in TIME (July 2, 1984) 88. Copyright © 1984 Time Inc. All rights reserved. Reprinted by permission from TIME.

celebrity—nothing about the people in the aftermath of the war, their concerns, isolation, or their true relationship to Argentina and Britain. Discontinuities are valuable because they point up the world's variety as well as the special force or its isolated parts. But to rely on them for truth is to lose one's grip on what is continuous and whole.

Journalism looks to where the ball is, and not where it is not. A college basketball coach, trying to improve the performance of one of his backcourt men, asked the player what he did when he practiced on his own. "Dribble and shoot," came the reply. The coach then asked the player to add up the total time he dribbled and shot during a scrimmage game, how many minutes he had hold of the ball. "Three minutes in all," came the reply. "That means," said the coach, "that you practice what you do in three minutes out of 40 in a game." Which means in turn that for every player, roughly 37 out of a possible 40 minutes are played away from the ball.

Journalism tends to focus on the poor when the poor make news, usually dramatic news like a tenement fire or a march on Washington. But the poor are poor all the time. It is not journalism's ordinary business to deal with the unstartling normalities of life. Reporters need a *story,* something shapely and elegant. Poverty is disorderly, anticlimactic and endless. If one wants truth about the poor, one must look where the ball is not.

Similarly, journalism inevitably imposes forms of order on both the facts in a story and on the arrangement of stories itself. The structures of magazine and newspapers impose one kind of order; radio and television another, usually sequential. But every form journalism takes is designed to draw the public's attention to what the editors deem most important in a day's or week's events. This naturally violates the larger truth of a chaotic universe. Oddly, the public often contributes its own hierarchical arrangements by dismissing editors' discriminations and dwelling on the story about the puppy on page 45 instead of the bank collapse on page one. The "truth" of a day's events is tugged at from all sides.

Finally, journalism often misses the truth by unconsciously eroding one's sympathy with life. A seasoned correspondent in Evelyn Waugh's maliciously funny novel *Scoop* lectures a green reporter. "You know," he says, "you've got a lot to learn about journalism. Look at it this way. News is what a chap who doesn't care much about anything wants to read." The matter is not a laughing one. A superabundance of news has the benumbing effect of mob rule on the senses. Every problem in the world begins to look unreachable, unimprovable. What could one lone person possibly accomplish against a constant and violent storm of events that on any day include a rebellion of Sikhs, a tornado in Wisconsin, parents pleading for a healthy heart for their child? Sensibilities, overwhelmed, eventually grow cold; and therein monsters lie. Nobody wants to be part of a civilization that reads the news and does not care about it. Certainly no journalist wants that.

If one asks, then, where the larger truth is to be sought, the answer is where it has always been: in history, poetry, art, nature, education, conversation; in the tunnels of one's own mind. People may have come to expect too much of journalism. Not of journalism at its worst; when one is confronted with lies, cruelty and tastelessness, it is hardly too much to expect better. But that is not a serious problem because lies, cruelty and tastelessness are the freaks of the trade, not the pillars. The trouble is that people have also come to expect too much of journalism at its best, because they have invested too much power in it, and in so doing have neglected or forfeited other sources of power in their lives. Journalists appear to give answers, but essentially they ask a question: what shall we make of this? A culture that would rely on the news for truth could not answer that question because it already would have lost the qualities of mind that make the news worth knowing.

If people cannot rely on the news for facts, however, then journalism has no reason for being. Alastair Reid may have forgotten that the principal reason journalists exist in society is that people have a need to be informed of and comprehend the details of experience. "The right to know and the right to be are one," wrote Wallace Stevens in a poem about Ulysses. The need is basic, biological. In that sense, everyone is a journalist, seeking the knowledge of the times in order to grasp the character of the world, to survive in the world, perhaps to move it. Archimedes said he could move the world as long as he had a long enough lever. He pointed out, too, that he needed a ground to stand on.

8. Print (Broder) vs. Broadcast (Friendly)

By ROBERT A. WITAS

Broadcasters clearly came out second best to their print brethren in a comparison of editorials from the two media at the opening session of the first ever joint convention of the NCEW [National Conference of Editorial Writers] and NBEA [National Broadcast Editorial Association.]

"There are some newspapers whose editorials set the agenda for the country," said Fred Friendly, retired president of CBS News, and now a professor at Columbia University.

"I don't know of any television stations whose editorials set the agenda for the country or even for their community," Friendly said.

But Friendly, whose assignment was to review the newspaper side in the session entitled "Print vs. Broadcast Editorials," laid much of the broadcasters' problems to limited air time that precluded in-depth arguments.

Washington Post reporter and columnist David Broder was supposed to make comments on the broadcast side but didn't do so in formal remarks because, he said later, he hadn't prepared any.

But Broder was anything but charitable in an off-the-cuff response to a question on his impression of broadcast editorials.

Broadcast editorials are, "to be polite, a very incipient art form in the broadcast media," Broder said.

"I don't get the impression that they (radio and TV stations) are investing very heavily in either talent or the backup for the talent they are using."

He said that most of the editorial comments he heard struck him "as an afterthought" and that broadcast editorials were "very much in the awkward stage."

Robert A. Witas is editorial editor of the Milwaukee Sentinel. This article originally appeared in The Masthead 36.3 (Fall 1984) 31-32. Reprinted by permission.

Broder had high praise for print editorials in his prepared remarks. He said that, while there had been a decline in the quality of regional and local political reporting over the years, he thought that "editorial pages have gotten even more interesting, diverse, less predictable and, notably, more lively in terms of the quality of writing." He said he had never heard of a case where broadcast editorials had an influence on local politicians as much as those in print.

Friendly credited editorials and not the politicians with bringing the Simpson-Mazzoli immigration bill "to the attention of the American conscience" and accurately predicted its prompt approval by the House.

Friendly noted that, two months earlier, House Speaker Thomas P. (Tip) O'Neill had said of the bill: "Who gives a damn about it? Just a couple of editorial writers."

"That's a pretty good epitaph to have on your tombstone," Friendly told the group.

Friendly said that, with a few exceptions, the news sides of newspapers didn't do a good job on Simpson-Mazzoli, and the news sides of TV and radio stations "never understood the bill or the problem." He called it "a great story of the power of the editorial press."

Friendly said that a great newspaper is "measured, first, by its agenda setting," and that "the credibility of the newspaper is really built, in the end, on its editorial page. It is the brain center, it is the intellectual heart and soul of the newspaper," Friendly said. "It can't be quite that at television stations and radio stations," he said. "There isn't time, there isn't space."

Friendly did credit broadcast editorials with being ahead of their time on some issues. He said he used to laugh at TV and radio editorials about sewers "and bridges that fall down" but that now he gave speeches on the importance of those issues.

Broder said that newspapers should be concerned about the "rightward tilt" of syndicated columnists, particularly if the country, as he suspects, is going into a long period of conservative government.

He said if the editorial page was to maintain its function of presenting adversary views, it was necessary for it to be as tough-minded and intellectually vigorous in its critiques of conservative government as those conservative elements and their kin have been of liberal government.

Both Friendly and Broder said that the difference among opinion, analysis and news is getting blurred in news sections and on editorial pages. It is getting harder to tell "where the news side drops off and where the editorial side begins," Broder said.

Friendly warned broadcasters of subtle devices, such as the "arched eyebrow," which can convey editorial opinion even when not intended.

9. What Is TV Doing To the Election Process?

By JOHN CORRY

What hath television wrought? The Reagan land-slide? The Mondale defeat? The abandonment of substantive issues? Arguments flourish. Politicians and scholars look back. They agree that television has changed the political process; they disagree on what this means. Clearly, television has altered party structure and revised election campaigns. A pretty face, if not a necessity, is an asset not to be despised. At the same time, no one seems quite sure how this works. What on television registers on our psyches, and what only passes us by? What, in fact, is television?

For one thing, it is not print. Old rules of journalism do not always apply. Newspapers do not exist without reporters; television needs nothing except itself. In the absence of someone to write for it, a newspaper is only blank newsprint or perhaps a shopper's guide. Television can get by with only its own technology and a subject on which to focus. The medium supersedes the correspondents who report the stories. They may be intelligent and informed, blessed with superior knowledge. Television makes them supporting actors in an ongoing drama, and so we know them by their styles. Sam Donaldson seems abrasive, while Diane Sawyer cultivates a terrible earnestness, and Chris Wallace a knowing smile.

Candidates occasionally rail at style, but no one since Spiro Agnew has taken it very seriously. It no longer seems to matter. When candidates complain about print, they complain about what someone has written. Error is disputed. When candidates complain about television, they complain, literally, about how they appear. This becomes murky. The day after the

John Corry is a critic at The New York Times. This article originally appeared in The New York Times (November 18, 1984) 27, 30. Copyright ©1984 by The New York Times Company. Reprinted by permission.

election, Walter F. Mondale said at a farewell news conference, "I've never really warmed up to television, and,
in fairness to television, it's never warmed up to me."

Mr. Mondale was onto something here, but it was
hard for him to be precise. He was talking about his
television image, and image is hard to define. After the
news conference, Martin Kaplan, Mr. Mondale's chief
speech writer, was asked if anyone could have beaten
Mr. Reagan, and instantly he replied: "Robert Redford.
Maybe Walter Cronkite." Part of the folklore born in
this election is that Mr. Reagan won only because of
television. His smile, charm and generalities were supposed to play well. Indeed, they did play well, but it
is patronizing to the people who voted for Mr. Reagan
to say they did so only because they were beguiled. It
supposes that Americans perceive government and
politics the same way they do *Dallas.*

Perhaps they do, of course, but how do we explain
Richard M. Nixon? He was the least telegenic candidate
imaginable, and he seemed to dislike television as
much as Mr. Mondale. Nonetheless, he beat George
McGovern, a personable man, with 61% of the vote. Mr.
Reagan, the Great Communicator, only got 59%. How
do we explain the portly, dew-lapped Speaker of the
House, Thomas P. O'Neill Jr.? He is terrific on television; he even appeared on *Cheers.*

It does seem clear that candidates now use television as much as it uses them. Using television, John
Anderson proved that a presidential candidate could
start a party from scratch and still be modestly credible. The Rev. Jesse Jackson, who spent nothing on
television commercials, proved that a candidate could
campaign in Syria, Cuba and Central America. Television cameras followed. When Mr. Jackson returned
from Syria with Lt. Robert O. Goodman Jr., Mr. Reagan
invited them both to the White House. This may have
been moral and patriotic; it was also politically ef-
ficacious. The evening news programs that night
featured Mr. Reagan and not Mr. Jackson.

Indeed, one of Mr. Reagan's great contributions to
our television knowledge this year was the finding that
an incumbent could defeat, or at least run a tie with,

the evening news. Network news broadcasts, almost by definition, are adversarial. This has nothing to do with ideology; it has everything to do with what plays well on television. Challengers almost always play better than front runners or incumbents; they are more interesting. There is empirical evidence for this in *Over the Wire and on TV,* which the Russell Sage foundation published last year. Michael J. Robinson and Margaret A. Sheehan analyzed the 1980 election coverage by CBS. (CBS was not purposely singled out; it just seemed easier to deal with a single network.)

The study confirmed what serious viewers of television probably suspected: President Carter received more "negative" coverage than did candidate Reagan. Similarly, television treated Senator Edward M. Kennedy nicely before he said he would be a candidate for the Democratic nomination, but not so nicely when it appeared that he might win the nomination. When it was clear he would not win, he was treated nicely again.

This year something very much like that happened to Senator Gary Hart. Mr. Hart ran a distant second to Mr. Mondale in the Iowa caucuses. Television commentators, cheered by the possibility of a contest, immediately anointed him as a contender. Could he do it, could he not? When it appeared that perhaps he could, the commentators looked again. Was the Senator's name Hart or Hartpence? Was he 46 years old or 47? Giving the commentators all the best of it, it may be argued that they think it only proper to apply a more rigorous reporting to candidates who look as if they might win. The effect, however, is the same: it is hard for a front-runner to look great on the 7:00 news.

More often than not, however, Mr. Reagan did look great. There he was at the DMZ in Korea, peering through binoculars. There he was in Normandy, talking to the boys of Pointe du Hoc. At the same time, it is a mistake to think that political reporting on television is all visual; a good deal of comment accompanies the picture. The visual part of Mr. Reagan's campaigning, however, often seemed more pronounced. Flags flew, placards waved, balloons ascended skyward.

Sometimes Mr. Reagan seemed to be running for the title role in *Patton.*

This was calculated, of course, but that's the way the game is played. Knowledgeable viewers conceded all future battles for the best visuals to Mr. Reagan on Inaugaration Day in 1981. When the Mormon Tabernacle Choir sang "The Battle Hymn of the Republic," he cried. This was real. It also signaled what lay ahead. The paradox of television campaigns, full of artifice, artificiality and advance men, is that what is real always works better than what is only calculation. Combine calculation—massed flags, say, or even assembled veterans of Normandy—with a candidate who responds with honest emotion and the effect is compelling. This is a nonpartisan rule. Mr. Jackson's speech at the Democratic National Convention may have been the most compelling television spectacle of the campaign. Network news directors, working from advance copies of the text, illustrated Mr. Jackson's speech with pictures of delegates. Network artifice enhanced Mr. Jackson's emotion. Some of the delegates were weeping. Some sober viewers wept, too.

The problem with this, media critics say, is that television can manipulate us any way that skilled practitioners choose. Modern campaigns use polls. Do not think of these as simple devices measuring yes or no responses. Perceptual polls and mapping techniques use discriminant, correlational and variance analysis to measure our souls. They tell professionals what we feel. Do we perceive the candidate to be lacking fairness, judgment or compassion? Do we think him insufficiently warm, informal or tough? Television, artfully used, can offer correctives. Few of them will have anything to do with issues.

Thus, when Mr. Mondale began appearing before crowds in his shirt-sleeves, even on chilly days, it was possible that a perceptual poll had found him to be looking too remote or too weak. Shirt-sleeves would help change the image; a man in shirt-sleeves might even look tough enough to deal with the Reds. When Mr. Reagan suddenly appeared in the company of the poor or disadvantaged, it was possible a poll had found that he seemed to lack compassion. Proximity to the poor on television would suggest that he cared, and it would be far more palatable than an increase in social spending. Television images, carefully arranged, can serve multiple purposes.

Meanwhile, media consultants refine, learning from each election. Already, one assumes, they are calling for tapes of the television debates between Senator Bill Bradley and Mary V. Mochary. Debates between men and women are treacherous, but Mr. Bradley had aquitted himself well. Media consultants will study his performance. Political positions will have nothing to do with this; the consultants will learn from his technique.

Obviously, television politics is growing slicker, although how the slickness will affect us is still unclear. Some thinkers say that already it is too late: television now shapes all our political perceptions; television is our only source of information; television allows us to respond only to vague and mushy messages. Actually, this is an elitist theory, most often put forward by people whose candidates have just lost. Conversely, it is also put forward by media consultants whose candidates have just won; their livelihoods depend on its acceptance. Either way, it supposes that Americans do not get information from, nor have their perceptions shaped by, their families, jobs, churches, synagogues, neighborhoods and associations. It also supposes that Americans no longer listen to the radio or read magazines or newspapers.

In fact, they do. The popular wisdom that most Americans get most of their news from television may not even be true. A 1981 study by the Simmons Market Research Bureau found that two-thirds of all adults read at least part of a newspaper every day, and that about one-third of all adults regularly read a news magazine. Meanwhile, fewer than one-third of all adults watch television news, either local or national, on any given day. On the other hand, we do know that television is doing something; we're just not sure yet what.

10. Remarks to the APME Convention

By RICHARD REEVES

The future of newspapers should be, probably has to be, the same as our past. What we must remember is what business we are in. That business is news. We invented it and defined it. American journalists in large measure put together the organisms that became the models for gathering, evaluating, and disseminating news, and we called those organisms newspapers. Beginning in the middle of the 19th century we began the process in this society (and, to a certain extent, created a model for other societies) of democratizing information: changing what people knew and when they knew it and therefore changing the way they lived and governed themselves.

The product of that time is what we now call "news." It was the period in which the names of American newspapers changed. Before, say, 1840 they had always had such names as *The Advertiser* or *The Commercial.* Then, new newspapers began to be called names such as *Herald, Journal, Tribune* and *Times.* We changed our own view of our function and in doing that created news. We have stumbled along since then, doing well sometimes, doing badly sometimes— and the world beat a path to our business.

Now (starting some years ago) other people are trying to get in: television, teletext, shoppers. And all of them are trying to redefine our business. They are trying to redefine news. They are trying to change the definition of what news is. It is my feeling that the future of our business will rise or fall on how well we let them do that, how we adjust to these attempts to redefine what is news in this society.

Richard Reeves is a syndicated columnist with Universal Press Syndicate. These remarks were originally delivered to the APME Convention, Miami, Florida, November 28, 1984. Reprinted by permission from a transcription edited by the author.

We make a fundamental mistake, I think, in beginning to imitate them. Newspapers recently have been imitating television rather than vice versa; they have shifted to publishing much softer news. That is a mistake because these people (our competition) are trying to take us a heck of a lot farther than just softer news. If we forget our history and functions, if we accept their definition of what news is, there will be no room for us at all. It is true that society is changing, and we are not going to be able to run the information business quite the way we once did. But in the process of meeting and resisting those changes, it would be very foolish to forget who we are and what it is we do.

Television does different things. TV networks and stations are now in the process of redefining or of trying to redefine news after a period of accepting themselves as electronic newspapers. This comes after 30 years in which television news was developed by people whose backgrounds were essentially print, who had been trained in the traditions and the kind of reactions that most of us were trained in. (Walter Cronkite is an obvious example of that kind of person.) Now television, and what is called news on television, is passing into the control of people who are essentially technical and who are supervised by people whose backgrounds are totally commercial. That is, the people who run television stations, and increasingly television networks, are people who began by selling advertising, by selling commercial time. They have no sense of what the news business is; news is just another thing that fits in their screen for a time.

The results of that transformation in television can be seen at any time. We can all see it tonight. Television had half-hour news programs and tried to expand them to an hour. They couldn't do that so they decided to cut it back to a 15-minute news program (which is basically what they run now) with headlines often determined by where a camera was at a certain time. The 15 minutes of daily news and commercials is followed by a back-of-the-book or their version of a feature section. If you looked at television news two or three years ago or five years ago and compared it to what it is now, you'd find it is quite different. TV

news is now much softer. It is described by the people
who put it on, people such as Van Sauter of CBS News,
who says what he is looking for is "moments." Well,
"moments" is not a word that any of us had anything
to do with defining or creating. "Moments" are those
visual instants when a camera happens to be where
somebody is starving to death or burning himself to
death or meeting a loved one after years or finding a
lost puppy. We've all done those stories, but never with
the momentary impact of live, moving pictures. They
were below-the-fold for us, but they are becoming the
principal focus of television reports each night. And
during this same period—the last five years—television
has gotten out of the documentary business. There are
no more long news pieces on television, no more of the
kind Edward R. Murrow once did, the kind Bill Moyers
or Edwin Newman did. Each time CBS, for instance,
announces that it is expanding its documentary unit,
if you look closely you will see it has fewer people—to
the point where it has no people anymore. The emphasis is now on *60 Minutes,* which is news packaged
as drama. Beyond that, what television really wants
to do is package drama as news, so the news program
of the future might look a hell of a lot more like *Fatal
Vision* than it will look like the nightly news. I see that
one of the networks (I've forgotten which one) is producing a mini-series on the Wayne Williams murders
in Atlanta. A screenwriter named Abby Mann, I see,
is going to make the argument over eight hours of
prime time that in fact Williams was the victim of a
conspiracy among the officials of Atlanta. Of course,
the screenwriter Abby Mann knows all this, as he
pointed out in the interview I saw, because he spent
four nights in Atlanta talking to people. If we adjust
ourselves too much to compete with screenwriters who
become "experts" by spending four nights in Atlanta,
we are going to be in real trouble.

My feeling is that television should be accepted, not
as part of journalism or as part of our business, but as
the environment in which we live. And that it should
be covered—not joined with—it should be covered like
the weather. We should cover NBC News or ABC News
or CBS News in the way we cover the White House.

We should set up pressrooms to cover television. (Maybe we could even cover it a little better than we cover the White House.) Television is an important part of our society, but it is not a part of our business. I think that was true in the past and will be much truer in the future. Watch what television people are actually doing as they feel that they are restrained by the traditions and ethics that we grew up with and made part of our craft over a couple of hundred years. The last election is an example. Television lets subjects define the news. That's to a large extent what the phrase "media event" means. What is on television about the White House has nothing to do with Sam Donaldson, whatever he says. Ronald Reagan decides what will be on television about the White House and about the campaign. Television allowed that to happen, for big reasons and small reasons. One of the small reasons is that people like Sam Donaldson are not about to get before the camera—when they are asked by Peter Jennings to explain what it really means—and say, "How the hell would I know? I haven't been within a quarter mile of the President. We've been shooting with long lenses the whole time."

The networks should be treated as newsmakers, not as colleagues, and certainly not as the definers and gatherers of news in the society. I would extend that argument and say that it is much more true with local television operations than with network TV. Do we really want to live in a world, are we willing to work in a business, where news is defined by the Harry Hotcombs in local news operations? They are *not* news operations, and most of us watching them know that. They are something different, and we should cover them and talk to our community about who they are and what they are doing. But who they are and what they are doing is not us; it is not what we do and certainly not what we should be doing.

The great plummets in the credibility of journalism recently are not unrelated to the fact that they coincide with the rise of television news. Yesterday I saw Steven Brill, the publisher of the *American Lawyer,* who had just come back from spending a week interviewing the jurors in the De Lorean case. One of his conclusions, he said, was that press coverage (which largely meant television coverage because we have allowed television to call itself the press) in no way affected the jurors because they don't believe anything in the press. So whatever the press said about De Lorean before the trial began, the jurors were not affected by it.

I don't know as much about my next subject as you people because you are on the front line in ways that I'm not, but I will give my own impressions about the roles of those non-news newspapers which I call shoppers—they have different names in different places— and the kind of teletext computer world which I gather we're going to hear more about. Again, I think it is a problem of who decides—who defines—what is news in the society and whether we should abandon the traditional definitions in an effort to fight the new competition. The new competition in the case of shoppers and computers is going to define news as advertising shopper news and data. Someone recently said to me that we newspapers are going to lose "all the small print." Well, if advertisements and data (the small print) are defined as news, then there is no room for the general interest newspaper as we know it. So it seems to me that what we have to do is clear in the sense of making sure that this new definition does not prevail in the society. We have to remember who we are and what it is we are trying to fight for or sell. Among those things is localism. It is a newspaper's job to create a local community and to present the ideas and the events and the interpretation that people talk about at the supermarket and at the water cooler. It becomes particularly critical in terms of creating the community of information when you are competing against splintered media, personal computers and whatnot wherein everyone does not share the same information at the same time. It is the sharing of information at the same time—what you know and when you know it—that really creates conversation and in a larger sense communication within a society. It is the newspaper's role to do that. We should know what our business is and what it is not. It is not pseudo-news, and it is not bits of information that individuals will pull up on a screen, and it is not "moments." It is news.

11. On Rising to the Occasion Of Popular Mistrust

By JAMES DAVID BARBER

Creed Black's speech pulls attention to the question of what effect the news has on the public. Is that a proper question for press and television professionals to address? I think so, but others don't. Others, among them some of the best in the game, think concern for public impact threatens the integrity of the enterprise by the temptation of toadying. That is the view of the pearl casters. They throw out gems, to the applause of their peers. If the swine fail to catch them, so be it; in that case, the problem resides in the swine, who should be reformed by their schools and churches into an audience worthy of the wisdom the media purvey.

A good many journalists, having been to college, caught this diseased orientation from professors, who are notable for their disdain of the whole idea of concern for what their adolescent auditors may or may not carry away with them into the world of commerce.

Lawyers and doctors are meant to be held to harsher criteria. The eloquent attorney who, however, loses most of his cases suffers a certain drop in credibility, as does the graceful surgeon whose patients keep dying.

The mission of journalism is to make reality interesting—not in the air but in the mind. By analogy to Bishop Berkeley's falling tree in the unknown forest, the journalist without impact is an irrelevancy, like someone shouting "Fire!" in an empty theater. Why then the resistance to this concern?

I think it springs psychologically from a combination of lethargy and existential dread—one fears that either one's repose in the comfort of habit or one's confidence in one's human significance will be shattered. But that is also why long-time neurotics resist psychoanalysis: the hope of liberation is blocked by the

James David Barber is James B. Duke Professor of Political Science & Public Policy Studies at Duke University. This article is a Credibility Seminar document (December 1984). Reprinted by permission.

fear of emptiness. A poor excuse. Finding out the news's impact might open up new creative possibilities. If not, the good old ways remain available.

The news as a civic phenomenon addresses the citizenry in four modes, which can be symbolized by typical names of newspapers:

The Herald, that is, the arouser, the trumpet blast of the angel at the masthead, the Paul Revere banging on the shutter in the moonlight. The "alarum without" in Shakespeare.

The Sun, that is, the warming presence at the breakfast table, the community comforter, the daily friend who brightens the spirit and gives basketball scores.

The Record, that is, the informer, the messenger telling what he knows that we do not, the fact-finder and fact-giver.

The Beacon, that is, the guiding light of public sentiment, the trend-setter, the interpreter, given to appending explanatory counsel of an improving kind.

Despite the inadequacies of research on the subject (which are legion), the impacts of the news in America may be approximated.

As arouser (*The Herald*), the news is weak. The culture values civic participation. Half the eligible electorate does not vote. Watergate largely failed to arouse the 1972 electorate. *Civic* lethargy abounds, though American energies pour out into other activities.

As the voice of community (*The Sun*), the news is weak also, or at least not well appreciated, as the decline in credibility attests. Most major institutions in the nation have suffered such decline in credibility, which is, however, little comfort to the press.

As informer (*The Record*), the news is weakest of all, if the criterion is the learning of information, not just bringing it into the presence of the citizen. Americans are extremely ill-informed—not in comparison to the past but in comparison to the demands of the times. The basics of the Constitution, the simplest elements of political geography, the most widely covered current events penetrate to the mentition of minorities of Americans.

As a guide of sentiment (*The Beacon*), the media are very powerful. After an event, polls jump in the direction journalism discerns/estimates/predicts. Cf. the immediate and subsequent polls on "who won" the 1984 presidential debates. Regarding politics, the journalist as tastemaker has overtaken the journalist as reporter or explainer.

How might a conference, composed as ours is, best contribute to an advance on these problems? Not, it seems to me, by designing audience/readership research. Not by developing practical steps toward enhancing press credibility in the local community. Not by contriving, in the manner of Jeane Kirkpatrick, to solve a problem by deciding who is to blame for it. Not by surveying only the entrails of our personal experiences, poetic visions, and indexed anecdotes. And surely not by supposing that no such problems exist.

Rather we might begin to explore, in a manner both realistic and imaginative, *ways print and television journalism might enhance its credibility both to the public and to itself.* We could try to figure out how to become at the same time trusted and trustworthy, influential and authoritative, attractive and deserving of attention. Key to that endeavor is the question: *what are the most promising alternatives to our present modes of doing news?* The rich resources members of the seminar bring to this inquiry suggests we might succeed, in posing thesis and antithesis, not in order to stay stuck there, but to move on to synthesis—more likely syntheses. I am not proposing a session of positive thinking; there should be plenty of space for breast-beating and finger-pointing. But also a close look, with journalism's skeptical but curious eye, at some of the apparently promising departures from practices grown old, if not necessarily stale.

The challenge is to rise to the occasion of popular mistrust, not by denying or evading it, but by considering how to render it at once passé and unjustified.

"The greatest need of our time is to clean out the enormous mass of mental and emotional rubbish that clutters our minds and makes of all political and social life a mass illness. Without this housecleaning we cannot begin to *see.* "Unless we *see* we cannot think. The purification must begin with the mass media. How?"

—Thomas Merton

12. Reporting the News Isn't Always a 'Friendly' Job

By ANDREW BARNES

MIAMI—It may be indicative of the current mind-set of newspaper editors that we asked ABC television's abrasive Sam Donaldson to come tell us about our bond of trust with readers.

Donaldson, nothing abashed, accepted.

There has been talk at editors' gatherings that the public's perception of the media as raucous and rude must be television's fault—after all, it couldn't be *us*. Donaldson, not surprisingly, said no, television reporters are good guys, too, the only difference is that they have a camera running when they ask their tough questions, and so we all see how they behave.

And he defended aggressive questioning of public officials, even the President of the United States. "If anything," he said, "the questions should be tougher."

As the speeches from the podium and the conversations in the hallways of this annual meeting of the Associated Press Managing Editors Association went on this week, the question was framed again and again: Do you, dear reader, want your newspaper to be "friendly?"

By "friendly" is meant, if I've got it right, a newspaper that speaks politely to its readers and the people it reports on, that involves readers with contests and explanatory columns (perhaps such as this one), a newspaper that is mindful of the damage it can do, and considerate of those pulled into the news.

Frame the question that way and it's like motherhood and sunshine, everybody's all for it.

Me, too. Of course we must have a paper that avoids rude blunderings and admits its mistakes.

But I submit that in a great deal of this soul-searching we have missed one of the basics. Readers buy newspapers for the news.

Andrew Barnes is editor and president of the St. Petersburg Times. This article originally appeared in the St. Petersburg Times (December 2, 1984) D4. Reprinted by permission.

In reporting and writing the news, there will sometimes be "collisions between the private person and the public purpose," as Bill Green of Duke University put it.

He posed a hypothetical situation. Is it newsworthy, he asked, when the mayor's son, 19, is caught shoplifting a small item in a local department store, and found to have a marijuana joint?

It would be "friendlier" to the mayor and his son to say no, it's such a small offense and putting it in the paper would disrupt the lad's young life, not to mention the mayor's political career, and for what?

I submit that of course it's newsworthy, just as it would be if one of my sons were to do the same thing, heaven forbid.

"These are heavy decisions you make," Green said, "and they are irretrievable."

"The thing that worries me," Green went on to tell the editors, "is the public perception of how you are handling them. You don't come out very well.

"The public believes you go too far. The public does not understand the First Amendment, for which you reach too often."

The key, Green argues, is that we explain why we must sometimes invade privacy, and even hurt individuals. "Our free press is not consistently enough a responsible press."

From the number of times these questions came up, it seems clear other editors, like me, are worried by the calls and letters we get, seemingly increasingly, asking what business we have putting a story in the paper that will make a bad situation worse.

Drake Mabry, an editor in Des Moines, said he feels accused of "insistent and inconsiderate intrusion into moments of private grief."

"Do we edit for our audience, or for the families of the victims?" Mabry asked. "Is there a difference?"

It will be a relief to get back to helping put out a newspaper. Talking about it has a wearing circularity. But these are terribly difficult questions, which we who edit newspapers have to solve, a piece at a time.

The last word (for the moment—this topic isn't going to go away) goes to David Lawrence, an editor in Detroit:

"Getting at the truth usually means we must forego being loved," he said. Still, "a good friend tells you the truth, and so does a good newspaper, even if it hurts."

That doesn't mean leaving out news of successes, and of happiness. We must also rejoice. We must make tough decisions with compassion, as Lawrence said. But that must not be an excuse for failing to print the news. "You ought to be able to trust a good newspaper."

13. A Time for Barkers

By RUSSELL BAKER

There was an entertaining dustup among the news people at CBS last week after Phyllis George was made co-anchor of the network's *Morning News* with Bill Kurtis.

Miss George was previously in the sports division and, once upon a time, was a Miss America, and her lack of journalistic experience produced some criticism among the professionals at CBS News. Richard Salant, though now retired from the presidency of the news operation, said her appointment "demeans" the news division and suggested the *Morning News* be put in CBS's entertainment, record or toy division.

Whereupon Miss George's agent, Ed Hookstratten, spoke for the wisdom of the age in which we live. "The newsies," he said, "sometimes have a tendency to take themselves a little too seriously and not completely understand what the broadcast medium is all about."

Because I am a "newsie," my heart is with the Richard Salants of the world, but the journalist's obligation to face reality compels me to side with Hookstratten.

When he says the "newsies" don't completely understand what the broadcast world is about, he is obviously commenting on journalism's reluctance to confront the extraordinary change that journalism itself has created in subjecting the country to total media saturation.

The result is now as clear as last fall's election, or last week's big news show, the hijacking of the Kuwaiti airliner and its six-day run on the TV screens and front pages.

I am referring to the emergence of the nation as audience.

Russell Baker is a columnist for The New York Times. This article originally appeared in The New York Times (December 12, 1984) A31. Copyright © 1984 by The New York Times Company. Reprinted by permission.

In the past there was something vaguely referred
to as "the public" or "the American public." Possibly
out of careless language habits, the existence of this
"public" encouraged the notion that it was concerned
with "public matters," which were usually rather
uninteresting subjects such as foreign policy, library
fines, garbage collection and so on.

Many journalists still practicing, even on television,
grew up with the idea of "the public." Print journalists
thought of that public as a "readership." At election
time, this "public" or "readership" was said to be an
"electorate," and journalists assumed it was their duty to make sure the "electorate" was "informed."

Without an "informed electorate," democracy
would be imperiled. So went one of the basic axioms
of civics class that most journalists continue to believe
despite 200 years of evidence that democracy can survive almost anything so long as its beneficiaries are
kept reasonably ignorant of what is going on.

All these traditional journalistic ways of thinking
about Americans—as "the public," "the readership,"
"the electorate"—hang on persistently because, as
Hookstratten points out, even at CBS News they don't
"completely understand what the broadcast medium
is all about."

What it's all about, of course, is "audience." The
brutal economics of television compel it to exalt audience above all else. In television, value is measured
in terms of audience size.

Audiences assemble basically to enjoy perfor-
mances. When "the public" turns into "the audience,"
it tends to tire quickly of subjects like foreign policy,
library fines and garbage collection, and demand
theater. This explains why people who know how to
create theater now occupy so much of our attention.

The hijacking story of the Kuwaiti airliner is the
standard case. A band of desperadoes trained in the
by-now familiar arts of hijack theater dramatize
themselves and fulfill the news industry's incessant
need for audience-grabbers for six whole days, and to
what effect?

Two senseless murders—inevitably called "execu-
tions" in the melodramatic parlance that fetches

audiences—may provide cautionary news for those planning to travel in Arab lands, but the event is otherwise entirely without meaning for a "public." Its only content is for an "audience," which craves theater.

While the hijack show was playing last week some 30 people were killed when kung fu devotees battled unemployed youngsters in Madagascar, and in Sri Lanka some 100 people were murdered by rampaging soldiers angry about plots to subdivide the country. These events were no less significant than the hijacking and far more deadly, yet they were staged without the slightest touch of theatrical know-how, and so bombed with the audience.

Mr. Hookstratten knows what's happened. Today all the world's a stage, the public's only an audience, and the journalist is like the guy who used to stand outside tents working his mouth to draw a crowd.

14. Writers on Journalists: A Version of Atheism

By ROBERT B. HEILMAN

I.

Novelists and dramatists have never had a very high tolerance for journalists. In this there is no doubt some snobbery: the vocation of literature, which hopes to be *ars longa*, condescending to the trade of writing that lives for a day. But this hostility comes less from class pride than from self-defense. To most writers, journalists are critics, that is, blundering carpers, sure to miss the point of the literary work, to ignore its virtues, to harp on its vices, and thus kill the market. The artist's response to the reviewer is given a neat turn in Samuel Beckett's *Waiting for Godot* (1952). The major characters, Didi and Gogo, get into a name-calling match, trading a series of abusive terms such as "Moron!"—"Vermin!"—"Abortion!"—"Morpion!"— "Sewer-rat!"—and "Cretin!" Gogo has the final word of abuse: "Crritic!"—to which Didi can only say, "Oh!"; and the stage direction adds, "He wilts, vanquished, and turns away." In Beckett's view, Didi can find no dirtier term to come back with.

The present theme, however, is not the artist's response to the critic, but the way in which novels and dramas have been presenting reporters and editors for at least two hundred years. The presentations reveal certain lines of opinion that remain strangely constant. Repeatedly, regardless of location or era, observers detect self-interest under a mask of disinterestedness, self-ignorance that appears in complacency and in cliches of attitude and expression, formulaic thought, and elementary style.

As early as Tobias Smollets's *Humphry Clinker* (1771) we find the charge that a victim of the press can-

Robert B. Heilman is Professor Emeritus of English at the University of Washington at Seattle. This essay originally appeared in The Georgia Review 39.1 (Spring 1985) 37-54. Reprinted by permission of The Georgia Review and the author. Copyright ©1985 by Robert B. Heilman.

not fight back effectively. When one man complains
of a newspaper's violent attacks upon a government
minister and of the minister's failing to reply, another
says that patience is better than litigation. If you sue,
the publisher "screens the anonymous accuser" (or, as
we say now, "protects his source") and profits from the
publicity. "The multitude immediately takes him [the
publisher] into their protection, as a martyr to the cause
of defamation, which they have always espoused...and
the sale of his paper rises in proportion to the scandal
it contains." How very modern. Further, the man who
sues the publisher "is inveighed against as a tyrant
and oppressor"—words that remind us again of our
times, when defendants often call libel actions attacks
on freedom of the press. Smollett heads right into that
point. His character says bluntly, "The *liberty of the
press* [his italics] is a term of great efficacy; and like
that of the *Protestant religion*, has often served the purpose of sedition." No one would use such terms today,
but Smollett spots a strategy that is still used: the cry
for freedom often fronts, perhaps unconsciously, for
something else. Matthew Bramble, Smollett's irascible Welshman, declares that "the liberty of the press,
like every other privilege,...must be restrained within
certain bounds," for, once it is taken to be "a branch
of laws, religion, and charity, it becomes one of the
greatest evils that ever annoyed the community. If the
lowest ruffian," he goes on, "may stab your name with
impunity in England," how can you attack Italy "for
the practice of common assassination?"

Eighty years later, Thackeray's *Pendennis* (which
deals with magazine rather than newspaper people)
shows us the title character and others getting into
journalism because they are broke and can't do
anything else. Some of them become name droppers
(one journalist, for instance, claims to have saved the
life of a French lord and to have taught him English,
as well as to have given requested advice to the King
of Belgium and other big shots). Here, as often
elsewhere, Thackeray portrays general human
frailties—phoniness, pretentiousness, eagerness for
attention—rather than flaws peculiar to journalists.
However, he does describe a London paper that attacks

a rival because the rival allegedly utters "forgeries
against individuals, and calls in auxiliary cutthroats
to murder...reputation[s]"; one of its writers is called
"the eunuch who brings the bowstring, and strangles
at the orders" of his paper. Thackeray also snapshots
a government figure who is a news-leaker (more than
a hundred and thirty years ago!), and paints fully a
scissors-and-paste journalist who cribs from other
papers while posing as an eyewitness reporter. Finally, he slips in a dry mention of an "independent county paper, so distinguished for its unswerving principles
and loyalty to the British oak, and so eligible a medium
for advertisements." That last phrase points to an
economic motive with which we, too, are familiar.

II.

Though the mid-nineteenth century is sometimes
thought to be a watershed between a dirty old and a
cleaner new journalism, in the 1870s and '80s several
distinguished writers portrayed journalists in need of
soap as much as those of Smollett a century earlier.
In his "parliamentary" series (adapted for television
in our time as *The Pallisers*) Anthony Trollope
describes one journalist very fully: Quintus Slide—a
suggestive name, recalling "slick," "slime," and "sly."
Slide, who first shows up in *Phineas Finn* of 1869, edits
the *People's Banner*; he is always roaring about "the
wrongs of the people" and screaming that "the ruling
powers were the 'people's' enemies." He offers a deal
to Phineas Finn, a young member of Parliament: if
Phineas will aid some cause dear to Slide, the paper
will guarantee him "unbounded popularity during life
and...immortality afterwards." Slide assures Phineas
"that in public life there's nothing like having a horgan
to back you." In "the 'Ouse" you can do "nothing, if
you're not reported." He even wants Phineas to write
for the paper; when Phineas refuses, Slide replies, "I
shall know how to punish this."

In *Phineas Redux* (1874), Slide, though still
bleeding for the "rights of the people," has found it expedient to shift political parties. This angers a
subscriber, who says he now reads the paper "just for
the joke of it." Slide replies, "As long as you take it,...I

don't care what the reason is." Trollope joins Smollett in noting the bedrock truth: the circulation motive.

When he receives a libelous letter which implicitly accuses Phineas of adultery with a peer's wife, Slide wants to print it because "the morals of the aristocracy...would be at a low ebb indeed if the press didn't act as their guardians." He must defend "purity of life, and...do our duty by the public without fear or favor." Phineas manages to get an injunction against publication—his only way out since, as Trollope explains, "Editors of papers are self-willed, arrogant, and stiffnecked, a race of men who believe in themselves and little in anything else, with no feeling of reverence or respect for matters which are august enough for other men." Slide, who has been gloating over the free publicity he would get by publishing the scandalous letter and follow-up articles, is enraged. Trollope explains again: "Newspaper editors sport daily with the names of men of whom they do not hesitate to publish almost the severest words that can be uttered; but let an editor himself be attacked, even without his name, and he thinks that the thunderbolts of heaven should fall upon the offender." Every detail of bad conduct must "be laid open to the light, so that the people may have a warning." Trollope adds, "That such details will make a paper 'pay' Mr. Slide knew also; but...only in Mr. Slide's path of life" does a man find "that virtue and profit are compatible." Hence Slide regards the injunction as "an evil on the public at large," and he plans revenge. He assures Phineas, "I'll crush you."

So Slide evades the injunction by printing the contents of the letter and other matters which make Phineas look like a sexual wrong-doer. Although Slide "really did believe that what he was doing was all done in the cause of morality," Trollope makes it clear that what Slide wrote was "full of lies," but that "Mr. Slide did not know that he was lying, and did not know that he was malicious." Here Trollope is making a subtle and important point—the self-deception of the man who supposes that his attacks on an opponent really come from love of virtue. Consequently, Slide in no way sees himself as "stabbing his enemy in the dark," for "the anonymous accusation of sinners in high rank was, on behalf of the public, the special duty of writers and editors." It happens, however, that the public rather likes a Byronic hero, and the attacks on Phineas fail. Then Trollope tires of Slide and makes him write his paper into a losing libel suit and get fired. At last look he thinks of "seeking his fortune in New York." Thus the Big Apple, to English eyes, a hundred and 10 years ago.

The Slide story, which I have greatly shortened, is one of our completest pictures of a certain type who combines self-interest, self-righteousness, and self-deception; who identifies "duty by the public" with a pursuit of one's own ends, right and truth with one's own motives and profit; and who believes that the journalist is the final arbiter of all matters, and hence that any opposition is an objective evil requiring punishment—in a word, the retaliatory spirit.

While such a spirit may seem to belong only to the Victorian dark ages, many newspaper readers in our own day will think of instances in which some figure deemed worthy of interviews does not "cooperate" and hence tends to acquire an unfavorable image through the press. An extraordinarily overt case of the retaliatory spirit appears in the *Seattle Post-Intelligencer* of May 18, 1983, where Steve Rudman complains about the fact that the baseball pitcher Gaylord Perry "has decided not to talk to reporters any more":

> That's Gaylord's prerogative, but...Gaylord should be advised that the people he is not talking to are the very people who will decide if and when he is inducted into the Hall of Fame.
>
> Some of those people have long memories. Some of those people might decide to let Gaylord languish a while before letting him into Cooperstown.

That does sound a little like Quintus Slide redivivus.

III.

Back to the nineteenth century and across to Norway. Henrik Ibsen's *An Enemy of the People* (1882) portrays some Norwegian cousins of Quintus Slide—Hovstad, an editor, and Billing, his assistant. Hovstad's paper has a name like Slide's *People's Banner*; it is the

People's Courier. In *An Enemy of the People* the main
figure is Dr. Thomas Stockman, staff physician of the
baths in a spa town, who discovers that the water is
polluted by industrial waste. He expects to be hailed
as a local savior; instead, his discovery poses so great
an economic threat to the town, which lives on the spa
business, that everyone turns against him. He is
declared "an enemy of the people," and he and his family are made outcasts. But when Stockman first makes
his discovery, editor Hovstad is delighted, for, like
Quintus Slide, he has his own fish to fry: he can use
the scandal to attack the men in power—"that ring of
pig-headed reactionaries."[1] A "journalist of my radical
leanings," he says, "can't let an opportunity like this
go by. The myth of the infallibility of the ruling class
has to be shattered" to assist "the liberation of the
powerless, oppressed masses." Hovstad will stand his
"ground as a strong, self-reliant man" against the "wor-
ship of authority in this town." Dr. Stockman is
delighted to have the "independent liberal press" with
him, and Hovstad's assistant, Billing, thinks that the
pollution story will start "the revolution breaking like
the dawn." The editors plan to "keep drumming it into the public that the mayor's incompetent, and
that...the whole administration—ought to be placed in
the hands of the liberals." Hovstad assures Stockman
that his article on the baths is a "pure masterpiece."
Billing sees it coming out "like a lightning-bolt" and
adds, "Hurray! It's war—war!"

But editor Hovstad, the crusader for truth and the
people, begins to see things differently when the
Mayor—who is, ironically, Dr. Stockman's brother—
assures him that the pollution danger is small, that
the cost of relaying the pipes to the baths would be pro-
hibitive, and that the necessary two-year closing of the
baths would be an economic hardship. The fearless
editor easily changes sides; now he "dare not print"
the doctor's article because the doctor "has the will of
the majority against him." An editor must "work in
collaboration with his readers"; his "duty to society"
compels him to break with Stockman (although twice
he insists that this action is due "partly" to his "consideration for [the doctor's] wife and his distressed

children"). When Dr. Stockman publicly disparages the hidebound majority, Hovstad, now heckling the doctor, demagogically exclaims, "That's an insult to the common man." He even boasts that his "roots run deep in those masses that [the Doctor] despises," and it is he who invents the title phrase, "an enemy of the people."

Ibsen's main target is a group conformity which resists truth, and he sees the editor as basically the chief defender of the very status quo that he claims to be against; hence his hypocrisy and demagoguery. Ibsen's final satirical blow is that the editor turns out to believe only in the lowest-common-denominator motive. Dr. Stockman's tricky father-in-law has quietly bought up baths stocks; thus he puts pressure on the doctor, whose campaign against the baths will wipe out a possible bequest to his wife and children. As soon as the editor hears of the stock purchase, he comes running back to Stockman. He now thinks that Stockman started a baths rumor only to depress the stock and make a killing. Hovstad wants in on the deal, and this time he is ready to ride out any public storm that may arise from this new reversal of position. He is incredulous when the doctor throws him out.

What Trollope's Quintus Slide and Ibsen's Hovstad finally share is commonplaceness of mind: they think that everyone is an operator with a price. Their own profit line is populism. Slide goes for the common man's conventional morality and keeps an eye out for misbehavior by uncommon men, while Hovstad goes for the common man's rights and keeps an eye out for flaws in the rulers. But in the end both go by majorities; their best eye is for circulation, and both can quickly change directions when it is expedient. If crossed, both are retaliatory.

IV.

Such characters provide the background for a witticism by Oscar Wilde in 1882, the year in which Ibsen created Hovstad. Wilde, in a letter from Boston as he is about to leave for New Orleans, writes: "They talk about yellow fever, but I think that anyone who has survived the newspapers is impregnable."[2] A decade later another Englishman in America felt the same. In 1893 Rudyard Kipling built a house near Brattleboro, Vermont, which, according to biographer Angus Wilson, "was also to be a fortress against the invasion of the American press." The press was unfriendly because Kipling made cracks about it; the Kiplings were bitter because the press "intruded on their privacy." Besides, Kipling felt that American reporters belittled whatever they wrote about: "They can by merely writing about it, knock all the beauty, honor, wit, wisdom, and reverence out of everything in the world, and leave behind only the smell of an over-heated ante-room or of a hollow tooth. Yet, individually, heaps of them are fascinating."[3] Even as Kipling distinguishes between the private personality of the reporter and the disfiguring of it by professional attitudes, he carries further a hint in Trollope by pointing to what is usually called journalistic skepticism—that is, an addiction to lowest common denominators.

Just about this time Lewis Carroll wrote to his sister, "I think *newspapers* are largely responsible for the bad English now used in books."[4] Here we shift from journalists' moral style to their verbal style. A few years later the Fowler brothers were planning, as they themselves described it, "a sort of English composition manual, from the negative point of view, for journalists and amateur writers. [Many of them] cannot write a paper without a blunder or cacophony or piece of verbiage or false pathos or clumsiness or avoidable dulness." The authors and their publisher (Oxford) considered various titles to catch the twofold audience of the book—schoolboys and journalists—finally settling on *The King's English* (1906).[5] It grew into the various editions of the Fowlers' *Modern English Usage.* Over a half century later Evelyn Waugh, writing Nancy Mitford on grammar and usage (as he often did), was damning the use of *aggravate* in the sense of "annoy." He quotes Fowler: "This use should be left to the uneducated. It is for the most part a feminine or childish colloquialism, but intrudes occasionally into the newspapers."[6]

The year 1906 saw not only the first Fowler volume but G.B. Shaw's drama on medical men and methods,

The Doctor's Dilemma. Here we find something of a shift of emphasis in the literary portrayal of journalists. What had caught the eye of Smollett, Thackeray, Trollope, and Ibsen was journalistic self-interest, often masquerading as devotion to the public interest. What catches the eye of Shaw is a special phase of self-interest, that is, self-ignorance, often combined with ignorance of other matters. Writing primarily about doctors and their problems, Shaw brings in a reporter when a painter, Dubedat, is on his deathbed and wants to talk to the press. Shaw describes the reporter in a full stage direction which bears quoting:

>...a cheerful, affable young man who is disabled for ordinary business pursuits by a congenital erroneousness which renders him incapable of describing accurately anything he sees, or understanding and reporting accurately anything he hears. As the only employment in which these defects do not matter is journalism (for a newspaper, not having to act on its descriptions and reports, but only to sell them to idly curious people, has nothing but honor to lose by inaccuracy and unveracity), he has perforce become a journalist.

The reporter thinks an artist's studio is "where he has his models"—an instance of the lowest-common-denominator thinking that Kipling attributes to American reporters. When a doctor uses the word "tubercle," the reporter hears it as "cubicle." Corrected, he says, "Oh! tubercle. Some disease, I suppose. I thought he had tuberculosis." He gets Dr. Ridgeon's name as "Pigeon." Walpole the surgeon takes over: "youd (sic) better let me write the names down for you: youre (sic) sure to get them wrong. That comes of belonging to an illiterate profession....Now attend (Pointing to notebook.) These are the names of the three doctors. This is the patient. This is the address. This is the name of the disease." When he says that the patient "may die at any moment," the reporter says, "I *am* in luck today." He wants to photograph the surgeon, and asks, "Could you have a lancet or something in your hand?"--Shaw's jest at photographic clichés which still hold.

When the dying artist is brought in to stage a deathbed scene, the reporter says to him, "I thought you might like to let us have a few words—about—er—well, a few words on your illness, and your plans for the season." The dying artist is an unconventional man: he tells his wife that she must *not* wear mourning and that she *must* remarry as soon as possible. The reporter, pleased, says that it "shewed a very nice feeling, his being so particular about his wife going into proper mourning for him and making her promise never to marry again." The point is not so much that he hears the opposite of what was said as that he hears spoken words entirely in terms of the cliches of his trade and his time. What he expects determines what words he hears. He now hopes to interview Mrs. Dubedat on "How It Feels To Be A Widow." With this delicate project he anticipates Barbara Walters by 80 years.

Perhaps the keenest of Shaw's insights is that what a reporter takes in, even in matters of fact, is largely determined by his own preconceptions. Gertrude Stein, commenting on her 1934 tour of the United States, makes the point most succinctly: "It was useless to expect much of reporters; they had their own stories already written in their heads, and were only interested in catching quotes that could fit in with these. They never really heard what was said."[7] Almost 50 years later another American describes similar experiences more fully. Thomas Sowell, the black economist, records how preconceptions about him have led to more than a dozen instances—he spells them out—in which opinions, attitudes, and even actions attributed to him by the media were inconsistent with, and often the "*direct opposite*" [his emphasis] of the facts available in the record. He adds, "People are constantly telling me how surprised they are at reading something I have written, because it is so different from what they have been led to believe by the media." He specifies exactly how the media minds worked: he was misrepresented because of "the presumption [in matters of race] *that no honest disagreement is possible* [his emphasis] on the orthodoxy promoted by the civil rights leaders and liberal politicians." Then he adds a note on the

pragmatics of journalism: "The time pressures of the
media and the need for excitement to attract readers
and viewers promote the creation of stereotypes,
bogeymen, and scapegoats."[8] Hence also, no doubt, the
familiar rule that only bad news makes good news.
Philip Lawler writes that "when a new disaster is
predicted the popular media rush to publicize it, never
wondering how soon it will be proved spurious. When
the bubble is burst and sanity is restored, the story is
relegated to the bowels of the newspaper. When the
Club of Rome issued its pessimistic *Limits to Growth*
in 1972, popular coverage was intensive. But when the
same group reversed its findings in 1976, no one
noticed."[9]

Americans writing on the American press are
paralleled by an Englishman reporting on an English
reporter. Walter Allen, who modestly calls himself a
literary journalist, has recently written about an experience of 1937. The *News Chronicle* was making a
survey of group opinions, and Allen was interviewed
as a representative of the "educated young." The interviewer was A. J. Cummings, the "star writer" of
the paper. Allen writes:

I sat back and waited to be interviewed. He
talked about himself. He had recently interviewed
Stalin and was full of it. He poured scorn on H. G.
Wells's interview with Stalin. He said: "The difference between H. G. Wells and me is that H. G.
sits on his arse all day."...He went on to tell me how,
before he was president, Roosevelt had entertained
him on his yacht, and how he, Cummings, had outlined to Roosevelt the principles of the New Deal.
All this with great solemnity. In the two hours I was
with him he did not ask me anything. Later he told
us, through the *News Chronicle*, what the educated
young were thinking. From all of which I learned
one thing, which the experiences of later life have
reinforced: that it is the besetting sin of successful
journalists to confuse themselves with their bylines.[10]

That portrait of a journalist, notably the name-
dropping, is fascinatingly similar to the fictional portraits in Thackeray's *Pendennis* of almost a century
earlier.

Shaw's picture of reportorial inaccuracy is echoed by Evelyn Waugh when he writes to Nancy Mitford about a "long article in an American paper saying how beastly I am—sound in principle no doubt but bang wrong in all facts, like all American journalism" (August 10, 1948). Shaw's picture of reportorial clichés becomes sharper in Miguel de Unamuno's imaginative 1930 account of Don Quixote's returning home after his knightly failures. The Don's worst "torment" would be "a swarm of reporters enveloping him and subjecting him to questionnaires and interrogations. I can hear one of them asking, 'And to what, Sir, do you attribute your celebrity?' "[11] Moving from the Spanish philosopher to a Russian playwright and novelist, we find the inquisitorial style presented more savagely: in 1927 Michael Bulgakov wrote a science fiction story in which the chief character is an inventor-professor. Bulgakov's biographer, summarizing the story, writes, "Newspaper men hound the professor as though he were their prey; a reporter, Bronsky, with his 'speaking newspaper,' has all the power of a demagogue over the crowd."[12] Here the stress is on the exercise of power, and the use of the word "prey" suggests that we are in a domain outside of scruple. A case in point has to do with Louis-Ferdinand Céline, who suggested that the publication of his pro-German and anti-Semitic views was a violation of confidence. On this his biographer remarks tartly: "If as a well-known writer you write a long letter to the editor of a paper—even if it is a personal letter to someone you know—and this letter contains your general opinions about certain issues of the day, you must be pretty ignorant about journalists if you feel surprise when your letter is prominently published."[13] Some 120 years earlier, the famous quarrel between Dickens and Thackeray had its roots in the same issue of privileged material. Dickens was on the side of the journalist Edmund Yates when Yates wrote a sort of flippant debunking piece about Thackeray in the journal *Town Talk*. Yates especially angered Thackeray by making use of private conversations at the Garrick Club, to which both belonged. The episode makes us think, in our own day, of people who believe that they are talking off the record and then find themselves in the headlines.

We could internationalize a charming English stanza by Anon:

> One cannot hope to bribe or twist,
> Thank God, the British journalist;
> But seeing what the man will do
> Unbribed, there's no occasion to.

V.

What is eye-catching about these chance findings is their consistency through time (two centuries) and space (six countries). True, most of the writers are English, but that is because I work primarily with them; still, there are several Americans, a Spaniard, a Frenchman, a Norwegian, and a Russian. Such persistent and widespread comments appear to represent more than subjective responses. At least they alert us to a number of ironies in the situation.

It is ironic that people who choose a profession based on the public use of words often reveal an uncertain verbal sense. One sees "reknowned" in *The New York Times* and "asterix" in *The Seattle Times*, and everywhere between the coasts "graffiti" and "media" are used as singulars more often than as plurals, "mitigate" for "militate," etc. The one rule of composition that everyone seems faithful to is that a paragraph should contain only one sentence. Even undergraduate reporters have at times a disconcerting air of being essentially uncoverers of misdeeds—a role that makes the linguistic medium of little importance. In my own five years on a small-city paper in Pennsylvania I had drummed into me from the beginning that the job had two rules: get the facts right and get the English right. Those principles seemed rather unfamiliar to student reporters who would now and then seek information from me when I was holding a university administrative job.

It is ironic that a profession committed to fact should evoke so many outcries about errors in fact, making most of us dread the approach of a reporter as much as that of a policeman. If the misrepresentation which we fear occurs, the correction, if any, too often tends to be *sotto voce*. (It's an old joke that if an error makes you look bad, it will shout at readers from the front-page rostrum, while the correction will be a whisper back among the recipes and garden hints. But I report with pleasure that many of America's better papers have recently been printing corrections not only on a major news page but often in a relatively fixed location within the paper and in a different typeface that attracts attention.)

It is ironic that a profession which at times attracts or produces gifted writers should depend so heavily on cliches—verbal and attitudinal. The word *tragic* is daily applied to every kind of misfortune, however routine or mechanical. Cliched attitudes produce the same kinds of stories again and again—pathetic stories of illness, accident, and hardship; and happy stories of sudden riches, especially in these days of state lotteries. Reporters' questions somehow elicit standardized answers. How often victims are reported as saying, "Why did this happen to me, why, why?" I believe that the human race by and large is sensible enough to know that irrational unpleasantnesses do happen, and that most people would not ask such a question unless, so to speak, cliched into it. Likewise with newly divorced prominent persons, who have to come up with the hackneyed "We remain good friends."

It is ironic that freedom of the press (a subject dear to Smollett and Trollope), essential as it is, should seem in some ways to inhibit free discussion of it. If you raise theoretical questions about it, you are likely to be rated a would-be censor or dictator. But few freedoms are absolute—that is, in no way contingent upon the needs, values, and other principles of the society in which the freedoms are exercised—and we might expect to hear cries of "freedom endangered" only in the event of unmistakable efforts to thwart it. Instead, the press gives us rather frequent alarmist outbursts over alleged attacks on freedom. Every time a pornographer or libeler gets nailed in some way, perfectly decent columnists and editorialists rush in, shake their heads, and predict the disappearance of truth from the public prints. Such constancy of complaint might, alas, risk the wolf-wolf effect.

It is ironic that freedom of the press, like motherhood, may be used. The politican who cheers for it can expect a good press. Likewise the leaker of inside information. He may be a man of principle, a man with a program of his own, an envious or resentful or revengeful man, but he can seem uniquely honest. He can choose glowing publicity or safe anonymity. If the reporter defending anonymity gets a mild contempt rap, his own and other papers will present him as a martyr and hint at Pulitzerhood. Listening to a whispering leaker is a little different from admirable work. Investigative reporting raises eyebrows only when the presumably disinterested muckraker converts someone else's misdeeds into his own best seller. One would feel easier about it if the profits went into a fund for the relief of indigent reporters.

It is ironic that a profession's defensible wish to survive economically and to turn a profit should often display so prominent a facade of simple public servitorship. Material well-being is a reasonable end; it need not be gilded as knight-errantry. As various of our literary observers have noted, however, the press seems always to have had a weakness for high moral frontage. Recently it has discovered a new noble end to serve—"the people's right to know." Really? "Right to know"—everything about everything? At any time? Regardless of circumstances? Of side effects? Of impact on processes of law and statesmanship? Of damage to individuals? Surely this is a dubious absolute. For one thing, it runs directly counter to that other right that has been discovered recently, the "right to privacy." My sympathy is rather on the privacy side, but I am not at all sure that it is any more an unconditional right than the alleged right to know. Simply to assert these rights is to beg very complex questions. The papers, of course, are rather charmingly inconsistent. When for whatever reason—and it may be a good one— they decide not to air a given subject, they are a little absentminded about our right to know. What their position often boils down to in practice, perhaps without their knowing it, is something like this: *we* alone have the right to decide what *you* have a right to know. Or, alternatively, *you* have a right to know if and when *we* say you have.

Tom Stoppard sums the thing up neatly in his comedy *Dirty Linen* (1976). A Parliament ethics committee, after investigating some sexual free-loading in the House, finally decides that private life is a private matter, provided that it does not break the law or injure others. The motion to this effect ends with this notable phrase: "that this principle is not to be sacrificed to that Fleet Street stalking-horse masquerading as a sacred cow labelled 'The People's Right to Know.' " "Stalking-horse" as "sacred cow"—that wit does it beautifully.

VI.

When a journalist tells us how he struggles for our right to know, he turns his workhorse or stalking-horse into a noble white horse. He not only mounts and caracoles in public but constantly praises his own horsemanship. Journalism is the only profession which has a built-in public-address *and* public-relations system. In pointing to its own virtues, no other profession can reach so wide an audience and do it daily. No judge can tell a courtroom what a fine trial he is running. Business can praise themselves, but only by paying sizable advertising rates. Teachers, like people in many walks of life, can only hope that a good deed or quality will be noted (sure as they are of splendid exposure when their frailties become known). Most professions have organs in which they can tell themselves how splendid they are, but only journalism has an organ which tells this to the world.

Self-interest is widespread, and no one expects to end it. But we do grouse when self-righteousness implies an absence of self-interest. Surely this is one reason why a profession which we acknowledge to be indispensable has evoked steady dissatisfaction for two centuries. It is a little hard to live with a private body which claims unconditional freedom to determine what the public body shall be informed about; which cries aloud at any suggestion of limit or restraint; which seems to believe its practitioners free from common human frailties, and hence to begrudge admissions of error.

These traits, beliefs, and attitudes may all hang together around some unifying center. Such a center is charmingly presented in another novel by Anthony Trollope: *The Warden* (1855), which opens the series on ecclesiastical life in the cathedral town of Barchester (i.e., Salisbury). John Bold, a reformer, thinks that some trust funds at the cathedral are being misused; he files a suit, and through an old friend (the journalist Tom Towers) gets the powerful daily, the *Jupiter*, to attack the church—especially Mr. Harding, the warden of an old men's home at the cathedral. (The *Jupiter* was easily recognized by Trollope's readers as the *London Times*, which was then often called "The Thunderer.") An innocent churchman suggests a protesting letter to the editor, but the "more worldly wise" archdeacon says no indeed, you can't win that way. The paper will twist your answers, pick on your mistakes, and make you look still worse. "A man...cannot successfully answer, when attacked by the *Jupiter*. In such matters it is omnipotent. What the Czar is in Russia, or the mob in America, that the *Jupiter* is in England." Sounding like a Smollett character, the archdeacon goes on to point out that the *Jupiter* will "take up any case...right or wrong, true or false" if this "will further its own views." So the *Jupiter* goes on abusing the poor old warden for rolling in wealth "stolen from the poorer clergy."

When Bold's suit is thrown out on a legal technicality, Bold, now knowing the innocence of the warden, tries to get Tom Towers to call off the *Jupiter*'s attacks on him. Trollope then devotes a gently ironic chapter to the *Jupiter* (Ch. 14), calling its office "that laboratory where, with amazing chemistry, Tom Towers compounded thunderbolts for all that is evil and for the furtherance of all that is good, in this and other hemispheres." Here are made "those infallible laws...which cabinets are called upon to obey; by which bishops are to be guided, lords and commons controlled, judges instructed in law, generals in strategy, admirals in naval tactics." From here "issue the only known infallible bulls for the guidance of British souls and bodies. This little court is the Vatican of England. Here resides a pope, self-nominated, self-consecrated—

ay, and much stranger too—self-believing!...hitherto afraid of no Luther; a pope who manages his own inquisition, who punishes unbelievers as no most skilled inquisitor of Spain ever dreamt of doing."

Trollope comments: "It is a fact amazing to ordinary mortals that the *Jupiter* is never wrong. Parliament is always wrong:...Why should we look to [the ministers] when Tom Towers without a struggle can put us right? Look at our generals, what faults they make;...All, all is wrong—alas! alas! Tom Towers, and he alone, knows all about it." Hence "none but fools doubt the wisdom of the *Jupiter*; none but the mad dispute its facts." Tom Towers quietly enjoys a sense of omnipotence. He loved to "listen to the loud chattering of politicians, and to think how they were all in his power—how he could smite the loudest of them."

Needless to say, it is hard to ask such a character to stop his attacks on Warden Harding of Barchester. Towers lectures Bold for attempted "interference" with the press. He "took such high ground," Trollope says, "that there was no getting on it." Towers says that the "public is defrauded" if "private considerations" have any influence. Trollope then apostrophizes Tom Towers as "thou sententious proclaimer of the purity of the press" and makes Bold quite disillusioned by his old friend. In fact, he lets Bold have the closing words on Tom. Bold calls Tom "a prig and a humbug" and tells us, "He was ready enough to take my word for gospel when it suited his own views...but when I offer him real evidence opposed to his own views, he tells me that private motives are detrimental to public justice! Confound his arrogance! What is any public question but a conglomeration of private interests? What is any newspaper article but an expression of the views taken by one side?... The idea of Tom Towers talking of public motives and purity of purpose!"

Finally, Trollope makes full and clever use of the idea of divinity that lies in the name, the *Jupiter*. He bursts into a rhapsody: "Who has not heard of Mount Olympus,—that high abode of all the powers of type, that favoured seat of the great goddess Pica,...from whence...issue forth fifty thousand nightly edicts for the governance of a subject nation?" Best of all is Tom

Towers' visible physical being. He walks "with his coat buttoned close against the east wind, as though he were a mortal man, and not a god dispensing thunderbolts from Mount Olympus." This is a good line, and Trollope develops its potential to the fullest in a sentence which is a great finale to the Mount Olympus chapter. Again Towers is on the street: "and so he walked on from day to day, studiously trying to look a man, but knowing within his breast that he was a god."

"Knowing that he was a god." Maybe that beautiful phrase sums up the whole problem that we have been glancing at. Let us recheck several details. Some of the foibles or vices attributed to journalists are, as Thackeray first pointed out, general human frailties—proneness to err in both language and fact, reliance on clichés, preference for scandal and disaster, opportunism, commonplaceness of mind. But journalism, as we have noted, seems to regard its members as, or to act as if they were, exempt from such liabilities. Now it is just such an exemption which is a basic attribute of the divine. Again, no Olympian can be called to account for what, to earthlings, may look like mistakes or even malfeasance; an Olympian cannot be expected to be contrite or do penance. Total freedom from penalties and bounds is a true mark of the Olympian, who knows not the limits on privilege that mark all other modes of life. There are no restraints on divine will. The god is omnipotent. Hence he can be a great creator; *ex nihilo* he has created the "people's right to know."

Quintus Slide and many of his fictional peers were sure they had a transcendent rightness which justified everything they did; Olympians need not seek vindication. But they can be vindictive; vengeance is mine, saith the Lord. If the journalist knows in advance what he is going to write, as several observers believe, that too betokens divinity: it is the gift of foreknowledge. If, as Kipling complains, journalists take a jaundiced and reductive view of human conduct, that is because to the all-seeing eye, the human depths are more visible than they are here on earth. If a journalist disparages persons and institutions of whom we think highly—well, the reason is clear: thou shalt have no other gods before me. If C. S. Lewis "can't abide the journalistic air of being a specialist in everything, and of taking all points of view and always being on the side of the angels,"[14] surely that is a futile revolt against the divine attribute of omniscience and against devotion to even the lesser deities. And doubtless Leonard Woolf was glimpsing an Olympian altitude when he said of the old liberal editors of the *Nation*, just before World War I: "They were so highminded...that I always felt myself to be a bit of a fraud in their company."[15]

No doubt many of us are made to feel that way by having contact with one who knows within his breast that he is a god. Freedom from imperfection, invulnerability to judgment and moral debtorship, freedom of the will, freedom from limitations, together with omnipotence, creatorship, foreknowledge, retaliatory power, omniscience—all that, in people who look like other human beings, is sometimes hard for the other to bear. No wonder if ordinary humanity has an occasional eye for the god's clay foot. No wonder that some mortals fall into atheism, at least some of the time.

Footnotes

1 Quotations are from Henrik Ibsen, *The Complete Major Prose Plays*, trans. Rolf Fjelde (New York: Farrar, Straus & Giroux, 1980), pp. 283-386.

2 H. Montgomery Hyde, *Oscar Wilde: A Biography* (New York: Farrar, Straus & Giroux, 1975), p. 73.

3 Angus Wilson, *The Strange Ride of Rudyard Kipling: His Life and Works* (New York: Viking, 1977), p. 190.

4 Anne Clark, *Lewis Carroll: A Biography* (New York: Schocken, 1979), p. 249.

5 Peter Sutcliffe, *The Oxford University Press: An Informal History* (Oxford: Oxford Univ. Press, 1978), pp. 151-52.

6 *The Letters of Evelyn Waugh*, ed. Mark Amory (New York: Ticknor & Fields, 1980), p. 592.

7 Janet Hobhouse, *Everybody Who Was Anybody: A Biography of Gertrude Stein* (New York: Putnam, 1974), p. 178.

8 Quotations are from Thomas Sowell, "Media Smears: One Man's Experience," *The American Spectator*, 15 (May 1982), 17-20.

9 *The American Spectator*, 15 (April 1982), 35.

10 Walter Allen, *As I Walked Down New Grub Street* (Chicago: Univ. of Chicago Press, 1982), p. 91.

11 Miguel de Unamuno, *Ficciones: Four Stories and a Play*, trans. Anthony Kerrigan (Princeton: Princeton Univ. Press, 1975), p. 210.

12 A. Colin Wright, *Michael Bulgakov: Life and Interpretations* (Toronto: Univ. of Toronto Press, 1978), p. 56.

13 Merlin Thomas, *Louis-Ferdinand Céline* (New York: New Directions, 1980), p. 177.

14 Humphrey Carpenter, *The Inklings* (Boston: Houghton Mifflin, 1979), p. 133.

15 Leonard Woolf, *Downhill All the Way: An Autobiography of the Years 1919-1939* (New York: Harcourt, Brace and World, 1967), p. 93.

Questions for Study and Discussion

1. The ASNE poll indicates that "three-fourths of all adults have some problem with the credibility of the media." Should the press worry about that 75 percent, or should it rejoice that the other 25 percent seem to regard the press as credible?

2. The participants discussed the hazards of using unnamed sources. What circumstances might require unnamed sources? What standards should the reporter apply to determine such circumstances? How should the reporter involve the editor in such decisions? Should reporters explain in stories why sources remain unnamed?

3. How can the press convince public officials to speak openly? How can public officials convince each other to speak openly?

4. The public sees reporters and TV crews as rude and intrusive. What steps can the press take to minimize this reaction? Does newsgathering necessarily require rude procedures?

5. James David Barber calls presidential press conferences "the impolite delivery of cream puffs to the President." Do you agree with this assessment? How could correspondents sharpen their questions and seem polite at the same time? By what means can the press set press conferences in the context of ongoing events without seeming to offer "instant rebuttal?"

6. The participants agreed on necessary connections between profitability and credibility. What compromises must an unprofitable newspaper make to survive, and how can such measures affect credibility? How can press leaders explain financial necessities to the public without further exciting their cynicism about the motives of the press?

7. Responsible newspapers print corrections prominently, yet some readers regard corrections as evidence of inaccuracy in papers. How can newspapers convince the public that printing corrections reflects a dedication to accuracy?

8. TV news programs lack air time for extensive corrections. How can stations correct errors effectively?

9. An old adage says that other people's grief sells newspapers. Discuss the conflict between this supposedly favorite subject and the right to privacy. Consider John Chancellor's remark that "death in America now needs to be validated...on television."

10. The television executives at the conference seemed to equate credibility with popularity, while the print representatives denied this equation. What does this difference in viewpoint say about the two media? Is popularity a valid test of credibility?

11. Journalists profess standards of fairness, completeness, balance, and accuracy. Would viewers and readers choose these same standards, and would they agree on the meanings of these four magic words?

12. Do time constraints make these standards irrelevant to television? Do they apply to news on public television and radio?

13. Should the media put more stress on "good news?" Could they convey the bad news in a less pessimistic way?

14. If you had attended this conference and had to perform Martin Nolan's role as the final summarizer and exhorter, what aspects of the discussion would you have emphasized? What advice would you have given to these media stars to improve their profession? What advice would you now give to other leaders of the press to combat the problems of credibility?

Some Approaches to Heightened Credibility

Judging from the survey findings as well as the focus groups, the approaches to heightening the credibility of newspapers cannot be narrowed to a few steps. Instead, many large and small steps will be necessary. Each newspaper will seek the right combination to serve its readers. Moving closer to readers does not mean any compromise of sound journalistic principles or integrity. Here are some approaches:

Practice good journalism
Be fair, unbiased, accurate, complete, factual, professional, aggressive and compassionate.

Be accessible
Be perceived as accessible by promoting and demonstrating openness. Be accessible through telephone calls, readers' representatives, letters to the editor, columnists from the community, writers with whom readers identify, speakers' bureaus, community involvement, public service projects.

Respect people
Treat people in the news with empathy, and that does *not* mean any less aggressive pursuit of the news. When people make the effort to contact your newspaper, make a corresponding effort on their behalf.

Gain (or regain) your franchise as a people's advocate
Demonstrate that newspapers are a watchdog for the people, not a remote and, to some, frightening institution. Show that your investigations help people; increase the visibility of reporters and editors; get to know your readers through reader forums and system-

---

This piece originally appeared in Newspaper Credibility: Building Reader Trust: An ASNE Research Report (1985) 11. National study conducted by Minnesota Opinion Research, Inc., Minneapolis. Reprinted by permission.

atic research. Promote all this so people know what you're doing.

Target efforts to improve credibility among certain groups

Include everyone in attempts to improve credibility, but concentrate on four groups with unusually high distrust of the media:

- *Sophisticated skeptics:* Address their reservations about the motivations and competence of newspaper people.
- *The less-well-informed and suspicious:* Address their distrust of opinions in newspapers and their suspicion that newspapers are tools of those in power.
- *Minorities:* Address their lack of confidence in newspapers. Make sure your newspaper's staff and management are as representative as possible.
- *Young people:* Address their lack of support for press rights and privileges.

Be aware of sensitive topics and reporting practices

Be more thoughtful about coverage of all sorts of people, particularly women, young people, senior citizens, people on welfare, minorities, political and religious conservatives. Pay more attention to coverage of international conflicts, the abortion issue, criminal trials, human tragedies, and national security issues. Be sensitive to public doubts about some investigative reporting practices and the use of unnamed sources.

Protect your local news franchise

Cover local news thoroughly and well so people continue to rely on newspapers for the news that's closest to home. Establish strong local-orientation programs for new staff members.

Educate the public about press rights and privileges

Let people know that press rights are, in fact, the people's rights, that those rights exist because the press is on their side. Promote this message nationally as an industry effort and locally, particularly to young people.

Reassess policies regarding fact and opinion, then educate the public about them

Make sure policies about fact and opinion are consistent and easily understood. Display coverage of controversial issues so readers are aware that different sides of those issues are being covered. Explain how "analysis" and "interpretation" stories can help people cope with an increasingly complex society. Explain the role of newspaper columnists. Educate people about endorsements of political candidates. Explain that newspapers bend over backwards to be fair in news coverage when they endorse.

Bibliography of Sources On Media Credibility

ABEL, John D. and Wirth, Michael O.
"Newspaper vs. TV Credibility for Local News," *Journalism Quarterly* 54 (1977) 371-375.

ADAMS, William C.
Television Coverage of International Affairs (Norwood, New Jersey: Ablex, 1982).

ALTER, Jonathan (with Lucy Howard and Nancy Stadtman)
"The Media in the Dock," *Newsweek* (October 22, 1984) 66-72.

ALTHEIDE, David L.
Creating Reality: How TV News Distorts Events (Beverly Hills, California: Sage, 1976).

ANAST, Philip
"Attitude Toward the Press as a Function of Interests," *Journalism Quarterly* 38 (1961) 376-380.

APME (Associated Press Managing Editors)
Credibility Committee Report 1984 (Philadelphia, 1984).

BAGDIKIAN, Ben H.
The Media Monopoly (Boston: Beacon Press, 1983).

BAKER, Robert K.
"Functions and Credibility," in John C. Merrill and Ralph D. Barney, eds., *Ethics and the Press: Readings in Mass Media Morality* (New York: Macmillan, 1975) 176-186.

BAKER, Russell
"A Time for Barkers," *The New York Times* (December 12, 1984) 31A. Reprinted in this volume as Essay 13.

BALK, Alfred.
A Free and Responsive Press: The Twentieth Century Fund Task Force Report for a NATIONAL NEWS COUNCIL (New York: Twentieth Century Fund, 1973).

BALON, Robert E.; Philport, Joseph C.; and Beadle, Charles
"How Sex and Race Affect Perceptions of Newscasters," *Journalism Quarterly* 55 (1978) 160-164.

BARBER, James David.
"The Journalists' Responsibility: Make Reality Interesting," *Center Magazine* 18:3 (May/June 1985) 11-15.

BARBER, James David
"On Rising to the Occasion of Popular Mistrust," Credibility seminar document (December 1984). Reprinted in this volume as Essay 11.

BARNES, Andrew
"Reporting the News Isn't Always a 'Friendly' Job," *St. Petersburg Times* (December 2, 1984) D2. Reprinted in this volume as Essay 12.

BARRON, Jerome A.
"Access to the Press: A New First Amendment Right," *Harvard Law Review* (June 1967) 1641-1678.

BECKER, Lee B.; Cobbey, Robin E.; and Sobowale, Idowu
"Public Support for the Press," *Journalism Quarterly* 55 (1978) 421-430.

BECKER, Lee B.; Whitney, D. Charles; and Collins, Erik L.
"Public Understanding of How the News Media Operate," *Journalism Quarterly* 57 (1980) 571-578, 605.

BISHOP, Robert L. and Schultz, Sue A.
"The Credibility Gap: Is It Widening?" *Journalism Quarterly* 44 (1967) 740-741.

BLACK, Creed C.
"Our Image Problem: A Paradox," address to the

American Society of Newspaper Editors convention, May 9, 1984. Reprinted in this volume as Essay 6.

BLAKKAN, Renee
"A Former Editor Looks at the Warts of the Press," *Advertising Age* (January 30, 1984) M44-45.

BOCCARDI, Louis D.
"The American Press: Too Tough or Too Tame?" Press Enterprise Lecture Series 20 (Riverside, California, February 5, 1985).

BOGART, Leo
"Comment on 'Public Attitudes Toward Freedom of the Press,' " *Public Opinion Quarterly* 46 (1982) 187-190. Responds to Immerwahr and Doble 1982 and to Kalven 1982.

BURGOON, Michael; Burgoon, Judee K.; and Wilkinson, Miriam
"Newspaper Image and Evaluation," *Journalism Quarterly* 58 (1981) 411-419, 433.

CANAPE, Charlene.
"Putting Stock in TV Business News," *Washington Journalism Review* (November 1982) 38-41.

CARTER, Richard F. and Greenberg, Bradley S.
"Newspapers or Television: Which Do You Believe?" *Journalism Quarterly* 42 (1965) 29-34.

CHANG, Lawrence K. H. and Lemert, James B.
"The Invisible Newsman and Other Factors in Media Competition," *Journalism Quarterly* 45 (1968) 436-444.

CHARNLEY, Mitchell V.
"Preliminary Notes on a Study of Newspaper Accuracy," *Journalism Quarterly* 13 (1936) 394-401.

CIRINO, Robert.
Don't Blame the People: How the News Media Uses Bias, Distortion and Censorship To Manipulate Public Opinion (New York: Random House 1972).

CLARK, Peter B.
"Newspaper Credibility: What Needs to be Done,"
Michigan Business Review 25 (January 1973) 1-6.
Reprinted in John C. Merrill and Ralph D. Barney, eds.,
Ethics and the Press: Readings in Mass Media Morality (New York: Macmillan 1975) 168-175.

CLARKE, Peter and Evans, Susan H.
Covering Campaigns (Stanford, California: Stanford
Univ. Press, 1983).

COBBEY, Robin
"Audience Attitudes and Readership," *ANPA News
Research Report* No. 29. (Washington, D.C.: American
Newspaper Publishers Association, December 15, 1980.)

COLLINS, Keith.
*Responsibility and Freedom in the Press: Are They in
Conflict?* (Washington, D.C.: Citizen's Choice, 1985).

COONS, John E.
Freedom and Responsibility in Broadcasting (Evanston,
Illinois: Northwestern University Press, 1961).

CORRY, John
"What is TV Doing to the Election Process?" *New York
Times* (November 18, 1984) 27, 30. Reprinted in this
volume as Essay 9.

COSE, Ellis
"Our Elitist Journalism," *Newsweek* (June 3, 1985) 14.

CUNNINGHAM, Richard P.
"With the Ombudsmen, The Eight Most Common Complaints," *Editor & Publisher* (March 19, 1983) 40.
Reprinted in this volume as Essay 2.

DENNIS, Everette E.
Understanding Mass Communication (Boston:
Houghton Mifflin, 1981.)

DIEHL, William K.
"Evil Empire?" *The Masthead* (Spring 1985) 15-16.

EDELSTEIN, Alex S. and Tefft, Diane P.
"Media Credibility and Respondent Credulity with Respect to Watergate," *Communication Research* 1 (1974) 426-439.

EINSIEDEL, E. F. and Winter, James P.
"Public Attitudes on Media Ownership: Demographic and Attitudinal Correlates," *Journalism Quarterly* 60 (1983) 87-92.

EPSTEIN, Edward Jay
"Journalism and Truth," *Commentary* 57 (April 1974) 36-40. Reprinted in *Current* (June 1974) 3. Reprinted as "The American Press: Some Truths About Truths," in John C. Merrill and Ralph D. Barney, eds., *Ethics and the Press: Readings in Mass Media Morality* (New York: Macmillan, 1975) 60-68.

ERSKINE, Hazel Gaudet
"The Polls: Freedom of Speech," *Public Opinion Quarterly* 34 (1970) 483-496.

ERSKINE, Hazel Gaudet
"The Polls: Opinion of the News Media," *Public Opinion Quarterly* 34 (1970-71) 630-643.

FIELDER, Virginia Dodge and Weaver, David H.
"Public Opinion on Investigative Reporting," *Newspaper Research Journal* 3:2 (1981) 54-62.

FISHER, Marc
"Newspapers Trying to Win Back Trust of Readers," *The Miami Herald* (November 29, 1984) F2.

FOREMAN, Gene
"Confidential Sources: Testing the Readers' Confidence," *Social Responsibility: Business, Journalism, Law, Medicine* 10 (1984) 24-31. Edited by Louis W. Hodges, Washington & Lee University, Lexington, VA. Reprinted in this volume as Essay 4.

FRIENDLY, Fred W.
The Good Guys, the Bad Guys and the First Amendment:

Free Speech vs. Fairness in Broadcasting (New York: Random House, 1976).

GALLUP, George, Jr.
"Americans Favor Tougher Controls on the Press," *Editor & Publisher* (January 19, 1980) 7.

GALLUP POLL
"The Public Appraises the Newspaper: A Report to Client Newspapers of the Gallup Poll on the Credibility of the Press, Including Higher Circulation Prices," *ANPA News Research Bulletin* No. 2. (Washington, D.C.: American Newspaper Publishers Association, February 19, 1974).

GANTZ, Walter
"The Influence of Researcher Methods on Television and Newspaper News Credibility Evaluations," *Journal of Broadcasting* 25 (1981) 155-169.

GERGEN, David
"The Message to the Media," *Public Opinion* 7.2 (April/May 1984) 5-8.

GREENBERG, Bradley S. and Roloff, Michael E.
"Mass Media Credibility: Research Results and Critical Issues," *ANPA News Research Bulletin*, No. 6. (Washington, D.C.: American Newspaper Publishers Association, November 6, 1974.) Reprinted in *News Research for Better Newspapers* 7, ANPA Foundation (July 1975).

GREENE, Bob
"By Any Other Name," *Esquire* (September 1981) 23-24.

GRIFFITH, Thomas
"Credibility at Stake," *TIME* (March 11, 1985) 57.

GROTTA, Gerald L.
"Attitudes on Newspaper Accuracy and External Controls," *Journalism Quarterly* 46 (1969) 757-759.

HARRIS, Louis
"Confidence in Institutions Rises Slightly," *The Harris Survey,* No. 92 (November 17, 1983).

HARRIS, Louis
"Does the Public *Really* Hate the Press?" *Columbia Journalism Review* 22:6 (1984) 18.

HARTUNG, B.W. and Stone, Gerald
"Time to Stop Singing the 'Bad News' Blues," *Newspaper Research Journal* 1:2 (1979) 19-26.

HASKINS, Jack B. and Miller, M. Mark
"The Effects of Bad News and Good News on a Newspaper's Image," *Journalism Quarterly* 61 (1984) 3-13, 65.

HEILMAN, Robert B.
"Writers on Journalists: A Version of Atheism," *The Georgia Review* 39:1 (Spring 1985) 37-54. Reprinted in this volume as Essay 14.

HENRY, William A., III
"The Dangers of Docudrama," *TIME* (February 25, 1985) 95.

HENRY, William A., III
"Journalism Under Fire," *TIME* (December 12, 1983) 76-93. Reprinted in this volume as Essay 3.

HOVLAND, Carl I.; Janis, Irving L.; and Kelley, Howard H.
Communication and Persuasion (New Haven, Connecticut: Yale University Press, 1953).

HUNTLEY, Chet
"A Disturbing Arrogance in the Press," *Montana Journalism Review* 17 (1974) 25-28. Reprinted in John C. Merrill and Ralph D. Barney, eds., *Ethics and the Press: Readings in Mass Media Morality* (New York: Macmillan, 1975) 143-149.

IMMERWAHR, John and Doble, John
"Public Attitudes Toward Freedom of the Press," *Public*

Opinion Quarterly 46 (1982) 177-187. Responses by
Bogart 1982 and Kalven 1982.

IMMERWAHR, John; Johnson, Jean; and Doble, John
*The Speaker and the Listener: A Public Perspective on
Freedom of Expression* (New York: Public Agenda Foun-
dation, 1980).

ISAACS, Norman E.
"The New Credibility Gap - Readers vs. The Press,"
ASNE Bulletin (February 1969) 1.

ISAACS, Norman E.
"It's Up to Editors to Close the Credibility Gap,"
Presstime 5:2 (February 1983) 27.

JACOBSON, Harvey K.
"Mass Media Believability: A Study of Receiver
Judgments," *Journalism Quarterly* 46 (1969) 20-28.

KALVEN, Jamie
"Comments on 'Public Attitudes Toward Freedom of the
Press,' " *Public Opinion Quarterly* 46 (1982) 190-194.
Responds to Immerwahr and Doble, 1982.

KINSELLA, James
"Journalists Clash Over Credibility Gap," *Editor &
Publisher* (May 25, 1985) 22, 36.

KNIGHT, Jerry
"Self-Criticism Not a Journalistic Pastime," *The
Washington Post* (August 13, 1984) WB1.

LAPHAM, Lewis H.
"Can the Press Tell the Truth?" *Harper's* (January
1985) 37-51.

LAWRENCE, David Jr.
"Points on Credibility: Newspapers, It's Your Serve,"
Washington Journalism Review 7:2 (February 1985)
49-51.

LEE, Raymond S. H.
"Credibility of Newspaper and TV News," *Journalism Quarterly* 55 (1978) 282-287.

LEE, Robert D.
A Free and Responsible Press: A General Report on Mass Communication: Newspapers, Radio, Motion Pictures, Magazines, and Books (Chicago: University of Chicago Press, 1947).

LEMERT, James B.
"News Media Competition Under Conditions Favorable to Newspapers," *Journalism Quarterly* 47 (1970) 272-280.

LICHTER, S. Robert and Rothman, Stanley
"Media and Business Elites," *Public Opinion* 4,5 (October/November 1981), 42-46, 59-60.

LIPSET, Seymour Martin and Schneider, William
The Confidence Gap: Business, Labor, and Government in the Public Mind (New York: The Free Press, 1983).

MARKHAM, David
"The Dimensions of Source Credibility of Television Newscasters," *Journal of Communication* 18 (1968) 57-64.

MATUSOW, Barbara,
The Evening Stars: The Making of the Network News Anchor (Boston: Houghton Mifflin, 1983).

McALLISTER, William H., III
"The Effects of Bylines on News Story Credibility," *Journalism Quarterly* 43 (1966) 331-333.

McCOMBS, Maxwell E. and Washington, Laura
"Opinion Surveys Offer Conflicting Clues as to How Public Views Press," *Presstime* 5:2 (February 1983) 4-9. Reprinted in this volume as Essay 1.

McCROSKEY, James C. and Jenson, Thomas A.
"Images of Mass Media News Sources," *Journal of Broadcasting* 19 (1975) 169-180.

MEYER, Philip
"Elitism and Newspaper Believability," *Journalism Quarterly* 50 (1973) 31-36.

MILLER, Mark Crispin
"How TV Covers War," *New Republic* (November 29, 1982) 26-33.

MINNESOTA OPINION RESEARCH INC. (MORI)
Newspaper Credibility: Building Reader Trust (Washington, D.C.: American Society of Newspaper Editors, 1985).

Modern Media Institute
The Adversary Press (St. Petersburg, Florida, 1983).

MORGAN, Neil
"Roundtables Provide Forum for Dynamic Community Action," *ASNE Bulletin* 677 (May 1985) 21, 23.

MOSIER, Nancy R. and Ahlgren, Andrew
"Credibility of Precision Journalism," *Journalism Quarterly* 58 (1981) 375-381, 518.

MULDER, Ronald
"Media Credibility: A Use-Gratification Approach," *Journalism Quarterly* 57 (1980) 474-476.

NIMMO, Dan and Combs, James E.
Nightly Horrors: Crisis Coverage by Television Network News (Knoxville: University of Tennessee Press, 1985).

NOVAK, Michael
"Why the Working Man Hates the Media," *More* (October 1974) 5-8, 26. Reprinted in John C. Merrill and Ralph D. Barney, eds., *Ethics and the Press: Readings in Mass Media Morality* (New York: Macmillan, 1975) 108-117.

PATTERSON, Eugene
"TV and Print Can Learn a Lot From Each Other," *St. Petersburg Times* (February 3, 1985) D3.

PITTMAN, Robert
"TV has Changed the Audience," *St. Petersburg Times* (February 3, 1985) D1.

POWELL, Jody
The Other Side of the Story (New York: Morrow, 1984).

PURVIS, Hoyt H.
The Press: Free and Responsible? (Austin: University of Texas, 1982).

RADOLF, Andrew
"Becoming More Credible," *Editor & Publisher* (February 9, 1985) 7, 9, 32.

RADOLF, Andrew
"A Credibility Shocker," *Editor & Publisher* (April 6, 1985) 9, 54.

RANNEY, Austin
Channels of Power: The Impact of Television on American Politics (New York: Basic Books, 1983).

REAGAN, Joey and Zenaty, Jayne
"Local News Credibility: Newspapers vs. TV Revisited," *Journalism Quarterly* 56 (1979) 168-172.

REEVES, Richard
"Remarks to the APME Convention," November 28, 1984. Reprinted in this volume as Essay 10.

ROPER, Burns W.
Evolving Public Attitudes Toward Television and Other Mass Media 1959-1980 (New York: Television Information Office, 1981).

ROPER, Burns W.
Trends in Attitudes Toward Television and Other Media: A Twenty-Four Year Review. (New York: Television Information Office, 1983).

ROSENBLATT, Roger
"Journalism and the Larger Truth," *TIME* (July 2, 1984) 88. Reprinted in this volume as Essay 7.

ROWAN, Ford
Broadcast Fairness: Doctrine, Practice, Prospects (New York: Longman, 1984).

SARGENT, Leslie W.
"Communicator Image and News Reception," *Journalism Quarterly* 42 (1965) 35-42.

SCHALELEBEN, Arville
"What Survey Do You Believe?" *Saturday Review* (May 12, 1962) 72-73. Responds to Tebbel 1962.

SCHMUL, Robert
The Responsibilities of Journalism (Notre Dame: University of Notre Dame Press, 1984).

SHAW, David
"Public Finds News Media More Fair than Accurate," *Los Angeles Times* (October 11, 1981) 1, 20, 21.

SHAW, David
"Public Relies on TV for News of World, Papers for Local Coverage, Survey Finds," *Los Angeles Times* (October 13, 1981, Late Final Edition) 3, 22.

SHAW, Eugene
"Media Credibility: Taking the Measure of a Measure," *Journalism Quarterly* 50 (1973) 306-311.

SHAW, Eugene
"The Popular Meaning of Media Credibility," *ANPA News Research Bulletin* 3 (October 22, 1976) 1-17.

SHOEMAKER, Pamela J.
"Bias and Source Attribution," *Newspaper Research Journal* 5 (1983) 25-31.

SHOEMAKER, Pamela J.
"Deviance of Political Groups and Media Treatment," *Journalism Quarterly* 61 (1984) 66-75, 82.

SIMMONS, Steven J.
The Fairness Doctrine and the Media (Berkeley: University of California Press, 1978).

SIMON, Scott
"A Pride of Media Lions Goeth Three Falls," *Quill*
(March 1985) 10-13.

SINGLETARY, Michael W.
"Components of Credibility of a Favorable News
Source," *Journalism Quarterly* 53 (1976) 316-319.

SINGLETARY, Michael W. and Lipsky, Richard
"Accuracy in Local TV News," *Journalism Quarterly*
54 (1977) 362-364.

SMITH, C. Fraser
"Reporting Grief: Marine Families Review the Press Invasion," *Washington Journalism Review* (March 1984)
21-22, 58.

SMYSER, Richard D.
"Minorities, 'Sourcerers,' the Role of Editors and 'Gen-
tle Truths,' " ASNE Presidential Address, Washington,
D.C., April 10, 1985, excerpted in *ASNE Bulletin* 677
(May 1985) 35-36.

STAFFORD, Charles
"The Problem Is Tied to Reporters' Poor Manners,"
Presstime 5:2 (February 1983) 9-10.

STAFFORD, Charles
"Journalists Sink Teeth into Issue of Credibility," *St.
Petersburg Times* (January 27, 1985) A1, A10. Reprinted
in this volume.

SUSSMAN, Barry
"Public Has Sharp Complaints about News Media, Poll
Says," *The Washington Post* (August 16, 1981) A1-2.

SUSSMAN, Barry
"News on TV: Mixed Reviews," *The Washington Post
National Weekly Edition* (September 3, 1984) 37.

TANNENBAUM, Percy H. and McLeod, Jack M.
"Public Images of Mass Media Institutions," *Paul J.
Deutschmann Memorial Papers in Mass Communica-*

tions Research, Scripps-Howard Research (December 1963) 51-60.

TEBBEL, John
"What News Does the Public Believe?" *Saturday Review* (March 10, 1962) 43-44. Response by Schaleleben 1962.

THELEN, Gil
"Newsmaker Panels Combine Simplicity of Organization with High Impact," *ASNE Bulletin* 677 (May 1985) 20, 22.

TILLINGHAST, William A.
"Source Control and Evaluation of Newspaper Inaccuracies," *Newspaper Research Journal* 5 (1983) 13-24.

TOBIN, Richard L.
"Monopoly Newspapers and the Credibility Gap," *Saturday Review* (May 9, 1970) 57-58.

WESTLEY, Bruce H. and Severin, Werner J.
"Some Correlates of Media Credibility," *Journalism Quarterly* 41 (1964) 325-335.

WESTLEY, Bruce H. and Severin, Werner J.
"Some Correlates of Media Credibility: Research Results and Critical Issues," *ANPA News Research Bulletin* No. 6. (Washington, D.C.: American Newspaper Publishers Association, November 4, 1974).

WILSON, C. Edward and Howard, Douglas M.
"Public Perception of Media Accuracy," *Journalism Quarterly* 55 (1978) 73-76.

WITAS, Robert A.
"Print (Broder) v. Broadcast (Friendly)," *The Masthead* 36:3 (Fall 1984) 31-32. Reprinted in this volume as Essay 8.

WRIGHT, William F.
"TV Newsman Dumps on TV News," *Editor & Publisher* (April 14, 1984) 13, 32. Reprinted in this volume as Essay 5.

YANKELOVICH, Skelly, and White, Inc.
"Tracking the Attitudes of the Public Toward the Newspaper Business," *ANPA General Bulletin* No. 66 (December 20, 1978); *ANPA News Research Reports*, No. 19 (April 20, 1979); and No. 20 (May 25, 1979).

ZANNA, Mark P. and Del Vecchio, Steven M.
"Perceived Credibility of Television News: A Matter of Viewer's Attitudes and the Position Taken by the Media," *European Journal of Social Psychology* 3 (1973) 213-216.

ZEECK, David
"What Role Can Journalism Schools Play in Credibility?" *APME News* (September 1984) 13-15.

FORUM
"Six editors respond to study, 'Newspaper Credibility: Building Reader Trust,' " *ASNE Bulletin* 679 (July/August 1985) 20-22. Short pieces by JoAnn Huff Albers, William B. Brown, Robert H. Wills, Judith G. Clabes, Jay T. Harris, and Joann Byrd.

USA TODAY
Opinion: The Debate: News Credibility (April 12, 1985) 12A, contains articles by Mario Cuomo, Judy Markey, Carol Richards, Ernest Van den Haag, and Carter Wrenn.

This bibliography draws heavily on a compilation by Minnesota Opinion Research Inc. Special thanks to Cecilie Gaziano for volunteering it, and to Eric Goldstein of the Gannett Center for corrections and additions.

DATE DUE

APR 14 1988		
1-25-89		
APR 09 1993		
MAY 05 2003		
APR 21 2008		

HIGHSMITH 45-220